Genius!

Genius!

Nurturing the Spirit of the Wild, Odd, and Oppositional Child

Revised Edition

George T. Lynn with Joanne Barrie Lynn

Jessica Kingsley Publishers
London and Philadelphia

First edition published in 2004
This edition first published in 2006 by Jessica Kingsley Publishers

116 Pentonville Road
London N1 9JB, UK
and
400 Market Street, Suite 400
Philadelphia PA 19106, USA

www.jkp.com

Library of Congress Cataloging in Publication Data
Lynn, George T., 1945-
Genius! : nurturing the spirit of the wild, odd, and oppositional child / George T. Lynn with Joanne Barrie Lynn.— Rev. ed.
p. cm.
Includes bibliographical references (p.   ) and index.
ISBN-13: 978-1-84310-820-7 (pbk. : alk. paper)
ISBN-10: 1-84310-820-8 (pbk. : alk. paper) 1. Child psychopathology. 2. Child psychotherapy. I. Lynn, Joanne Barrie, 1947- II. Title.
RJ499.L96 2006
618.92'89—dc22

2005020171

British Library Cataloguing in Publication Data
A CIP catalogue record for this book is available from the British Library

ISBN-13: 978 1 84310 820 7
ISBN-10: 1 84310 820 8

Printed and bound in Great Britain by
Athenaeum Press, Gateshead, Tyne and Wear

We dedicate this book to Gregory Barrie Lynn

"Every child is born a genius." — *Albert Einstein*

Contents

Part I: Understanding and nurturing the positive genius of your attention different child

Part II: The seventh criterion in the field of nurturing: caregivers' practice of high-level wellness in their own lives

Part III: Special considerations

Figures

Tables

Dragons Dance
In the Eyes of My Son

They painted no eyes,
            the ancient Chinese scholars,
    painted dragons
        so near life
            that given sight
            they leapt from the scroll,
                soared
                through cloud and sky,
    lost in light at the sun's core

                You leap from my arms,
                    soar beyond me,
                rushing back in young panic
                        to fly again
                    from this ambiguous
                            safety—
                    I let you go,
                admiring your
                fire, my
                        lightened
                    arms
                embracing
                    other work

        Unpainted scrolls
            demand
            their eyes

Acknowledgements

This book is informed by the wisdom of many—professionals, parents, kids, and our community. We offer them our grateful acknowledgment.

We thank the Lake Washington School District for fifteen years of support, from the supervisors, teachers, principals, bus drivers, and support staff. Our thanks go especially to Dan Phelan and Becky Anderson, and to Richard Haines. Thank you all for the huge difference you have made in Greg's life.

We thank the parents of kids with odd genius whom we have met in local meetings, through thousands of emails, in the context of doing presentations, and as George's clients. We have found here such great heart, deep wisdom, and positive intention. And we acknowledge the people who run the service agencies that provide for our kids and have contributed to our knowledge about them. These include Mary Cochran McConnell and Jan Bleakney. We are truly all in this together!

The many layers of our community have been of great importance. Joanne thanks in particular poets Barbara L. Thomas and Judith Skillman, and writer Sondra Kornblatt for their friendship and expert critiques; and the people of Kirkland Congregational Church, for their prayers and loving support.

Those we wish to acknowledge most are the kids, many of whom have worked with George in counseling. They provide the basis for the composited case narratives in this book. They are an elite group—the kids in Special Ed, the arch nerds, the Goths, the punks. Some of them are veterans of several psychiatric hospitalizations. They inspire us with their resourcefulness in living with mental states that could disable less hardy souls. They show us the face of their genius. This is a great gift and we hope we do it justice here.

We thank our son most of all, for his courage and strength of character in wanting his Great Story told.

George T. Lynn
Joanne Barrie Lynn
July 2004

In the crucible

Preface to the first edition
by Joanne Barrie Lynn

I'm writing this preface at the very end of the project, right before publication. Ten days ago our son Greg graduated from high school, and stopped taking a beneficial medication that has side effects that dull him. His face and voice and body are energetic and animated again, and his vocabulary is again delightfully rich and outrageous. I can't predict what our future will bring, but for now Greg's personality is back, he has successfully completed a lengthy and difficult project, and all of us are quietly joyful.

Neurologically eccentric children require a higher degree of caregiving than neurotypical children, and as with any child, the inherent genius might or might not find its expression. In this book, we show the maps we've discovered and the routes we've traveled, to find this genius.

Genius is most comfortably appreciated at a distance. Close up, George and I live with the obsessions, the rages, the dangerous behaviors, and sometimes the misdirections from professionals. We seldom know how to deal with Greg, except through experience, and that has been mainly by the seat of our pants. We've made many mistakes. But we've been there, we've kept the faith. We learn whatever we can; we write what we know. The best we can do is make the emergence of genius as likely as possible. There are no guarantees.

What I bring to this project, apart from editing the manuscript, is the microcosm to George's macrocosmic view of eccentric neurology. George writes for and corresponds with the greater world community of parents and publishers, of doctors and researchers and academics. He is grounded intellectually and emotionally in his everyday work as a counselor, international lecturer, consultant and writer, learning about other children with neurology similar to our son's, and helping parents like us find the elusive path to family harmony. Though he is actively engaged at home in the difficult task of bringing up Greg, he has spent his workdays at his office all of Greg's life.

I spend my life at home, in the minutiae of nurturing Greg's genius, care-giving, cleaning up messes, dealing with meds, resolving the multitude of school issues, wrestling him out the door to doctors' appointments, hunting for low-stimulus activities that he can take part in without meltdown, translating him to schools and professionals, introducing and explaining him to the people in our small city who have known him by sight and reputation and short conversations for his whole life. Sometimes I have found time for my own work; often I have not.

Part of this microcosm is the telling of Greg's Great Story. It is in the small intimate details of a life that eccentric neurology is illuminated, and it is in these details—the good, the bad, the painful, and the sublime —that genius is recognized. Great Story (see page 84) must declare the pain and bondage of eccentric neurology, as well as its beauty and usefulness, or the release into genius is not seen to be the miracle that it is. Greg is in the midst of that great leap from child to adult, and the poems and short pieces I've written about him are pieces of the map of his road to his genius.

Genius isn't always obvious, or visible. Greg's genius with computers, for example, goes far beyond my understanding, and I have to take the word of his jaw-dropped computer teachers, to whom his genius is rare and highly noticeable.

I find Greg's genius primarily in his playfulness. I have my neurotypical father to thank for this. All my growing-up years I tap-danced in the kitchen with him, making puns, singing silly songs, competing in rhymes, telling tall tales, in sync with each other, our individual rhythms making harmony that bonded us through the hard times of parent and child.

My neurologically eccentric son gives me his playfulness with his voice. Talking to himself or me, happy or angry, silly or raging, his pitch roams up and down the octaves, words are accented to conform to the rhythms of his tics and pacing and sharp gestures, metaphors are vivid and unexpected, his vocabulary huge and passionate and feral. He learns by hearing, by talking to himself, explaining how he feels, describing the next step in whatever project he's engaged in. We play in parallel. All his life he has listened to my singing and poetry, except during the hard late-teen years, which aren't entirely over yet.

No one else seems to notice his spontaneous poetry, but this is how I measure the overall health of Greg's spirit, his genius. On his latest medication his speech was passionless, unaccented and sat on a monotone. He was easier to understand when he was medicated—and he was alive! —but he was not verbally interesting. A part of him was missing, the part that plays, the part that feels joy.

Families such as ours live in a crucible, that chemistry lab vessel made of a material, steel or platinum or porcelain, that doesn't burn away in a furnace. Chemists and alchemists have used crucibles for centuries to purify ores and other materials, burning out the dross and leaving the pure metal. George and I live in the furnace of our son's wild neurology, and our job is to contain him so that he can grow, without burning up in his own heat. And we must not burn out in the nurturing of him.

One important note: everything we write about Greg that we send out for publication, we read to him first. He can't tell us what or what not to write, but he has veto power over the publication of anything his father and I write about him. Usually he allows us to publish, sometimes with a few changes or omissions. In one article when he was eleven, he wrote a passionate short essay. By fourteen, like every teenager, he needed privacy as much as understanding, and allowed us to publish, "where kids won't see it"—grownups didn't count—and with no photographs that showed his face. In this book he has given permission for every word about him.

The importance of identifying the genius of 'attention different' children

Preface by George T. Lynn

In order for our children to grow up as free and productive human beings they (and we) need a *positive vision* of their lives and potential. My work as a psychotherapist for twenty-five years has taught me this fundamental reality about my own change process and that of my clients: you do not change yourself by focusing on your faults. You have to know your gifts and what you want for yourself in your life and you have to proceed toward this destiny with commitment. This principle of human development applies to both adults and children.

My first two books, *Survival Strategies for Parenting Your ADD Child*[1] and *Survival Strategies for Parenting Children With Bipolar Disorder,*[2] provided ways for parents and other caregivers to understand and help very difficult children who were difficult because of their brain chemistry—those who are "wild, odd, and oppositional." These two books described ways to survive the day-to-day stress of parenting our kids and to get them to adulthood in one piece. You have to have a foundation to grow on. You have to have a safe and strong launching pad.

This book provides strategies for daily survival, but its main focus is much wider than the first two works. It is about charting the journey after a successful launch. It is an attempt to answer questions I have received from many parents of very difficult children over the years of my practice: "What is in store for my child when he grows up?" "Is he doomed to failure or is there some hope?" "What is a realistic scenario for his positive development and what can I do to move him in that direction?" These are gravely serious questions that must be answered with respect, compassion, and accuracy. This book is an attempt to provide some answers.

The children I work with in my counseling practice instinctively respond well to hearing about the positive in themselves. They are instinctively able to be more resourceful in situations once they are told that they *can* be and are shown how. The journey begins in the doctor's office but does not end there. Appropriate medication to relieve a child's suffering and enable him to experience stability and cognitive focus is the first order of business, but it is only the first step.

Genius! provides a plan for nurturing the best qualities in your child. It is based on the premise that we all have an idiosyncratic contribution to make to the world and that we are guided to that gift by something called genius. It provides ways to sort out and strengthen your child's positive features without denying the presence of his challenges. It represents my evolution as a therapist from fighting fires to planning futures and my hope is that it provides inspiration for your own work as a parent in this direction!

Why the term "attention different"?

I use the term "attention different" (AD) to describe our wild, odd, and oppositional children, preferring to forego terms like "deficit" or "disorder." I will use standard diagnostic terms interchangeably with the term attention different throughout this book. But I favor the term attention different because it defines our children's perceptual styles more accurately than standard terminology, which connotes pathology. Using the AD moniker points to the fact that they *pay attention* differently than neurotypical children. Though their style of perception may cause them to have problems in the modern classroom, it is the classroom environment that is unnatural and "deficient" in terms of human learning, not the children who are sent there to learn.

- The attention deficit disorder (inattentive type) child is fixated on his inner reverie, his mind buzz, and the images that captivate him. His suffering is a result of his inability to follow what they are saying in class and tendency to be stuck in his inner world.

- In attention deficit hyperactivity disorder, the child's focus is caught by everything around him and his hyperactivity is a response to a search for the most interesting stimulus. He may be vexed by impulsivity and have difficulty staying on one topic long enough to complete the thought.

- The focal style of the child with Asperger syndrome is deep but not wide. He will learn all there is to know about his favorite subject but have very little common sense or frustration tolerance. He is also given to obsessive hyperfocus.

- In bipolar disorder, a child is swept away by the demands of his shifting emotional states. His intense focus on his own emotional and intuitive life may get him into trouble. He is inexperienced in the control of his own cognitive excitement.

- The child with Tourette syndrome is captivated by focus on his proprioceptive sensations or the heat of his overabundant energy. Fixated on his inner energy feelings, he may behave impulsively or not be attuned to people around him.

These peculiar ways of paying attention are distressing to parents and teachers who have to accomplish a task by the clock. Our children typically pay more attention to their own interests in the moment than to the requirements put on them by teachers. This does not make them deficient in any way. It makes them "inner directed." If they make it to adulthood, they will probably be rewarded for having the capacity for this kind of "resolve" or "determination." But first they have to make it through school.

In the following pages I suggest that there are some powerful positives that go with paying attention differently. There are things that you can do as a caregiver to take the quality of "deficit" out of this feature and make it an asset for your child.

Why I use the pronoun "he" and "him" throughout this book

You will notice that when I talk about AD children in the singular, I use the masculine pronouns "he" or "him." A note of explanation is useful here. I use this gender specifier as a convenience, not to indicate that all AD children are male. Depending on the pattern of the attention difference, there may be a higher percentage of boys than girls who share a specific diagnosis, or there may be a relative equality in gross numbers. The use of the masculine just makes the narrative less complicated.

The Spirit in the Bottle[1]

Once, long ago, a boy went into the forest with his father to cut wood. His father was poor and his axe was old. Late in the afternoon, when he stopped once again to sharpen it, he slipped and the axe gashed his leg.

"I'm fine, son," he told the boy. "But you must gather firewood. We'll have to rest here tonight before I can walk home on this leg."

So off the boy went, gathering wood. He looked for birds' nests too, for eggs for their supper. He saw a great oak and thought perhaps he could climb high enough to find a nest. But when he stepped onto a root, grasping a low branch, he heard a muffled voice. He looked among the roots and dug up a small half-buried bottle, covered in dark leather that was partly ripped off. There was a cork in the narrow neck.

The boy pulled aside the leather and peered into the bottle. "Oh!" cried a voice, and the boy jumped back, startled. But he didn't drop the bottle. He looked again and saw a small pale green spirit.

The spirit gazed mournfully through the glass into the boy's eyes and begged, "Release me kind sir I pray you, release me from the prison of this bottle!" The boy, without thinking, uncorked the bottle, and the spirit burst out, flashing with light, growing almost as tall as the oak.

"And now," cried the spirit, "to reward you I shall break your neck!"

"That's not a reward," the boy said to himself. "The spirit has tricked me! I'll trick him back.' He fell to his knees, holding up the little bottle.

"Oh spirit!" he said, "show me, one more time before I die, your great power! Show me how a spirit as enormous and powerful as you, can make yourself so small that you fit inside this trifle of a bottle."

19

"A trifle indeed," sniffed the spirit. "Watch and learn." He drew himself together, made himself as thin and small as the neck of the bottle, and dived in.

"*Thud!*" went the cork into the bottle. "*Smack!*" went the boy's hand, driving it in tight. "*Aii-ii!*" wailed the spirit, trapped again.

"Oh kind sir, let me out I beseech you! I can't live small forever! I will reward you with great riches, if you release me from my prison of a bottle!" The spirit wept and wrung his hands.

This time the boy thought carefully.

And then he pulled the cork.

Would you? Would you set free a pale green spirit who wanted to break your neck a minute ago? Would you trust this spirit, this time?

The boy did. He took a great risk.

"Ah!" breathed the Spirit, out in the air again, and this time no bigger than a sapling. "How wonderful it is to stretch! Thank you kind sir!"

"And my reward?" said the boy.

"Yes indeed, courage and kindness are rewarded," said the spirit, and gave the boy a thick white folded cloth, square, small enough to fit in his hand. "Touch this cloth to any wound, and the wound will heal. Touch it to metal and the metal turns to silver. This is a miraculous cloth. You should thank me."

"I thank you for not breaking my neck," said the boy, and ran through the forest to his father, with little firewood, no eggs, and the possibly miraculous cloth.

"Oh father!" said the boy, "let me heal you with the gift the spirit of the bottle gave to me," and he touched the cloth to his father's gashed leg.

"What is this!" exclaimed his father, eyes widening as he watched his leg heal, the flesh becoming smooth and whole.

"It is the gift for my courage and kindness," said the boy. Then he touched his father's axe with the cloth, and the blade turned to silver.

"Well," chuckled the father when he had heard the whole wonderful story. "My old axe won't chop any more wood, but it will still send you to school, my clever lad. You have great gifts for the world."

The boy grew up to be the most renowned doctor in three countries, known for his wisdom and kindness, and for his healing touch. And those closest to him knew him, too, as one who takes great risks, after careful thought.

Retold from the Grimm brothers

PART I

Understanding and nurturing the positive genius of your attention different child

Introduction

We know that something unknown, alien, does come our
way, just as we know that we do not ourselves make a dream
or an inspiration, but that it somehow arises of its own
accord.

Carl Jung[1]

The modern meaning of the term "genius," that it defines a person who scores in the upper 1 percent of the population on certain tests of intelligence (approximately IQ 135), has not been the meaning ascribed to the word for the past two millennia. The Greek philosopher Plato said that a person's genius is the spirit that guides expression of what he called the "seed self" or "daemon"—the "guiding force" of the child. Plato said that we come into life like an acorn, a tiny complete package of everything we have the potential to become. From this seed, our spirits may grow huge, full, and beautiful, as does an oak tree. It is our daemon, the great philosopher maintained, that guides our seed-selves to flowering. Later, in Greece, the term "muse" came into currency for describing a type of inspirational spirit that comes to us to guide us to our fulfillment, our growth from acorn to mighty oak.

Many cross-cultural myths carry the idea that one's genius is a kind of spirit guide. From the Grimm brothers' fairy tales, we get the story of "The Spirit in the Bottle." In this European myth, the boy finds the magic bottle at the base of a tree and opens it, releasing the spirit. The persona known as the "spirit" in the European versions of the story is called a "genie" in the Arabian version of the story of "The Genie in the Lamp."

I use these classical attributions to shape my meaning for this word: *genius is an unconscious pattern in the personality that guides a person toward the fulfillment of his particular potential*. Described this way, genius is one's creative guiding spirit, or genie.[2] Its character becomes known in a child's special interests, capabilities, vulnerabilities, and dream life.

The traditions of myth and language inform us that genius has two aspects: a positive aspect and a negative aspect. The spirit is initially malevolent and tells the boy he is going to kill him. But later, the spirit gives the boy a magic cloth that has the ability to both heal a wound and turn ordinary metal into silver. This is a beautiful metaphor for the place of genius in human beings: it has the ability to take us from suffering to healing, and from misery to prosperity, but it is hot material and must be handled with care and thought, properly contained, or it will take us over and destroy us.

Common characteristics and gifts of the genius of attention different children

In the pages that follow we will take a hard and loving look at the genius of the children we parent, the very "difficult" ones. In my counseling practice with attention different (AD) kids I am often struck by the perfection of the personality of the child who sits across from me. He or she may come in trailing a long list of diagnoses, but in the safety of counseling, the genius will show itself. It will reveal itself in what interests the child, what he is very good at doing, how he describes himself, and in the problem that brought him to me. Problems usually show the dark side of the child's genius.

There are some common patterns in the dark side of the genius of AD children. They tend to be tyrannical, oppositional, hyperfocused, obsessive, over-energized, socially inept, full of rage, and, at times, frankly psychotic. These aspects of the genius want it all and want it right now! Parents of AD children; those diagnosed with neuropsychiatric conditions such as attention deficit hyperactivity disorder (ADHD), bipolar disorder, autism and Asperger syndrome, or Tourette syndrome, know what it feels like to be banished because of the wild excess of the behavior of their children. Though they were once members of a social group, a church, a business community, or a neighborhood, their child's behavior has made them into social pariahs. They have been marginalized by the judgments of their community and extended family that they are to blame for their child's behavior. Friends drift away. People give them impromptu lectures on their parenting style. They come to dread social interaction and the disapproving looks of strangers. They become isolated. Their children also become social pariahs; lonely kids stuck playing on the computer all day. They are rejected for their inappropriate behavior by other children or exploited by those kids canny enough to recognize how easy it is to fool a kid who wears his heart on his sleeve.

The positive genius of our kids is proof of the fact that when trouble happens, human beings often develop compensatory strategies that are evolutionary *enhancements*. In my counseling practice I often get a strong sense that somehow, someway, a particular child, troubled as he is, is in the *right kind of trouble*. This is trouble caused by the presence of a certain genius that is both his guide and his demon. As much suffering as this genius causes, its presence also helps him work things out by teaching him that he has gone up the wrong alley in the maze and needs to go back to center. Suffering, far from being the enemy that threatens the child's life, is the soil in which his particular giftedness grows.

The positive genius of AD children is expressed idiosyncratically. Each child is different in the gifts that he has for the world. But there are also some powerful common denominators of AD genius. There are some characterological signatures that I have found to be very interesting.

The first of these is that AD children have *intolerance for absurdity*. They provide the function of *error detection* that "smart system" theorists such as Donald Michael say is essential to the growth of an organization or cultural group. They are our truth-tellers.

Growing up on the outside looking in, AD children enjoy freedom from "groupthink"—the tendency to identify with a group so tightly that you do not question the way things are. The AD child, being a chronic outsider, will make meaning of his life by casting a sharp eye on the absurd "common wisdom" of the group. AD children, as a rule, find school to be a most absurd experience and they do not suffer the situation quietly. They are truth-tellers.

Second, they *see deeply* into things that interest them. Each AD neurotype has its own way of doing this. A nine-year-old child with Asperger syndrome who is interested in the topic of artificial intelligence may have a college level knowledge of the issue. An adolescent challenged by bipolar disorder may show a powerful depth and skill in her poetry made richer by the experience of her mood swings. A twelve-year-old ADHD boy with a passion for motor cross racing may become a regional champion in his sport. True to his ADHD type, this boy feels the track conditions in his body and moves instinctively. The genius of these children expresses itself in the ability to be powerfully in contact with the object of its fascination.

Third, they have *wild creativity*. As a function of being who they are, and of being guided by their type of genius, AD kids cannot color between the lines. Their type of creativity begins as "what if?" questions and they are restlessly explorative. They are easily annoyed by propriety in this regard. Their creativity, in my clinical experience, tends to have different flavoring depending on the diagnosis, and to mobilize all aspects of the children to attain their personal goals.

The creative genius of children diagnosed with ADHD will show itself in talents in athletics, the performing and visual arts, and in entre-preneurial endeavors. Many of my ADHD adolescent clients are sports champions or team captains at the high school level. As performers or musicians they tend to be creative and innovative composers, and charis-matic on stage.

The creativity of children diagnosed with Tourette syndrome will show itself in their attacks on social norms and conventional ways of looking at beauty and invention. These features are seen in the music of Wolfgang Amadeus Mozart, who, according to eminent neurologist Dr. Ruth Bruun, showed many signs of having Tourette syndrome.[3] Mozart wrote music composed in his head that showed the total range of human experience, from joy to deep sadness. He was irreverent, oppositional, and wildly scatological. His raw creativity was matched by his constitu-tional wildness.

The creativity of children challenged by bipolar disorder is seen in the brilliant focus and intelligence they can put on whatever they find compelling. An American child challenged with bipolar disorder enjoys writing his own computer game in Japanese because this brings him closer to the technical and artistic foundation of the game's multimedia designers. Children on the bipolar disorder spectrum often have this powerful auditory–visual intelligence. Historically bipolar disorder is the condition most associated with artistic creativity. To quote the great (probably bipolar) poet Emily Dickinson, "Madness is divinist sense."[4] The "maddened" (bipolar) mind is close to the mind of God.

The genius of children who fit the Asperger syndrome diagnosis is usually seen in the child's enjoyment of a specialization in science, engineering, or the arts. Autistic writer Temple Grandin suggests that people with Asperger syndrome have a kind of creativity suited to their tendency to think in pictures.[5] They are not good at following conventional rules to get to their results, but are powerfully visionary and will get new ideas as "feeling-images." She profiles Dr. Albert Einstein as a person with Asperger syndrome, recounting that he developed the theory of relativity from a vision he saw while pondering the relationship between mass and energy. Parents of kids with Asperger syndrome tell me that their children are able to solve math problems in their head but cannot show on paper how they arrived at their results. The genius of children challenged by Asperger Syndrome does not like to bother itself with material not directly related to its principal interest.

Fourth, attention different children have prodigious skills for *purposeful action*. This capability is a natural result of having to apply so much will power just to get through each day. AD children can be tough, stubborn and powerfully goal-directed once they have identified what they want.

School does not give our children the venue to express their sense of purpose. Dr. James Hillman, the psychiatrist/philosopher who wrote the best-selling book *The Soul's Code: In Search of Character and Calling*, an examination of the personalities of the 100 most influential people in the twentieth century, contends that most of the eminent people in his study hated school.[6] Very little came easily to them. Their brilliance and quirkiness made the classroom an anathema to them—they could not stand it and so immediately came into conflict with teachers and other adults in their lives. The fact that their genius could not be constrained by the demands of school made them outlaws, and so being, made it necessary for them to survive by wits and grit. One gets a sense reading biographies of people like Thomas Edison (probably suffering from bipolar disorder or severe ADHD), Nikola Tesla (whose life showed the presence of obsessive-compulsive disorder), and Albert Einstein (Asperger syndrome), of this enormous purposefulness and refusal to be beaten down by circumstance and prejudice.[7]

Dr. Oliver Sacks, a neurologist who has devoted his life to articulating the gifts and interior lives of people with serious neurological disorders, writes:

> But it must be said from the outset that a disease is never a mere loss or excess—that there is always a reaction, on the part of the affected individual to restore, to replace, to compensate for and to preserve its identity, however strange the means may be.[8]

I believe that Dr. Sacks is seeing the genius in his interview subjects. He is seeing the ferocity of their will to live and express themselves despite their neurological limitations. He is glimpsing, at particular moments, their seed selves.

Aspects of the genius of AD children are:

- They are intolerant of absurdity, hypocrisy, and dishonesty.

- They possess wild and unconventional creativity and the ability to see deeply into what interests them.

- They are purposeful and persistent.

AD children provide the gift of renewing disturbance to the world

I attempt to get across two messages in this book. The first is that though a child's behavior may be extremely distressing right now, he can grow up to be a very successful adult if his genius is properly nurtured. I have watched quite a few of the AD kids I work with grow into young adulthood. I have seen them struggle. I am always happy to hear good news about them and I hear a lot of it. They rarely follow the beaten path. They suffer the difference. Many drama queens and drama kings number among them. But they survive and I am privileged to witness their genius beginning to flower.

My second message is that our cultural survival depends on having a plentiful supply of AD kids among us. We need their ability to disturb us as much as the natural ecology needs the force of hurricanes to stir up and renew the environment. The culture itself needs their dynamic and disturbing presence to survive and develop.[9]

AD children disturb the "way it's always been" and in so doing renew and heal human culture. The great systems physicist Ilya Prigogine gave us the idea that systems have a tendency to fall into entropy of their own accord and require disturbance to grow.[10]

The genius of AD children relishes disturbance. They shake things up and see the lie in the contention that "everything is under control." In reality, the natural state of things tends to be highly chaotic. It is the most disturbing people among us who name this lie that everything is or must be predictable. They teach us that the future does not come to us in a straight line, and that we would be better served to consider all the possible outcomes.

Attention different children are natural candidates for the role of system disturbers and it is in the classroom that they first express this gift. Our children are in good company when it comes to their ability to disrupt the world that their schoolteachers try to create for them. The lives of AD-probable people such as Victor Hugo, Vincent Van Gogh, Nikola Tesla, Thomas Edison, Winston Churchill, Albert Einstein, and Eleanor Roosevelt showed this dislike of school and the ability to disrupt things there.[11] This is august company indeed!

Hugo and Van Gogh have been described as manic-depressive. Tesla, the odd genius who discovered alternating current fits the obsesive-compulsive Asperger model. Edison fits the ADHD profile and may have been manic-depressive. Churchill showed signs of attention deficit disorder and dyslexia. Einstein's intense visual style and Asperger-like personality makes him a natural in the Asperger pattern. One of Albert Einstein's teachers said, "His presence in the classroom is disruptive and affects the other pupils."[12] Another said "In school he was called 'Biedermeier', which means a little dull, a little simple, a little unclever."[13] Eleanor Roosevelt's reclusive brilliance showed aspects of attention deficit disorder, depression, and high anxiety. The young lives of these system disturbers were filled with many of the problems seen in the lives of all AD children.

Each diagnosis has a specific gift for cultural survival

Just as there are common denominators of genius that unite all AD children, there are common denominators of giftedness for each diagnostic neurotype profiled in this book. Kids in each diagnostic pattern have specific gifts that all of us need to survive as a community and culture:

- One of the primary contributions of the genius of ADHD children is their ability to exercise creative leadership. Executives such as Fred Smith, who started Federal Express, or David Neeleman, founder of the innovative airline Jet Blue, are examples. Presidents John F. Kennedy and Bill Clinton both show aspects of ADHD in their leadership styles and private lives. Both Presidents valued the qualities of open-mindedness, innovative thought and the ability to learn from error, in the selection of advisers. Both leaders also showed impulsivity in their private lives and were embroiled in questionable extra-marital activities.

- Recent research into the genotype of those who led the great transcontinental migrations of the Asiatic peoples to the North American continent 40,000 years ago, reveal that many may have possessed the DRD4, or risk-taking gene, a common feature in the genetic makeup of people diagnosed with ADHD.[14]

- Dr. Simon Baron-Cohen, who researches the thinking style of children with *autism and Asperger syndrome*, contends that the special genius of these kids is found in their ability to conceptualize systems.[15] Through extremely intensive focus on the way a system works, be it a computer, locomotive, or river, they are able to understand and change its behavior. The human mind tends to foreclose on a solution and relax into the comfortable illusion that things are working as well as they can. We are fortunate to have those among us who look past conventional answers to see entirely new possibilities for function. This assertion runs counter to the idea that the "special interest" diagnostic of Asperger is a symptom. More correctly, in terms of its social function, a special interest is a direct manifestation of the autistic's genius.

- The autistic mind seeks perfection of pattern, and to get to that place it must understand all there is to know about the object of its interest. Einstein's statement that his life was about "Understanding the thoughts of God" points to his passion for learning about the cosmos as a system; how it all goes together and interacts.[16] Thomas Jefferson's life showed features of Asperger abysmal social skills, sensory defensiveness, and in his ability to conceptualize political systems.[17] The US Constitution, which he co-authored, is a masterpiece of visionary practicality. It is a guide for good government as well as a statement of enlightened political philosophy.

- Just as society requires the presence of the ADHD neurotype to spearhead change and lead it into the future, it requires the knowledge of science and natural systems that is brought to it by the autistic and Asperger neurotypes.

- The survival of culture requires the occasional burst of unorthodox brilliance provided by people who fit the diagnosis for *bipolar disorder*. Children with bipolar disorder are the ultimate warriors, those who challenge the status quo with the force of tremendous emotional energy and bravado. When leaders of the transcontinental migration wanted to know what was on the other side of the hill, they called on the bipolars to find out. It could have been a rampaging mastodon or an easy meal, but it would be the people who thrived on the most extreme emotional, physical, and social challenge and intensity who would do the scouting.

- Systems warp when pushed to their limits, and require great disturbance to change and heal. People with bipolar disorder are the ones who provide the brilliant bolts of energy that are required for this growth, and for the survival of culture. The footprints of bipolar people are seen in every great change that human culture has experienced, good or bad. Included in their ranks are the tyrants such as Stalin and Nero, the literati such as Ernest Hemingway and Emily Dickinson, and the artists such as Van Gogh and Jackson Pollack.

- People with *Tourette syndrome* bring huge energy to the task of exploration and invention. They are very physical people and are original thinkers. They tend to be obsessive in pursuit of their goals. In indigenous cultures, they are the shamans, the medicine people, the oddest of the odd, those who can communicate with spirits. As inhabitants of the Restless Explorer archetype (see page 58), their spirits can be luminescent with energy, unforgettable. They are attracted by the forbidden, by closed doors, and by the power of nature. They have a genius for auditory perception and sensation. This is seen in their symptoms (the swearing and animal noises) and their musical artistry—Mozart is included among them. The child with Tourette syndrome is a person who is comfortable living on the edges of social propriety.

- During the great intercontinental migrations, it would be the Touretters who would be called to provide the spiritual meaning of the journey, and to heal those on the path. It would be the Touretters who would provide the "what-if?" creativity, the very original way of looking at problems that would save the day as the journey proceeded through new geography. It would be the Touretters (such as the very Tourettic Dr. Samuel Johnson, author of the *Dictionary of the English Language*) who developed the language system of the people, and who provided the music.

If the four genotypes addressed in this book—ADHD, Asperger syndrome, bipolar disorder, and Tourette syndrome—had not been in our gene pool, we would have to invent them in order for our culture to survive! Each pattern of genius brings its own gift to the whole, its own vital ingredient. It is important for us, as parents, to keep in mind that as strange as is the life of our small "hot house flower," that life and the genius it possesses are essential for the survival of the whole (see Box I.1).

The difference between the genius of AD children and that of neurotypical children

Both AD children and neurotypical children have genius. But there is a difference in how neurotypicals and AD children express their special capabilities and delights.

Neurotypical genius shows itself as the direct expression of love in the spirit of the farmer or "grower." Neurotypicals give the same attention to detail as farmers give to the health of their crops. Living the steward archetype, the genius of neurotypicals protects and nurtures the system. Neurotypicals live in clock time. They accomplish things on schedule. They provide the center of the culture—the hearth and the harbor. They nurture new inventions. They build freeways. They apply their genius to making life more comfortable. They are able to plan ways to spread compassion in the world, such as is seen with many philanthropic organizations.

The genius of the AD child reflects the wounds that he carries by virtue of his atypical brain chemistry. Because he lives in a state of internal chaos, he is comfortable with states of extreme feeling and may be able to manage himself in crisis settings better than neurotypicals. Not being able to contain his inspiration, not being able to color between the lines, he will be the one with the iconoclastic ideas. Both types of genius are needed for a system to prosper. Their productive interaction begins with acceptance of the fact that the genius of the AD child has a lot to offer to the mix! One type settles, the other pioneers.[18] Both types are needed.

A word about social eminence and genius

Looking in this book at the lives of famous people, the reader might get the impression that genius is always expressed as a "great contribution to humanity." It is not my intention to give this impression. Genius is simply the guiding spirit. Living life whole and healthy is the destination. Each AD child will reach this goal in his own way and in his own time. Genius is not measured by accomplishment. I use examples from the lives of famous people as a literary convenience. Famous people, in their joys and suffering, teach us lessons about their neurotypes. This does not mean that being like them is the only way to achieve genius. It just means they are exemplars of genius in a certain way. In bas-relief, they reveal the patterns of genius and in so doing help us spot these same patterns in our own children. An AD child, becoming an adult, may realize his purpose in life in pragmatic service to the community—as a police officer or garbage collector. Or he may enjoy a low-level scientific job and devote

Box I.1 In the Crucible: Blessed are the cracked

Blessed are the cracked,
> *for they shall let in light.*

Anonymous

I'm sitting by the window in Starbucks, watching my son stride stiffly across the street. He walks a little hunched, the dark waves of his shaggy hair falling over his face. As usual he is smoking. He is dirty and unshaven. His sweat pants are two sizes too big. People stare, most of them discreetly. Greg hates these stares. He is twenty.

"I'm a regular person," he says. He wants to be known for who he is and sees no need to look or act like everybody else. He can't see why he should take time away from his computers to shower and change his clothes more than every week or two.

His voice is a low rich monotone. His beautiful face has little expression. His gaze is fixed, and he has a hard time making eye contact. But when he tightens his focus and turns that gaze on you, you are transfixed.

Greg is diagnosed with high-functioning autism, Asperger syndrome, occasional psychosis, Tourette syndrome, obsessive-compulsive disorder, non-verbal learning disabilities. He has an IQ that can't be properly measured and a writing style that is terse, funny, informative, and sophisticated. Anyone who talks to him is intrigued.

But walking across the street he looks like danger, like the oddballs mothers warn their kids to stay away from. Last year when he was unmedicated and psychotic I was afraid of him, though he could sometimes pass as a regular teen. Now, properly medicated, he is no longer psychotic and I am no longer afraid. But the meds stiffen his muscles and bring out his autistic features and he looks odd. Everyone at school, on the street, in the malls and theaters, the beaches and bookstores and parks we go to, everyone looks at him askance.

his weekends to invention and hanging with his "weird science" buddies. The important thing is that he gets a fair shot at realizing his potential, whatever it is. And the reality is that his contribution as an AD adult will be exceptional and unusual, whatever vocation he chooses.

Creating a "field of nurturing" to bring out the positive genius in your AD child

The "master game" for you as a parent of a child like this is to keep the child alive and on track emotionally until he is old enough to have the observer perspective (see page 38) and resourcefulness to take care of himself. This is a doable task, but a difficult and thankless one. The performance of it will take you through your own rite of passage—you will meet your own demons of disappointment, rage, and futility.

You will be required to behave in extraordinary ways, both to shield your child from the revenge of culture, and to help him develop his strengths so that he does not fall into self-destructive behavior or depression. My experience as a psychotherapist informs me that there is a way to heal the wounding of extraordinary brain biology, so that it becomes a force for forming the child into an exceptionally positive human being—one who derives the full benefit of his particular genius. I have been privileged to observe this "map" for the unfolding of genius in the lives of the amazing families who come to my counseling practice. Though in most cases it is clear that medication is needed to maintain stability, it is the quality of the child's experience with people close to him at home and school that make the difference. If certain criteria are not present, the positive effects of even the best medication may be undermined. In fact, medication is only part of the solution. The ecology of the child's life itself must be carefully managed so that his potential is released.

In order to accomplish this task you need to approach it with a certain attitude and certain child-rearing practices. I have carefully noted the practices of the parents who seem to prevail in this great struggle with brain chemistry, and encoded them into a personal system I term "the field of nurturing."

The seven criteria of the field of nurturing

The field of nurturing is a social and emotional context that gives the AD child a positive sense of who he is and what he can accomplish, as well as the confidence to deal with the more exhausting aspects of his atypical neurology. It denotes a social and emotional environment in which caregivers:

1. recognize the AD child's genius and understand how genius expresses itself in this child's symptoms and gifts

2. are attuned to the child

3. give the child an explanation of his difference, a Great Story (see page 84) that moves him forward

4. provide him with a community and mentors in his life

5. attend to physical factors, including medication

6. help the AD child remember how to behave resourcefully

7. practice high-level wellness in their own lives.

I sum up these criteria as a checklist in Appendix I and invite you to assess the absence or presence of these features in your own family. I approach this task with a great deal of humility—I am not a perfect parent and would not score perfectly on the checklist. But this kind of instrument is a useful way of looking at the map for change. You may be halfway or two-thirds or nine-tenths of the way there! It is useful to get a picture of where you have been and where you are going.

Caregiver heal thyself

In chapters 7, 8 and 9, I discuss the last criterion in the Field of Nurturing, which is that caregivers take care of themselves on emotional, spiritual, and physical levels. In these chapters I suggest that you, as a caregiver, must have ways to express your *own* genius and realize your *own* purposes if you are going to contain your child's willful, brilliant, self-centered genius. Parenting an AD child isn't for wimps and you need to be strong in body and heart to deal with the challenge.

These chapters are written from the heart. I live these chapters as the father of a profoundly involved, brilliant, and spiritually beautiful attention different son. And I pass along not only the relevant research and strategies for taking care of yourself as a parent but also my personal experience of what has worked for my wife and co-author, Joanne Barrie Lynn, and me in our task of raising Gregory. Gregory has approved all the narrative in this book about his life. Once again, I acknowledge his gift to me—the wisdom, brilliance, meaning, and purpose that there is, potentially, in every child's life, no matter how odd his behavior may be.

Keep your eye on the prize: observer perspective

Before describing the field of nurturing, it is important to take a moment to identify your immediate goal as the parent of an AD child. This is to create as many moments of *observer perspective* as possible in your child's life. Observer perspective is the ability for him to *see himself in the context of his situation*, to own his part in the problem, and understand how others fit into the picture. This is the "Aha!" moment expressed by the child as "I see the consequences of my behavior." It is the achievement of observer perspective that opens the road to your child's positive genius (see Figure I.1).

Observer perspective: the ability to see ourselves in context

I have seen this quality in the most "profoundly involved" kids. Invariably the development of observer perspective starts small. You have to be able to notice the little events that tell you something good is happening:

- He says "thank you" for some kindness.
- He apologizes for some mean thing he said.
- He offers to make restitution for something he has done.
- He accepts the need for medication.
- He shows kindness to animals or people.

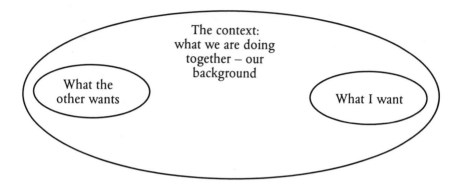

Figure I.1 The context: what we are doing together

Your search, as a caregiver, for markers of genius and evidence of observer perspective may be difficult. The obnoxious and destructive behavior of AD children exerts a powerful influence on how we see them. Despite the fact that the task is daunting, in practical terms the only way to help a child gain observer perspective is to attend to that small part of his psyche that contains his positive genius and to nurture that part one step at a time. It is my intention in the chapters that follow to show you how to "blow on the coals" of observer perspective in your child's personality so that more and more of his daily life expresses the broader view of life that this perspective affords.

CHAPTER 1

First criterion

Caregivers recognize the AD child's genius

I am the bird that flutters against your window in the morning,
and your closest friend, whom you can never know,
blossoms that light up for the blind.

Rolf Jacobsen, from "Guardian Angel"[1]

Six ways to recognize the genius of your AD child

The Greeks believed that one's daemon has an intention all its own, separate from the rest of the personality. A modern writer, psychotherapist Robert Moore, author of *Care of the Soul*, suggests that you can directly consult this aspect of your self, this personal guardian, for advice in times of crisis or when you need inspiration.[2] If you apply this idea in your relationship with your attention different (AD) child, you begin to better understand his behavior and motivation. His genius is the Prime Mover in his life and once you know its pattern, you are in the position to work with it to strengthen your child's personality and resourcefulness. The pattern of an AD child's genius, the face of his daemon, may be seen from six perspectives:

1. The "wound" of atypical neurology reveals a child's genius.

2. Study your child's early interests to glimpse his genius.

3. Understand your own childhood passions and challenges to discern your child's genius.

4. Understand you child's fears to identify his genius.

5. Observe your child's developmental history to identify his genius.

6. Imagine the AD child's archetype to get a sense of his genius.

The "wound" of atypical neurology reveals a child's genius

The neurological "deficits" identified in the child's diagnosis are necessary if he is to realize the benefits of his particular genius. As he struggles with the negative features of his diagnosis, he develops certain features of character and compensations that are part of his giftedness. Thus the "wound" of the deficit is required to grow the genius to its full potential. The idea that a wound is needed to liberate potential in people is as old as human history and is one of the most common themes of mythology. In the ancient Greek stories of Hercules, the Arthurian legends, and the modern genre of movies such as *Star Wars*, a heroic figure is wounded and that wound becomes the basis for a quest. First there is a withdrawal from civilized life, then a series of challenges that must be overcome. There is the return, at the end, to society, success, nobility, and redemption. Myth tells us that the wound allows us to see things that we could not see before. And this new perspective always lifts us higher in our lives and our potential. When you consider it, something like a wound is required for every stage of growth, beginning with the "wound" that the spermatozoon inflicts on the ovum, opening to new life.

The French verb "to wound" is *blesser*. There is a similar derivation in Old English – the root of the word being "blod" (blood). So we see that there is an ancient idea that a wound is needed to let in the energy necessary to make us whole. Our question becomes how can we, as parents of AD children, bring our kids up so that the wounds they carry strengthen them? What conditions can we set up to give our children the best chance of realizing their personal genius?

Looked at this way, a wound to the brain, such as the neurobiology that a child inherits, may either hobble his ability to be successful or be a force that strengthens him in the struggle—a kind of psychological "isometric" that equips him to meet the challenges that he faces. The child's behavior may be so violent or disruptive that it overwhelms the resources of those who love him. Or the right conditions may be present and the destructive force of the wound is turned to the child's advantage. Modern medicine does a good job of attacking symptoms in neuropsychiatrically involved children. But it is a mistake to believe that once symptoms are quelled, the child becomes neurotypical or normal.

For some AD children, the wound is a requirement for expression of the gift. Take the example of the great nineteenth-century inventor, Nikola Tesla. Tesla, as noted earlier in this book, was a contemporary of Edison. Tesla discovered alternating current and invented the induction motor. He also experienced obsessions, hallucinations, phobias, and strange states of mind. Writer Clifford Pickover describes Tesla's boyhood:

> To escape his tormenting dreams and visual weirdness, Tesla would spend hours creating imaginary mental worlds. In these parallel universes, he would make new friends, go on wonderful journeys...
>
> When it came to the construction of sophisticated devices, he often performed a "virtual reality" simulation in his mind's eye without ever touching a workbench. Tesla wrote "When I get an idea I start at once building it up in my imagination. I change the construction, make improvements and operate the device in my mind. It is absolutely immaterial to me whether I run my turbine in my thought or test it in my shop. I even note if it is out of balance."[3]

Tesla's probable wound was that his psyche inhabited that strange place between Asperger syndrome and schizophrenia. This wound was required for release of his gifts into the world. If antidepressant medication such as Prozac, or antipsychotic drugs such as Abilify, were available in the 1890s, we may never have had the benefit of alternating current!

True to the form of genius inspired by a wound, there are also negative impacts from the gift. In Tesla's case, his probable Asperger syndrome carried a naïveté that contributed to his letting Edison fool him into giving his patent for alternating current to Edison to run his dynamos. Edison had earlier promised Tesla $50,000 for the task and after it was delivered, reneged on his word, telling Tesla (a native of Serbia) "Tesla, you don't understand our American humor."

THE AD WOUND GIVES BIRTH TO GENIUS IN MODERN AD KIDS: MARK, ANDY, AMY, AND CARLA

Moving from Tesla, the nineteenth-century Asperger genius, we come to Mark, an eleven-year-old modern-day boy also diagnosed with Asperger syndrome. A central feature of his diagnosis is the presence of a "special interest." Mark, as is the case with many Asperger kids, has an activity that consumes most of his energy during the day and to which he relates obsessively. An Asperger child might be into railroad trains, or computers, or heating systems, or bugs. Mark is into *blood*.

Though he has few friends at school (who wants to talk about blood?), Mark did not voice loneliness when we discussed his social situation in counseling. Talking about emotions (another thing children with Asperger detest) took too much time away from talking about blood. He could give me statistics on blood diseases, what caused them, and how they are treated medically. He loved science and biology and was anxious to complete several applications of his theories with regard to the prevention of blood diseases on his computer at home. He was very good at doing the math required for his projects in his head, but could not show his work at school.

Mark's calling is probably medicine. Probably research. This is probably the arena into which he will direct his guiding spirit. Now he has other problems.

He has very poor social skills, is highly anxious, and tends to be a whiner. His mother hates his whining. His affect is flat. He talks in a monotone, delivering little lectures about things that interest him, and he is not interested in engaging others in his topics. You do not get much emotional response from him. And he needs extremely predictable routine in his life. Just getting from class to class is an issue for him.

Mark's primary challenge is that he has a difficult time maintaining continuity. His short-term memory for faces, emotional states, places, and what one is supposed to do in these places, is abysmal. His special interest gives him continuity. "Yesterday I talked about blood," he thinks to himself. "Today I talk about blood." This sense of continuity keeps at bay the terror that he is about to forget who he is and what he is doing. This is the central terror of many children with AD cognitive states. And as annoying as it is, the expression of his genius for blood helps him stay sane.

Not until adolescence will more of his personality emerge. He will still be clueless as to others' emotional states, but his character will come out and he will be accepted as he is, an odd genius.

His "symptoms" are aspects of both the wound and his genius. Mark is most happy doing the work he loves to do, blood work. He will be happiest around others interested in this topic, and with this community his genius will be expressed tenfold, his gift powerfully manifested in the world. Some research suggests that all great scientists are obsessive-compulsive, as Mark is. When people obsess, their uncomfortable, "dysfunctional" state of mind is the only way to generate the heat necessary for the breakthrough of new ideas.

It is understandable that the great commotion of Mark's Asperger syndrome labels it as an enemy, a sickness, and a disorder. Indeed, genius does challenge our expectations and hopes for our children and our deepest fears. It is a formidable force in a child's personality, but not a malevolent force if understood and guided. If you see the situation in all its complexity, you see the presence of the child's genius right from the beginning, and you realize that the understanding and acceptance of this genius, and how it pushes the child's life, is essential to his healing. Healing in this sense is defined as the process of becoming whole—to be able to deal successfully with challenges to stability and expand one's life joyfully into the world. In this sense disorder gives rise to healing.

There are other examples of how the genius of AD children is fueled by their symptoms.

Andy is twenty years old. You would never know it to look at this drop-dead handsome kid, but most of his life he has suffered from a painful feeling of not really belonging to the human race, of being a total outsider. He is diagnosed with bipolar disorder. This feeling is common among adolescents with this diagnosis.

In the past couple of years, however, things have been changing in Andy's life toward the positive. He has become a tour guide for high school groups traveling to Mexico. He discovered on a trip south with friends around age 18, that his wound, the feeling of being an outsider, has equipped him to be the ultimate traveler, guide, and raconteur. His insecurity has made him an able social chameleon. He can fit in anywhere and is totally in his element not knowing what the next day will bring.

Amy, 15, a poet with bipolar challenges, shows the promise of becoming a very successful writer. She is troubled by restlessness and feels a powerful loneliness. She alienates other children with her explosive behavior and violent mood shifts. She is terrified of her own emotional states, not knowing what kind of a person she will be tomorrow. But when Amy is writing she does not feel these emotional states. In fact she experiences joy and a sense of flow with people and things around her. Thus the anxiety that is her central symptom pushes her relentlessly toward personal success and personal healing through the practice of her art.

Andy and Amy are "born to the breed" of persons with bipolar disorder—they show typical gifts as well as the typical challenges spoken of by Dr. Kay Jamison, a leading authority on bipolar disorder.[4] Jamison contends that mania can be conducive to creativity because it allows afflicted individuals to work long hours without sleep, to focus intensely, to experience a variety of emotional and cognitive states, and to make bold assertions without fear of the consequences. In this sense, the disorder *is* the genius.

Dr. Alice Flaherty, a neurologist and writer on the subject of why some people are *compelled* to write, suggests that bipolar disorder and temporal lobe epilepsy are conditions seen in the best writers in human history.[5] I would echo her contention from my experience as a psychotherapist. Almost all of the children I work with who are diagnosed with bipolar disorder are prolific writers or visual artists.

Finally there is Carla, a bright ten-year-old diagnosed with Tourette syndrome. True to her type, she is obsessive, and in her case she obsesses about the orderliness in her room. Everything is lined up perfectly. She helps set the table for dinner and insists on everything being exactly the way it was last time. Everything must also be very clean! If her parents counter her obsessionality in any way she has a huge meltdown.

But there is another side to Carla. She has an eye for art and loves to visit art shops and galleries. She always finds the most interesting pieces in the establishment and is able to discuss why she likes each find. The wound of her obsessive compulsion moves toward her genius and powers it in a way. Her genius takes the archetypal form of "The Aesthetic" or "Artist." She loves clean form, balance, that which gives the eye a peaceful feeling. Her genius might lead her to art or design or a similar vocation. And she will probably be as meticulous and annoying with her obsessionality when she grows up as she is right now. In Carla's case and in all the children described in this section, the "defect" or inherited wound of the child is part of his or her basic genetic resource kit. The child's genius includes the wound and the gift as bone and muscle, inseparable from each other.

Box 1.1 In the Crucible: "Tide Pool"

I find Greg's genius everywhere, as a mother does. He is deeply curious and intelligent. I've delighted in his exploration of the natural world since he was four, examining crabs and starfish on the wild Pacific coast.

Tide Pool

Crabs eat voraciously, pinching bits
from other creatures' corpses
to stuff their hidden mouths,

stalked eyes always on the hunt.
When I drop a shucked mussel
my son scrambles

sideways around the barnacled rim
of this startling cosmos,
small avid hunter,

stuffing his eyes.

Study your child's early interests to glimpse his genius

Genius shows itself at an early age for most AD children and gives us a signature of its presence. I remember Gregory, sitting at age three in front of a phone outlet with a screwdriver clutched in his little hand. He sat there for more than an hour staring at the outlet and then, as if on signal, attacked it with the tool. At the last minute, we prevented him from destroying the outlet in the "interest of science." Now Gregory is heavily into computers and most fascinated by how they move data from one place to another. His odd behavior as a toddler was a clear precursor to the expression of his genius for computers seventeen years later. Not only was he interested in their mechanics but also in the power that came from moving energy and data efficiently. His actions as a three-year-old were a specific expression of his genius.

Box 1.2 In the Crucible: Locks and lies

What is prohibited is what attracts Greg, and he can't stay away from it. When he sees a password or locked door, he can't rest until he gets it open, or finds out what is on the other side of it. Since he was twelve he has been careful about his hacking skills, and we've learned to trust him to respect all locks on all doors. He in turn is learning to trust that we will not unnecessarily keep him from exploring what he wants to explore. It's always a dynamic discussion.

When Greg hears a lie, he *has* to expose it. When he has a point to make he hammers away at it, insisting that you agree with him. He splits hairs, getting that point across, until his truths are half-truths, quarter-truths, an infinity of splintered reality. We bring him back to whatever shared truth we can find, and work from there to the point he wants to make.

Dr. James Hillman's study of 100 of the most eminent people in the twentieth century leads him to believe that the genius of these people showed itself in their fears and talents as very young children.[6] He cites many examples, among them Golda Meir, Prime Minister of Israel, who led her country to a thundering victory in its war with the Arab states in 1973. As a child growing up in Milwaukee, Meir, at nine years of age, organized a protest group against the purchase of expensive schoolbooks for children who were too poor to afford them. At age eleven she rented a hall and raised money to stage a meeting proclaiming the virtues of socialism for Yiddish people. This strange, rather isolated girl, was often criticized for her lack of academic success but she was able to move large groups of people through her speeches, which she said came to her "in her head" without preparation.

The parents of AD children tell me that their kids never enjoyed the toys other children liked. They wanted real things to play with and often these real things hinted at a future passion. Hillman describes the experience of pioneering geneticist Barbara McClintock, who won the Nobel Prize for her research. At the age of five she asked her father for tools to use in the laboratory. She was angry that he did not get tools an adult would use but rather those that fit into her little hands. She writes, "They were not the tools I wanted. I wanted real tools, not tools for children."

There are many other examples of this early emergence of special ability. Mozart, who Dr. Ruth Bruun believes meets diagnostic criteria for Tourette syndrome, was playing the piano at age three.[7] Nikola Tesla was fascinated with flying as a young boy and conducted several experiments, which involved jumping off the roof of his house, or the roof of a nearby barn, wearing fabricated wings. He survived these experiments but one cannot help wondering if they contributed to the grief he experienced from abnormal brain function later in his life—his obsessions, delusions, hallucinations, and strange sensory states.

Lecturing frequently to audiences of parents of AD children, I am given the opportunity to hear from them many accounts of how the genius of their kids is already showing itself. In the same breath, many of these parents anguish over the lack of acceptance of their children at school, and over the severe problems their kids have at home in regulating their dispositions, rage, tendency for hyperfocus, and oppositionality. It is as if the body of the AD child cannot yet contain either their gifts, or the pressures they experience from their own guiding spirits, and thus come into severe conflict with the people around them.

Understand your own childhood passions and challenges to discern your child's genius

The lives of these people also give us evidence that the acorn does not fall far from the tree. All the attention different conditions described in this book carry strong genetic imprints. Yet given this essential similarity in character, pushed by genetics, each child has a path all his own.

As dysfunctional as an AD child appears in the school years, there is an excellent chance that, given the right conditions, he will transmute his issues to grow into a brilliant life. I base this contention on my observation of the parents of my young clients. I find that more often than not, these parents describe themselves as having the same challenges as youngsters that their children now have. However successful a parent is, be he a prince or a pauper, in that parent's life I see the seed of genius for the child and the pathways that lie in potential for the child.

There is an eight-year-old boy diagnosed with attention deficit hyperactivity disorder (ADHD) who is having major difficulty in school because of his hyperactivity. The father, a successful executive, tells me (I have heard this remark many times) "He is just like I was when I was a kid." The boy, as gifted a visual-intuitive as his dad, is already beginning to find ways to escape the scolding from his teachers for his dreaminess and inattention—he looks at them blankly while running replays of movies he has seen in his mind, from the first scene to the last scene, *with dialogue*. The boy's genius for action and imagination is clear. Will he take a path to self-destruction or become a brilliant business leader, explorer, or paradigm challenger, as did his dad?

There is the single father of a ten-year-old girl who is diagnosed with Asperger syndrome. The man is a successful computer engineer who, like many parents of Asperger children, appears to possess the same patterns as his daughter, of flat affect, interest in machines and ideas, and intense observational ability. She is in trouble at school because of a dangerous lack of pragmatics and the inability to understand the emotional states of other kids. And, with all these issues, she has an intense interest in medical equipment. She continually attempts to enroll other kids in playing doctor with her (often to the point of being very annoying) so that she can practice the use of the equipment she has studied in medical books.

The father sees himself in his daughter. With all her problems, she also shows the gifts in her aptitude for science, mechanical ability, and imagination that may allow her to make a powerful contribution to society when she grows up. Because of learning from his own suffering, the father is able to get the right teachers into his daughter's life. She will not have to experience the pain he went through as a child.

Understand your child's fears to identify his genius

The great German poet Rainer Maria Rilke said, "Our deepest fears are like dragons guarding our deepest treasure."[8] The observation that fear disguises genius bears true to my experience of working with AD children.

There is Tom, a twelve-year-old boy diagnosed with generalized anxiety disorder. Tom often resists going to school because he cannot deal with the taunts and insults of bullies. Despite his parents' and teachers' counsel to ignore the things the other kids say, he constantly goes into meltdown when tormented by them. He is greatly anxious and maintains that certain words have special power to hurt him.

Despite his fears, Tom is accomplished in the martial art, Kendo, Japanese sword fighting. He delivers a slight bow whenever he enters my counseling room. After he decided I could be trusted, he began talking about his desire to live in Japan and study Kendo and meditation there. Tom finds great satisfaction in the premium that Japanese culture puts on personal honor. It is understandable that he is drawn to a culture that prizes this quality and that he is repelled by his school experience, which delivers little but humiliation in social settings and absurdity in the classroom. I wonder what his contribution will be if he is able to grow up without becoming severely depressed and anxiety-ridden. Perhaps he has something to teach his own people in the United States about honor, a quality that is often absent from our schools. Still, Tom's emotional life is endangered by his isolation. His genius must be recognized and nurtured if he is to survive.

There is Jack, a seven-year-old whose mother brings him in because he refuses to sleep in his own bed and devises an endless stream of ways to jump into bed with his parents. In session, Jack and I hit it off. It turns out that he is an avid historian of the Second World War. He loves to talk about all things military, bringing in facts and memorabilia about famous battles and important warriors and military leaders. Such strange behavior from such an anxious boy. Delving deeper into his psyche, I notice that he is actually quite interested in joining the Coast Guard when he grows up. This is a positive application of the Warrior Archetype (see page 57), toward protection not destruction. Jack, like many children who aspire to the Warrior Archetype shows high anxiety. Is his genius revealed by his anxiety? Does he in some way anticipate the stress, loneliness, even terror that must come to those who choose the path of the Warrior? Does his need to sleep in his parents' bed represent a resourceful attempt to take comfort now, while he can, before the important work of his life begins?

There are historical precedents for this idea that a child's genius shows in his fears. We find interesting parallels to the cases described above:

- Erwin Rommel, the German general, probably the best and most inspirational leader Germany fielded in the Second World War, was an extremely anxious boy, known as the "white bear" because he was so pale, dreamy, and slow of speech. Little Erwin would often avoid school because the other boys would tease him about his timidity. Was some aspect of his personality anticipatory of the horror of mechanized warfare that he would experience leading the German Army against Montgomery and Patton in North Africa years later? Was this same aspect noted in his sense of honor, a sense that implicated him in an attempt to kill Hitler, and that Hitler recognized in eventually demanding that Rommel should commit suicide (which he did) to remove him as a threat to the German leader?

- Robert Peary, who walked the Arctic wastes until he "discovered" the North Pole, was the only son of a widow. He stayed close to his mother, at home in the yard, to evade boys who called him skinny and teased him about his fearfulness.

Was his anxiety about leaving home a harbinger of his place in history as one of the world's great explorers?[9]

- Ingmar Bergman, the pioneering Swedish filmmaker, often confused fantasy and reality. Going to the circus as a boy of seven, he fell in love with a beautiful bareback rider, named her 'Esmeralda,' and concocted a story that she loved him, and that his parents were selling him to the circus where he would join her in her act. His classroom teacher, on hearing of his fantasy, thought him so deranged that she publicly humiliated him for it. Bergman also developed a longing to possess a 'cinematograph,' an early version of the motion picture projector. He states, on seeing *Black Beauty* through the device, "To me it was the beginning. I was overcome with a fever that has never left me. The silent shadows turned their pale faces toward me and spoke in inaudible voices to my most secret feelings." Were the peculiar delights of this strange boy evocative of his contribution later in his life? Did his genius ride with Esmeralda?[10]

- Samuel Johnson, one of the foremost inventors and humorists of the nineteenth century (he is the author of the *Dictionary of the English Language*), had to overcome a powerful obsessive-compulsive disorder and incurable hypochondria. He could not step through a doorway without performing a series of bizarre rituals. Johnson showed a number of other behaviors, which were evocative of the tics seen in Tourette syndrome. And he possessed a genius for words and the auditory domain, which is characteristic of the syndrome.[11]

- Charles Darwin suffered from an anxiety disorder and panic attacks. Coming back from his famous trip to explore the islands off South America, he developed physical symptoms such as heart palpitations, light-headedness, shortness of breath, nausea, and vomiting. He also suffered from severe anxiety and hysterical crying. These features were evident in Darwin as a younger man, before his famous expedition, and moved him toward the humanitarian protection of animals as a member of the antivivisectionist movement in England.

Darwin expressed dismay that his theory of evolution would offend his close friends, many of them devout Christians. Darwin's anxiety disorder made him a virtual recluse for the last years of his life but may also have been an essential aspect of his gift. He wrote at one point: "Ill health has annihilated several years of my life but has not saved me from the distraction of society." Research suggests that if it had not been for his illness, evolution might not have become the all-consuming passion that resulted in *On the Origin of Species.*[12]

Contending that a child's peculiarities shape his genius is not to say that he is "predestined" in a certain way. I have no evidence from my own practice for any theory of predestination. In fact, my experience as a psychotherapist indicates that people create their future one decision at a time. No one can say that this is the way one "ought to go," or that a person is born with a specific vocation that is held in the "mind of God" for the person. I am saying that genetics, heredity, and a child's life circumstances shape the expression of his gifts and may, in fact, be essential parts of the gift itself.

I am also saying that all of these factors may be part of the pattern we call the child's genius, which is both an expression of these energies and something quite different, quite apart. It is the muse that brought certain visions to Tesla and certain music to Mozart. It is the psychic "entity" (the daemon) that has an interest in a specific outcome for their lives.

Observe your child's developmental history to identify his genius

Dr. Carl Jung said that we achieve meaning by wrestling courageously with certain questions that confront our existence. The cosmos does not say, "Do exactly this with your life," but instead gives you predicaments to deal with; personal problems to solve that are yours and yours only. Jung was the first of many wisdom-bringers on this topic to observe that the "destination is the journey,"—that we become more conscious by deliberately confronting the problems that face us in life, and that the process of doing so is, in fact, how we become more whole. Jung termed this result "individuation."[13]

Between the ages of two and four, the child must answer the question "What are the limits of others over me?" This is the great stage of "no saying," the so-called "terrible twos." In the elementary school years, the child must face the question "How can I open my little world to accept others and interact with them safely?" This is the time of learning to say, "yes," which follows the time of learning to say "no." At around age twelve, the child must ask: "How do I fit into the world? What kind of a person am I?" At around age seventeen, the adolescent must ask: "Do I choose to be like my parents, establish a different value system, or put the question of my identity on hold until later in my life?"

If a child is hampered in the resolution of these questions by virtue of his neurobiology, he will suffer developmental delays in the expression of who he is and will show instability in his character, but his genius will still try to find a way to express itself. Oftentimes, genius seems to "ride bareback" (to borrow from Bergman's story above) on the child's particular personality, and use his idiosyncratic neurobiology to express itself.

One child may experience great difficulty saying "no" because his sense of self is neurologically underdeveloped. He does not have the executive function to pay attention long enough to get a sense of his own power. The term "executive function" describes the brain's ability to pay attention and make good decisions. Poor executive function is characteristic of ADD. So "no saying" continues through the elementary school years leading to a diagnosis of oppositional defiant disorder. Later in life, when executive function "grows in" (brain research indicates that the brain keeps developing this ability through a person's twenties), the experience this child has in opposing authority may be expressed in his choice of occupation as a successful trial lawyer or labor negotiator.

If a child cannot say "yes," cannot let himself experience love and the affirmation of others, a powerful loneliness may set in which will move him to seek ways later in life to connect with nature and others. He may evolve into the type of person who makes great discoveries in science because this is the way he gives to others and connects with them.

Another child may not be able to resolve these essential questions of "yes," "no," belonging, and identity, and may grow into his adolescence with very little sense of himself and who he is. This child may be hampered by the deep brain dysrhythmia seen in bipolar disorder. His internal sense of what is appropriate and inappropriate is thrown off. He lacks "boundaries," and is extremely impulsive. This child may be diagnosed with bipolar disorder and will find himself screaming into his adolescence, all speed and no control. This great instability may contribute to the child's ability to live in extremes of temperament and states of sensory deprivation or extreme stimulation. His genius will ride these features and later on express itself in his contribution as a writer, poet, artist, business mogul, or superstar.

Imagine the AD child's archetype to get a sense of his genius

In my book *Survival Strategies for Parenting Children With Bipolar Disorder*, I introduced the idea that the characters of attention different children often fit specific "archetypes."[14] The term "archetype" is based on the Greek to mean "the original model" or "the perfect example." Carl Jung used the term to describe essential aspects of the human personality. For example, decisiveness and wisdom taken together were said to form the "King" archetype. Love and leadership working together form the "Queen" archetype. Love, caring, and passion are qualities seen in the "Lover" archetype.

Writer Thom Hartmann's apt description of ADHD as a throwback to the "Hunter" personality cued me to look for archetypes in other conditions on the AD spectrum. Hartmann believes that the ADHD Hunter archetype may be a throwback to the time in human culture when hunters were vital to the survival of the tribe.[15]

The use of archetypal description helps us see the positive as well as the negative aspects of the genius of an AD child. Using the archetypal device is one way to identify the daemon in your AD child quite directly. A child's archetype may be seen as the "default setting" in his personality that gives him certain hopes, fears, motivations, challenges, and gifts. Jung said that archetypes spring from the "collective unconscious" in that they are seen quite similarly in all cultures. All cultures have mythological representations of "King" energy or "Lover" energy or "Trickster" energy. The individual forms of genius develop in children in these grand patterns.

Here are some examples of archetypes, ordered by diagnosis, of attention different children:

- I call bipolar disorder the *Warrior* archetype. A child on this spectrum has an understanding of his strengths (endurance, fire, intelligence) and vulnerabilities (egotism, hubris, rage, a tendency to be tyrannical).

  The fierce energy of the bipolar child encapsulated in this archetype is seen in the child's most shattering losses, as his hot temper trashes his important relationships. Brain scans show that living in this chronic state of "fight or flight" raises adrenaline in the child's brain and so gives him relief from the chronic depression he experiences. This same fiery energy gives him the will to reach his goals despite the cannon shots he takes from his unexpected shifts of mood.

  Balancing these challenges are the Warrior's gifts for fearless exploration of the darker aspects of human nature. Children with bipolar disorder are often gifted with the potential for remarkable artistic and intellectual brilliance, especially in the written or performance arts. These children spend a lot of time breathing the rarefied air of extremity and excellence. Bipolar candidates in history include George Gordon, Lord Byron, Friedrich Nietzsche, Edgar Allan Poe, Virginia Woolf, Frédéric Chopin, Gerard Manley Hopkins, James M. Barrie, and many other poets and writers. Children in this archetype often astonish me with their wisdom and accomplishment.

- I call Asperger syndrome the *Hermit* archetype, a mythical wandering teacher, never really grounded in our space and time. Hermits bring wisdom and new ideas to people, but they can be isolated. Gifted children with Asperger syndrome need friends, and they need help and effort in getting friends into their lives.

  The Asperger child is so anxious that he may become an iconoclastic loner. He is a captive of the unbearable social stress that he experiences and his need for absolute predictability. His personality shows the early marks of the "absent-minded-professor" temperament. Parents of Asperger kids will say that their child was born "grown up" in terms of his seriousness about life.

The scientific gifts of the Asperger Hermit archetype have always been an integral part of the progress of the human race. The oddness and isolation of the Asperger child, which is seen in his Hermit archetype, gives birth to his brilliant gifts. Albert Einstein is one example of a probable Asperger breakthrough thinker.

- In Tourette syndrome we see several archetypes. First there is the *Shaman*, or *Healer*. The Touretter's natural obsessionality would give birth to ritual, an important part of the survival of any culture. And their tics and strange utterances would have made them appear possessed by visitors from the spirit world. Many of the kids with Tourette syndrome I work with show a deep affinity with nature and are powerfully open to the suffering of animals and people around them. These children are natural candidates for the healer's role.

Know the Tourettic child and you also know the archetype of the *Restless Explorer*. Tourettic children may be extremely restless and physically overcharged. They love to explore. They are attracted by the forbidden, the closed doors, and by the power of nature. And they tend to have a genius for auditory perception and sensation.

Though diagnosis gives us a clue to a potential pattern, every child is different. There are gentle Touretters and combative Touretters. There are likeable kids with Asperger, and, using the language of the man who coined the diagnosis, Dr. Hans Asperger, "malicious" Asperger kids.[16] Some children diagnosed with bipolar disorder fit the "fight" aspect of the condition and spend all their time fighting with the world. Others understand that the most important thing is to be in control of your life. These children wrestle with the challenges they face at the same time that they put their gifts out in the world.

These archetypal descriptions must not be taken in any diagnostic or prescriptive sense. I use them to denote patterns of energy that I see in my clients. I find that when I speak to these energies, they speak back. If I am able to track the Warrior-like intensity of contempt for people, and desperate loneliness in the words of a bipolar teenager, he may let me talk with him for a moment and in that time he will *really* listen! In this place the child may feel secure enough to begin sharing the secrets of his genius with me.

A child's genius is particular to who he is as an individual. It is as idiosyncratic as a fingerprint. As we have seen his genius is shaped by his neurology, special gifts, and most excruciating challenges. It is his and his alone. But if you can also see his archetype you get a way to unify your vision of his genius—the whole picture comes to you, not just fragments of knowledge you have about him.

Box 1.3 In the Crucible: gifts, and their costs

His Tourette syndrome gives Greg wild rhythms and feral leaps of metaphor. His autistic side gives him the demand for the exact word, the precise cadences, and an underlying beat, strong and steady and monotonous as a heart. His occasional psychosis gives him bizarre visions with no boundaries, where he is not safe, but can see what the rest of us can't. I don't like or trust these visions, and I don't understand his chaotic rhythms and smashed metaphors.

On his latest medication his speech is mundane. His brain is cleared for the focus he requires in school, but he pays for his learning. We both pay. Even when I cringe at his hurtful words, or fear for his safety, or mine, even when I think he won't survive, I love his metaphors, his vocabulary, his rhythms and emphasis, his choral range, his rhymes. When he is medicated I miss his powerful and eccentric voice. I do not miss the hurt, the fear, the danger of his psychosis.

Finding the genius in the AD child's archetype: Aaron's story

Aaron is a fifteen-year-old boy who was brought to my practice by his parents to help him with problems associated with his diagnoses of Tourette syndrome and obsessive-compulsive disorder with psychotic features. He would not take medication. His family doctor suggested that Aaron might be showing signs of early onset schizophrenia, and was pessimistic about his chances of surviving adolescence. Coming into my office, he threw his long hair over his face, so that I could not see it. This, he immediately announced, gave him some protection from the air in my office for the time being.

Aaron's primary challenge was a fear of leaving his house, pushed by the belief that upon exposure to the air outside the house, he could become ill. He had only come to see me because his parents had threatened to commit him to a psychiatric hospital if he did not come in. I immediately acknowledged his courage for talking with me.

In addition to his severe agoraphobia, he would become extremely upset when his twelve-year-old sister touched anything in his view. This, he believed, contaminated the air in his home. A powerful obsessional state would result in which he had to get down on his knees and pray that God clean the touched object so that he would not get ill. At these times he was given to yelling at other family members. He would not go outside but when he was inside, he made life hell for everyone else in his family.

He would not go to school. A gifted musician, he played the saxophone, and would sometimes while away his time at home with music. He had a gift for computers and had recently taken to writing music. Aaron had no friends.

His parents came in with him for his first visit. They had the look of veterans of the parenting experience of raising a child with severe AD challenges. They talked carefully around him so as not to upset him. They were not weak people, just exhausted to the bone. I felt deep empathy for them. I knew the stress and crisis that had been their lot for years, from my own life as the parent of a very difficult son.

They were stuck in the place of plaintively arguing with Aaron to get him to attend one class a day at school and to consent to taking the antipsychotic medication his doctor had recommended. They were terrified of the expense of putting Aaron in a psychiatric hospital. They would have to sell their home just to pay for the first few months of his stay.

As daunting as Aaron seemed as a client, I felt a sense of earnest questioning behind his tough exterior, as if he were wrestling with some powerful personal dilemma that was driving much of his behavior, and that none of the professionals in his life had seen.

Aaron, as is the case with many AD children, was good at throwing "wild weasels" at the world. This is a term borrowed from US military slang for the type of aircraft that is sent over targets about to be bombed to draw enemy antiaircraft fire away from the bombers. Aaron's wild weasels consisted of his symptoms and his attitude. He was a scary character and he knew how to keep people away from him.

Our first session together went well because I was able to get to Aaron's *wound* before going anywhere else and spend time looking at it with him. As a therapist I knew that once this kind of rapport is achieved, a new energy comes into the room. The wound is sacred and so the place where the wound is acknowledged becomes sacred space.

In our first session together, Aaron shared something of the feelings of terror he experienced around going outside, and his uncontrollable urge to flee or freeze into position, which he termed "imprisonment." I simply listened and offered respectful questions to help him go deeper into the phenomenon of his life. His parents had told me that though his Tourette syndrome had been obvious from the time he was four or five, it had not been until age twelve that his more distressing behavior had shown up. This was a clue to look for the wound at around that age.

Many AD children in the US experience severe trauma at school at age eleven and twelve. This is the time when the school system pulls one-to-one services and puts the child into mainstreamed sixth grade. It is also at this time that AD children are thrown into the greater social system and must deal with the tender mercies of the bullies who patrol the school grounds. AD children like Aaron, with their social phobias and lack of social skills, are ill equipped to survive in this dog-eat-dog social setting.

Aaron related that he had always been different, more serious, and more easily offended than other kids he knew. He had a very poor ability to recover from social affronts and would often blurt something impulsively that would make the other kids think he was even weirder than he appeared, with his Tourettic tics and tendency to obsessionality. In the seventh grade he became the target of several of the school bullies who organized a psychologically cataclysmic humiliation of Aaron ganging up on him in one of the boy's bathrooms at school.

They had surrounded him as he tried to leave the facility, taunting him. Eventually they closed in on him, pulling off his pants and forcing him to run into the school's main hallway to escape them. By the time the hall monitor arrived, they were long gone. Aaron was devastated with shame.

When he came home that day, he was psychologically disorganized and was not able to recover the next day. After a few days he decided that these boys were so evil their breath had poisoned the air and that any prolonged exposure to it would make him ill.

The enormous wound of his assault had traumatized him deeply and caused him, for the first time in his life, to feel abandoned by everything good, even, he told me "abandoned by God." To make things worse, the school minimized the incident to his parents, who would have done something if they had known. Aaron was left to suffer alone. After several years, he still pondered the question of whether he lived in a just or cruel universe.

Working with him I noticed that his life did indeed show the archetype of Restless Explorer, the signature form of Tourette syndrome, but his exploration, due to the trauma he had experienced, had been to the inner precincts of his psyche. He told me that when he went into "imprisonment," he often experienced certain mystical insights and a sense of compassion for those around him. He needed the absolute boundary of the catatonic-like organization of his energy to experience this insight.

As we continued to meet, I began to get a picture of the central predicament that Aaron was dealing with, that showed in the intensity and interest he had in discussing the religious ideas of grace and redemption. His wound as a child born with Tourette syndrome had become unbearable in the face of the social cruelty he had experienced. And yet true to his type, the wound had forced him to a place where he could experience his genius, the aspect of himself that was involved in a wrestling match between his hatred of the world and his wondering if redemption is somehow possible.

This quest for redemption gave me another perspective on his archetype. A child in primitive societies who shows signs of what modern medicine would diagnose as Tourette syndrome, is often chosen to be trained as a Shaman or medicine person. Because of the extreme behavior of the child, he is considered able to have one foot in this world and one foot in the spirit world. In this way he is said to be able to function as an intermediary for healing sicknesses. Aaron's interest in the question of redemption and evil reminded me of the writings of many of the great mystics, including St. Thomas Aquinas and St. Paul. Seeing Aaron in these archetypal terms, I found myself engaged in intense dialogue with him about what he had learned about the questions of grace, and good and evil in human beings. I wanted to know if he felt it was possible that he was welcome in the universe and not just a throwaway. As we talked about this issue, Aaron became more aware and accepting of his "symptoms," in the form of his agoraphobia and obsessionality, for it was these powerful feelings that gave him the safety to do the exploration of his own trauma that was required for healing.

As he shared his life story with me, I began to get glimpses of his genius that showed itself as wildly creative, musically talented, odd, insightful, and powerful. To better understand his genius, I asked him to talk about what central values he was pursuing in his life. Children in mid-adolescence go through an identity crisis that usually resolves by age eighteen or nineteen. This crisis is often seen in the form of an attempt to resolve one important question. In Aaron's case, his psyche struggled to decide (to quote the fifteenth century philosopher Thomas Hobbes) if life is simply "poor, nasty, brutish, and short" or by-and-large, what you make it.[17]

I knew that a huge impediment to Aaron's release of his guiding spirit into the world was the feeling of distrust that had been caused by his original trauma in the boys' room. I knew that just once we had to go back there and heal the memory of that event, if he were to breathe freely outside his home.

Seeing in him the archetype of Shaman, I decided to use a technique borrowed from the Native American tradition to ease his suffering. I chose to use an abbreviated version of the Native American "soul retrieval" process to turn back the clock to that awful day in the seventh grade. I told Aaron that we needed to go back there for a short time and do some adjusting to that event. I told him that until that was done, there would be a part of him that was not accessible to him. I explained the Native American belief that parts of one's being or soul may sheer off during a traumatic event and that for healing to occur, these parts need to be recovered. Aaron accepted the process with some hesitancy.

I asked him to close his eyes and pay attention to his breathing. We did a short awareness scan and breathing exercise in which I asked him to imagine that with each in breath he was taking in good energy and with each out breath he was releasing all tension.

Then I asked him to imagine he was going back to the place and time of the incident in his memory, viewing it as he would a movie. I asked him, as he safely watched this scene, to freeze-frame the action, so that he could talk for a moment with the young Aaron who was being tormented by the bullies.

As we got into this part of the exercise, Aaron started crying and uttering threats and obscenities back at the other children he was seeing in his mind. I followed this for a few minutes, letting him speak while asking him to pay attention to his breath from time to time. Finally he calmed down and told me that in his mind's eye, young Aaron was now curled up in the corner of the bathroom weeping quietly to himself. I asked Aaron to go, in his mind's eye, to the younger aspect of himself, sit down on the floor next to him and talk to him. I asked him to reassure the younger self that he would grow up safely and that he (my client) would never let harm come to the young Aaron ever again.

I guided Aaron to ask his younger self if he would be willing to come back with us now. After some hesitation, the younger self in Aaron's imagination agreed to travel with us to the present time. I coached Aaron to put his younger self on his back and follow my voice, as I guided them back, in imagination, to my counseling room.

Once back and still in the light visualization trance, I asked Aaron to face his younger self in imagination, hold open his arms, and let the little boy "walk into your chest to live in your heart." I tapped a little chime I have in the office three times to note the completion of the process.

I noticed that Aaron's face was much more relaxed as he came back into everyday consciousness in the room. This is evidence to me that I was communicating with a protective part of him that needed a voice in his life now. This part protected him from outside threat but in the process also kept his genius "imprisoned." Though Aaron did not report dramatic change from the exercise, I noticed in the weeks that followed that I was hearing fewer complaints about him from his parents. He had gone out of the house for short stints a couple of times and was easing up a bit on his obsessional state around his little sister.

Sometime later we talked about school. He had been thinking of returning there to do one class, music, which he enjoyed. I learned that his chronic agoraphobia had improved to the point that he would no longer freak out being outside. The agoraphobia had been replaced by a touching obsession—he could not stand to have anyone touch him or get closer than three feet to him.

We puzzled about how to get what he wanted from school without having to get too close to other kids. He decided to ask staff to let him use the stage in the band room to play his saxophone at lunchtime for the kids in the adjacent lunchroom. He would come onto the stage from a side door and leave by that door and had the area to himself for his performance time.

Soon Aaron's playing was well known among his fellow students. He was a very handsome kid and his wild tousled hair and disheveled appearance appealed to several girls who found him intriguing. Toward the end of our work together, Aaron, still somewhat isolated at home and school, was now happily working with me to improve his social repertoire so that he could develop a friendship with a girl. He had gotten to the point of no longer seeing himself as accursed. His obsessionality was beginning to lift, and he even began to think about accepting antidepressant medication to treat it. He no longer felt the chronic, low-level paranoia that had pushed him deep into himself. He no longer experienced the sense of being "imprisoned" in that boy's room with his tormentors, unable to help himself.

Once I had an idea of Aaron's archetypes as Restless Explorer and Shaman, I was in the position to enter into dialogue with him and understand his strengths and vulnerabilities. In our work together, he marshaled the ability of his inner Shaman to travel deep inside himself and find healing. It had guided him through the essential rite of passage that left him knowing that though there are cruel people in the world, the world does not have cruel intent toward him and that finally it was safe to come home.

Recognize your child's genius and understand how it shapes him through his symptoms and gifts.

1. Recognize how the AD child's compensation for a "*deficit*" or *wound* in emotional or cognitive ability helps form his genius.

2. Study your child's *early interests* to glimpse his genius.

3. Understand *your own childhood passions* and *challenges* to discern your child's genius.

4. Understand your child's *fears* to identify his genius.

5. Observe your child's *developmental history* to identify his genius.

6. Put all your observations together to form a sense of your child's *archetype*.

CHAPTER 2

Second criterion

Caregivers are attuned to the AD child

The capacity for self-integration, like the processes of the mind itself, is continually created by an interaction of internal neurophysiological processes and interpersonal relationships.

Dr. Daniel Siegel, from The Developing Mind[1]

Family therapists use the term "family envelope" to designate the presence of cohesion, of a sense of positive "us" in families. The type of family envelope that is required for nurturing the genius of attention different (AD) children might be compared to the protective cocoon around a butterfly larva before metamorphosis. Medication, to use the butterfly metaphor, helps the child complete his program for development by giving him inner strength, inner tempering. But the "cocoon," the "chrysalis," the right family envelope, is also essential for the development of genius.

The importance of family attunement to nurturing the AD child's genius

There is a good body of research on the family environments most conducive to symptom remission in people diagnosed with schizophrenia and bipolar disorder.[2] This research demonstrates that the best environments are those in which family members have strong positive connections with each other and practice good communication skills. To quote the language of developmental psychology, family members are "attached" to each other; they have positive emotional connections and demonstrate that they like to spend time together.

Dr. Gabor Maté, in his book *Scattered*, shows that parents' maintenance of a loving connection with their children, a quality he terms attunement, is a requirement for the development of their brains. Attunement begins between the child and the mother in utero as the fetus listens to the mother's heartbeat. After birth, eye contact with the mother, her presence, verbal interaction, and positive non-verbal behavior, will enable the infant's brain to grow at an optimal pace. Her gentleness will communicate that he is welcome in the world. Maté shows that attuned parenting leads to optimal development of a brain structure located over the right eye called the "orbitofrontal cortex" or "OFC."[3]

The OFC is so important because it brings present perceptions and emotional reactions together with the memory of past experience to guide future behavior. If the mother–child attuned interaction is not present, the child may show developmental delays in the OFC, especially in its ability to curb impulsivity and pay attention. In order to develop strong OFC circuitry, the brain must enjoy peace from time to time and the relief from distress. It must feel at home.

One way to conceptualize the importance of the OFC is to say that its proper function results in the child's possession of "observer perspective"—the ability to see oneself and others in context—to balance emotional reaction with an understanding of others' intentions and needs. Observer perspective is the Holy Grail for healing the psyche of the AD child and releasing his genius. It means that he "owns" the choices he makes in his life and owns his part in the trouble he experiences. With good observer perspective, the wild, odd, and oppositional child is able to regulate the expression of his particular gifts, his energy, intensity, or emotionality.

Dr. Daniel Siegel, a noted writer on the topic of brain development and personality, echoes Gabor Maté's emphasis on the importance of attunement in his discussion of its role in the development of the child's core sense of self. Siegel is an authority on the "attachment" process. Attachment is said to occur through loving and dependable parenting provided by caregivers who are attuned to the child's developmental needs. Siegel states:

> Collaborative communication allows minds to "connect" with each other. During childhood, such human connections allow for the creation of brain connections that are vital for the development of the child's capacity for self-regulation.[4]

Dr. Siegel suggests further that it is the memory of the feeling of being in an attuned, nurturing relationship that enables the child to experience a "coherent, core self" and that this memory helps people develop the "emotional resilience to deal with states of dread, terror, or shame."

We are talking here of the importance of Great Story, of personal autobiography in the developmental process.[5] This will be covered in detail in the next chapter. Great Story is made possible by memory, and memory enables the positive expression of the child's genius. The ancient Greeks worshiped the goddess Mnemosyne, who was the goddess of memory. She is the mother (by Zeus) of all the Muses. Her association with memory has resonance to the subject of this chapter. The Greeks recognized that without the memory of nurturing caregivers, a person lacks a sense of internal stability. We need a reference point for empathy, confidence, and positive feeling. If we do not have that reference point, we may experience chronic insecurity. In Greek mythology, Mnemosyne also gave birth to Asclepius, the god of healing. The wisdom of Greek culture affirmed the primary importance of remembering a positive relationship, and of being positively attuned to others, in order to live successfully.

How 'feeling like a nobody' pushes oppositionality

Having a clear memory or "felt memory" (to use Daniel Siegel's term for the memory of the body) is not the strongest suit of our wild, odd, and oppositional children. In fact, given that many of them were extremely difficult to parent from the moment they came home from the hospital, there just may not be too many positive events to remember. Much of the problem is related to the under-development of the OFC, and to a resultant inability to have the confidence to say "Yes!" to anything. Lacking a sense of ground, a reference point, they gravitate to "Hell no!" as a primary response. They are very oppositional.

Many anxious children come in for counseling with a diagnosis of oppositional defiant disorder. The diagnosis is a list of behaviors, grouped for the sake of convenience, that describe a non-compliant child. Unlike other diagnoses, which may describe common *emotional* states for a particular condition, the diagnosis of oppositional defiant disorder describes a set of annoying and dangerous *behaviors* that are seen in certain children. I do not consider the diagnostic label useful for crafting a counseling strategy but I do find it useful as code for "anxious child."

Though the oppositional child may appear to be headstrong, spoiled, or willful, his behavior is not pushed by these qualities. In fact, just the *opposite* is true. The child's oppositionality is caused by his incomplete sense of agency in his own life—his feeling that he has no power to control events and must be controlled by them.

Oppositionality is part of nature's plan for self-protection during the developmental process. In order for the child to grow, he needs to differentiate himself from his parents and other adults in his life—to form a solid base for future development. A neurotypical child goes through a normal growth phase of "no saying" (the "terrible twos") that begins before age two and may go on for several years thereafter until he feels strong enough about himself to begin allowing the "yes" word from time to time. The exercise of no saying helps the child develop a sense of who he is as a person apart from his parents. This is a requirement for the development of his personality.

AD children show chronic oppositionality long past the time when the reflex to say "no" to everything should be less active in the child's life. Unlike the neurotypical child, the AD child's ability to pay attention is hampered by his brain chemistry. In order to develop a sense of personal identity, the child must be able to remember his experience and learn from it. He must be able to picture himself as a successful person with all these successes behind him. For the child to know himself, he must be able to see himself in his mind's eye and have a sense of personal history. Many AD children do not have the innate ability to create personal history. They are chronically fixed in the here-and-now with no "there-and-then" behavior to reference, to give present experience meaning. This state of being provokes high anxiety and great pushback: "I do not know how to choose but I do know how to say 'No!'"

The child who does not have this ability for awareness of self becomes a victim of every stimulus that pushes him this way or that. He cannot say, "This is who I am and this is what I decide."

The AD child also tends to be ultra-sensitive to stimulation—his brain signal receiver is turned way up. The combination of his OFC developmental lag, high anxiety, and hypersensitivity make his reaction to his parents hugely out of proportion to the real issues he is facing. Mild paranoia and the inability to see his own part in problems along with a reflexive anger results. A permanent power struggle is set up which will remain the *status quo* until the child is able to develop a sense of himself as a capable and independent person with his own life and destiny.

Children with neuropsychiatric diagnoses are greatly challenged by reflexive oppositionality, but the good news is that the brain continues to grow through adolescence and into young adulthood. A good relationship *now* will build his sense of self and self-efficacy. Siegel calls this "earned attachment." Contrary to folk wisdom, reducing oppositionality is not as much about imposing strong consequences as it is about *building relationships*. Research with the families of persons with severe mental illness suggests that anxiety, the criterion that pushes oppositionality, is reduced by a child's experience of attuned relationships at home and at school.

Characteristics of attuned families

In the attuned family, the qualities of acceptance and effective communication seen in the attuned mother–child relationship will also be evident in the positive contact among other family members. It will be this sense of attuned connection that will enable the brain to develop a good sense of observer perspective.

Research suggests that attuned families will demonstrate a set of interlocking behaviors and values.

First, attuned family members are concerned with furthering each other's well-being. People may argue with each other but they come together after the argument is done. The huge extended family portrayed in the film *My Big Fat Greek Wedding* demonstrates many qualities of attunement—they protect each other, they know each other, they support each other in the end.[6]

Box 2.1 In the Crucible: tracking "I love you" in the idiosyncrasies of speech

Journal:

Greg is nine. "Nighty-night-night-night," he warbles to me. His loon laugh segues to fart sounds. "I'm a gassy boy I lo-o-o-ve you Mommykins." He Bronx-cheers into the pillow, curving his neck like a cat under my stroking hand. I give him my nightly blessing, hoping he'll settle into sleep. He growls and purrs, then blows his nose on his fingers and wipes them in his long hair. I stifle a scold. Before he closes his eyes, his mind steams into high gear – "Why does ice float? How do molecules get hot?" He plumbs me to my depths until I turn off the light and give him his final tuck. He blesses my life.

I can track Greg's mood by his speech. One happy morning when he was fourteen he spoke with the accent and facial expressions of some non-human TV character. "Give me my breakfast, Mother Person, or I'll have to behead you." Mr. Bloodthirsty Star Trek Alien ate his oatmeal with brown sugar and quietly took his meds. He headed out into the misty rain on his bike. "Bye-diddly-*doo* liver-head love y'all!"

Second, attuned family members accept each other's foibles and there is a lot of positive communication. As we note above, AD adults and children do better in a family in which people have the ability to stay calm, focused, and positive. This finding makes sense in terms of the sensitivity of some AD children in picking up the emotional states of others. Because they cannot help but notice others' feelings toward them, they may instantly react, oftentimes very aggressively. This hypersensitivity may actually serve their genius later on in life because it will enable them to make very quick, gut hunch assessments of people and situations. But now the energy is raw and too powerful.

In *Survival Strategies for Parenting Your ADD Child*, I suggested that AD children tend to "stalk reactions" from adults.[7] They are driven to annoy people because, faced with their inability to maintain attention and happy mood, getting in a hassle with an adult is preferable to living with a feeling of isolation. A high degree of interpersonal emotionality raises adrenaline and gives one a sense of power and control. Unfortunately given the tendency the AD child has to instability, once his adrenaline levels begin to rise, he may have little ability to calm himself down—he becomes a guided missile with no recall capability.

Guidelines for building an attuned parenting style

Attuned families demonstrate a common set of behaviors that contribute to their effectiveness in dealing with high maintenance children. Use the eight guidelines listed here to improve communications with your child on a day-to-day basis:

1. *Be his consultant.* To help your child build his internal sense of self, get him to talk with you about what he is experiencing. Again, it is much more important that you listen to him than that you share your wisdom as a parent with him. To gain rapport and trust with him you must be able to get a sense of what he is experiencing. If, for example, he starts screaming at you when you require him to finish a particular project, ask "Are you mad at me because I didn't give you enough time to finish or because you had to go back to the beginning when I interrupted you?"

2. *Ask him why he does certain things.* To help an AD child be more successful, understand his motivation for obnoxious and self-destructive behavior and help him craft more effective ways for getting his needs met. One bright nine-year-old I have worked with in counseling told me that he aggravates his teacher "to see her face turn red." This is a clue to me that he

is experiencing a lack of stimulus satisfaction due to "stimulus flooding" in the crowded classroom. Another child ventured the comment that anti-social behavior was a way to get the teacher's attention, because his interpersonal skills were so poor he could not get it any other way.

3.   *Practice respectful communications.* Encourage family members to use affirmative descriptions of each other's behavior, more compliments than criticism. Discourage the use of adjectival descriptors such as "You're lazy and crazy," and encourage the use of behavioral language: "I love you but not your rude behavior."

4.   *Practice basic good listening skills.* Create a family culture in which people feel safe enough to accept that they could be wrong. Share the airtime. Paraphrase to make sure you know what the other was trying to say to you. *Listen to the child.* Let the child speak. Do not try to set him straight on the first expression of his defiance and oppositionality. Listen with your heart and let your feelings inform you about what is going on with him. Tap yourself on your own breastbone to bring your awareness to the part of you that loves him, and listen with the feelings that come up.

5.   *Do not get into power struggles, and keep expectations clear.* Anxious kids benefit from firm, non-punitive boundaries on their behavior at home and school. They need to know the rules and learn best in a structured, predictable, and interesting classroom. If an anxious child gets his back up about some demand from an adult caregiver, he will try to get the adult into a power struggle because he knows this struggle, it has a comfortable familiarity to him, and it gives him a sense of focus. The most successful parents stick to their guns and draw the line on prohibited behavior while helping the child focus on his issues and verbalize them. They do not get into power struggles. Choose your battles. Don't wear yourself out fighting over small things.

6. *Watch for bitterness and unresolved conflicts.* Attuned family members do not let things slide. If there is an issue, it is brought up. Address the problem before the sun goes down if you can.

7. *Know that physical punishment does not work.* The idea that spanking changes behavior is a fallacy when it comes to dealing with an oppositional AD child. In fact physical punishment is a direct assault, at a biological level, on the child's sense of attachment to you. Violating someone's physical boundaries to hurt him is instinctively sensed as a hostile and rejecting action.

8. *Do not be fooled by appearances.* AD children dread the feeling of vulnerability they experience from being buffeted this way or that by mood swing, impulsivity, or obsessionality. They are operating from "fight or flight" programming and have no way to sense if someone is friend or foe, so they attack all comers. Deep inside lives a very scared child. It is unfortunate for the child that his attempt to cope is as primitive as that of a scared little animal. Parents and teachers who see through the crusty and insulting exterior of the oppositional child to his "inner child" essence have a greater advantage in terms of communicating with the child.

The attunement model does not blame parents

It has become fashionable in the past twenty years among mental health practitioners to talk about how lack of attachment to a child by the mother causes behavior problems. Psychologists who claimed that autism was caused by "refrigerator moms;" cold mothers who deprived their children of human contact and the love necessary for normal development, first popularized this paradigm. This theory was especially popular among those who felt that environment was primarily causative in the development of the child and that genetics or brain chemistry had very little to do with how the child behaved. There is little doubt that attachment and maternally attuned behavior is important to brain development. But in the case of the AD child it may be the child's *neurologically driven* behavior that fractures attunement in his family. Most of my client parents report that they have loved their children from birth.

True, there are mothers themselves who possess mental health issues, addictions, or other impairments. Daniel Siegel's research provides evidence that adults who did not themselves come from attuned and attached family environments will have difficulty forming healthy attachments with their kids. But it is important to be careful about labeling neurologically different parents as "cold" or unattached. Autistic parents, for example, may have children (who in high probability will also be autistic) and may lack warmth in their parent–child relationships. However, looking closely one may discern that there is an attached relationship that exists "logical mind to logical mind." In these families, interpersonal communications may be very different from those in neurotypical families, but the exchange among family members is attuned and conveys strong feeling, expressed in true autistic fashion, with great understatement and reserve.

Oftentimes, doctors and other practitioners who subscribe to attachment theory will not prescribe medication for the child, based on the idea that psychotherapy is the best way to reduce dysinhibited behavior. The form of psychotherapy usually advocated involves restraining a raging or dysinhibited child until he stops screaming and thrashing about. This intervention is said to give the child a sense of loving "container" for the first time in the child's life—finally an adult cares enough to hold him even though he may fight the "therapeutic" embrace with all his might. There are no substantiated cases of children getting over neuropsychiatric conditions with holding therapy.

The complex reality is that attachment and attunement are deeply important for the development of the central nervous system, and the development of brain structures connected with attention and observer-perspective. The usefulness of considering this criterion, however, is found in the priority it puts on parents having an effective, attuned, relationship with their children *right now*. In order for a ten-year-old to develop neurological capacity, attunement needs to be happening between him and other family members in his *present* life. There is no point in going back in time to blame parents. In fact this may do great harm in that it makes parents and children feel like losers, broken, bundles of symptoms, incapable of even *holding* their own kids—to really get healed, someone else has to hold their kids.

Box 2.2 In the Crucible: walking the walk

As Greg grew up so many people told us how badly we parented him. Many of our friends and family have been enormously supportive of the difficult road we walk every day, bringing up this son. But so many people—doctors, teachers, neighbors, strangers, even dear friends—have told us how to do it the *right* way. If we had the sense God gave geese we would:

> bear down and get tough
> ease up on the kid
> heal our past lives together
> get him on Haldol/Risperdal/colloidal silver
> take him off meds and find him a
> > younger shrink
> > older shrink
> > crystal healer
> > life with Jesus.
> try the in-patient ward
> put him to bed with warm milk and a story
> throw him in a cage
> beat the Devil out of him
> post the household rules on the refrigerator
> set limits

and all would be well.

How attunement nourishes the emergence of the AD child's positive genius

In chapter 9 I describe how important it is that parents and caregivers have love in their lives. Love and attunement are very similar terms. One could not love another without being attuned to the other in the sense of being on the same "musical" note—there is *rapport*. But used in this sense, the term attunement takes on its specific dictionary meaning: to "be prepared for something." This quality of preparedness is not contained in the definition of love. It is implied by the word attunement. The attuned family is quite literally preparing for the emergence of the child's genius by modeling a certain frame of reference, a blueprint for human interaction.

The attuned frame of reference is the medium that soaks into the child's psyche as he grows. It contains the ideas that people should be respected, and that there are consequences for action that cannot be avoided and that must be faced. This frame of reference pulls out the child's resourcefulness and requires him to make decisions. It helps him develop observer perspective and it teaches him the Golden Rule.

Empathy is the Golden Rule in action. In my book *Survival Strategies for Parenting Children with Bipolar Disorder*, I suggest that developing empathy is a survival skill for children with the extreme genius seen in bipolar disorder.[8] The brain chemistry of this neurotype equips the child to make great contributions to culture and to have a very exciting life in the process, by way of the fact that he is driven to extreme experience. He can "boldly go where no man has gone before," to quote the famous *Star Trek* intro. But his tolerance for extremes is a two-edged sword in that he may lose control of himself in the process. If he develops empathy he will be well on the way to controlling the wildness of his genius (also known as his "genie" in the mythological sense). He will see the impact of his actions on others and himself. With awareness comes change.

When attunement holds sway as a family value, the AD child learns empathy. Caregivers in the attuned family are cognizant of the fact that because of his attentional "wounds" it is more difficult for him to be empathetic, so they keep themselves in a state of readiness to reach him and teach him. As he matures in this environment he has the benefit of this loving vigilance. He comes to identify one of the core features of himself as a person who is interdependent with others; that it is his connections that make him strong, not just his skills and abilities. Growing up attuned to mature and loving caregivers, he has a model for what it is like to be a person who is both powerful and connected to his community.

Lori's case

Given the upbringing of most parents today, it is difficult for them to see that becoming attuned to an oppositional child is the best way to decrease her oppositionality. It just seems to make more sense to bear down and get tough. Lori's case illustrates the small breakthrough in perception one dad had around this issue.

Lori was a very spirited, very oppositional, and very moody eleven-year-old. Her parents, Sam and Diane, had worked with me for several sessions to devise ways to decrease her oppositionality and moodiness. Sam was getting dispirited with the process and had mentioned that he was exploring the idea of putting her in boarding school. Despite these comments, I saw more potential in the situation and would continually encourage Sam and Diane to build their relationship with Lori and seek common ground wherever they could find it.

As things would have it, one incident brought the situation to a head. Lori and her dad had argued over homework. Frustrated with her inability to meet her homework schedule and angry at herself and her life, she had taken a sharp object, a trophy from school, and gouged holes in the walls of her room with it. Her father, confronted with the damage, had two choices, to go ballistic himself or to control his reaction and get creative. Sam decided on the latter course.

He said to his daughter, "It looks like you and I have some repair work to do together." Lori looked at him in amazement, struck dumb by the fact that her father was not getting angry as he usually did. Instead she saw the caring and fatigue in his eyes, and knew in that moment that his intention was good. All she could say was, "Yup, Dad, I guess so," as she dropped into deep sobs. Later, the two of them went to a local hardware store and purchased the materials needed for the repair, with a contribution from her allowance.

This was an important moment because it gave each of them the experience of a relationship that had eluded them. When they got in hassles in the future, they could use this positive experience to remind them what their life could be like together.

Sam had taken a risk in letting go the way he did. He had been raised to believe that swift and sure punishment was the only way to deal with this kind of situation. But in using the incident as a way to build a bridge with his daughter while modeling self-control, he demonstrated, in a learning moment for her, that people could deal with conflict and frustration and make the best of it. And especially that there is more strength in connection than in personal anarchy.

Later in life, Lori may experience the rewards of her ability to apply so much intensity to whatever goal she chooses. Now, as a child, she is learning that despite the fire she feels inside so much of the time, the forces of chaos do not rule the world. Her genius has a safe place in which to grow up.

Ensure that your child develops his cognitive gifts and success in his life by tuning in to him emotionally.

1. Emphasize the positive in communicating with the child. Use positive verbal and non-verbal behavior. Notice the good and praise it.

2. Practice good listening skills; paraphrase and restate for understanding.

3. Consult with him and let him be involved in making choices.

4. Do not let issues fester. Get on them right away.

5. Do not get into power struggles.

6. Know that physical punishment does not work.

7. Behave "like they do in psychiatric hospitals": cool, calm, collected, and in charge. Don't let him get your goat.

CHAPTER 3

Third criterion

Caregivers help the child discover a Great Story that moves him forward

I will be all right. Do not worry. I know my name now.
Haku in Hayao Miyazaki's Spirited Away[1]

We are challenged to find a positive vision for our children. We need that vision to evoke and nurture their positive genius. Good medical diagnosis and treatment is the first order of business but medical intervention is the beginning, not the end of the story.

Haku, one of the child-heroes of Miyazaki's beautiful anime movie speaks the lines in the epigraph above. Haku's name was stolen by an evil wizard and so he was bound to serve her. Once he discovered his true name, he also discovered his identity (he was a river spirit). And once he discovered his identity, he was free.

Miyazaki's story carries a truth about human beings: in order for us to survive emotionally and spiritually, we need to have a sense of positive personal identity. We need to know who we are, what we stand for, and what is the meaning and purpose of our life. There is a human imperative for self-definition in this way. We need to know our life story and we need to tell it to others. In Miyazaki's terms, we need to know our own name. Then, and only then, does our genius take full flight.

Daniel Siegel suggests that possession of what he terms "autobiographical memory" is essential to the development of a sense of self on a neurological level.[2] He points to developmental studies that reveal that the orbitofrontal cortex, the brain structure associated with observer perspective, requires the experience of personal story for proper development. Siegel says that in order for a child to develop a sense of self, a sense of coherent, meaningful experience, he needs the foundation of personal narrative. And, importantly, it is the presence of this narrative that enables the child to be flexible and adaptive in his reaction to stress. Siegel's work on the attachment (attunement) factor in human development informs us that the most successful parents help their children develop personal narrative through positive listening and retelling of events in the child's life—a process he terms "memory talk." Through this process the child's brain grows normally and his ability to deal with the stress of life is greatly enhanced.

Dr. Larry Silver, in his comprehensive guide to helping children with learning disabilities, *The Misunderstood Child*, says that children with learning disabilities are susceptible to passive identification with their disabilities—of seeing themselves as bundles of symptoms.[3] He cautions parents against validating their infirmity in this way, as this perception robs kids of the motivation and energy to change. Though they may know their diagnoses, they do not know their true names.

What you see is what you get. If all the child and his caregivers see is disability and symptoms, this is all they will get. If they see his potential, his true name, they move him toward realizing that potential. They give him the courage and the energy to move toward claiming what is his birthright—his genius and its gifts to the world. The attention different child needs this vision to heal himself and to keep his genius on the right track toward success.

As parents, we are desperate for a realistic positive vision of our children's futures. We look to our kids' doctors for a positive vision but most often we are sorely disappointed. Doctors are little help in this regard because their whole lives are structured around finding a symptom and knocking it out. They do not have the time or professional orientation to take a child in emotionally, really understand him, and identify his true gifts through his distressing behavior. Doctors look intensely at individual aspects of the problem and a good doctor will come up with the right mix of drugs to dose as many of a child's individual challenges as possible. But most doctors do not have time to meditate on the warp and weave of a child's spirit, or what storehouse of giftedness might exist within him.

Box 3.1 In the Crucible: acknowledging family strengths

Though some are supportive and helpful, not every professional gives parents the acknowledgement of being good. We are in that office because of problems, and any psychiatrist or neurologist or psychologist worth his sheepskin has dozens of solutions. If the solutions don't work, it's because we, the parents, aren't quite up to snuff—resisting, neurotic, pathological. *Go back to Mommy School and this time get it right.* They don't live our lives, can't imagine them, and seldom understand the extent and scope of our problems. Some of them have not brought up children. One psychiatrist with whom we butted heads lived alone with his dog, and his scorn at the chaos in our family life was visible. Not only didn't he see the importance of telling us that we were good parents (because we were) but he didn't help Greg understand the many strengths of his family. That would have helped us all.

Next we go to our children's teachers. We suppose that surely these people, trained as educators will be able to help us build our children's strengths and help us craft a long-term plan to bring out the best in them. Unfortunately teachers also have a specialized orientation. They have a curriculum to put into the children. If the child cannot absorb the curriculum, then the child's learning disability will be identified and remedied so that the curriculum may be properly installed. Teachers are also specialized traffic managers. They are not paid to educate children as much as they are to move them from one grade level to the next in an orderly fashion. There are just too many children for them to have time to look for the genius in an individual kid, especially a very challenging one. It takes soft eyes to do so, and the average school day proceeds along a merciless schedule that does not leave time to really take a child in and understand him. Complicating the situation is the fact that our children typically march to their own drummers and resist the learning designs of the educational system.

We parents have our own issues when it comes to holding a positive vision for our attention different (AD) children. We are tied down dealing with their excruciatingly dysfunctional behavior and we get very little support from the community. Add to this the fact that our kids may carry our issues—highly anxious children often have highly anxious parents—and we, too, are unable to envisage noble futures for our little troublemakers. Great pain is our constant companion, and suffering this pain we do not have the energy to see the positives in our children's psyches.

We do, however, have available to us a source of wisdom in this regard. And that source of wisdom is *mythology*—the stories, such as Miyazaki's *Spirited Away*, that humans have told each other for thousands of years about how people have transcended impossible situations. As the Hopi Indians of the American Southwest put it: in times of trouble we must go back to the beginning and tell our story. This gives us a bearing for the direction we must take. Just as a culture, or a people, needs myth to find its way in difficult times, individuals must consult personal mythology to find their way when beset by the trouble life brings to them.

The importance of mythology and Great Story for releasing our kids' genius

Dr. Jean Houston, a well-known modern philosopher and therapist calls myth "Great Story" to suggest that it works on both the cultural and individual levels to bring meaning and healing to people's lives. Examples of culture-wide Great Story would be the stories of the Garden of Eden, or the *Iliad* and *Odyssey* of Homer. These are tales of the struggles that human beings went through to achieve transcendence and growth, and typically contain a narrative that shows heroic figures meeting huge challenges, being thrown into darkness and despair as a result, and eventually triumphing over these challenges.

An individual Great Story is essentially the story each of us tells ourselves about our lives that gives meaning to our origins, struggles, successes, and failures. On an individual level a person might see himself as "a victim of circumstances," "a long-suffering patient," "a rescuer of the downtrodden," "a warrior of the heart who has gained wisdom from suffering," "a successful person who has pulled himself up from poverty by sheer hard work," or any number of other personal mythologies. Typically a personal Great Story answers the important three questions around which personal identity is formed: (a) "Who am I?" (b) "Who are all these others?" and (c) "What are we doing together?"

A child needs a Great Story to be able to identify the genius in himself. In *Survival Strategies for Parenting Children With Bipolar Disorder*,[4] I quote Jean Houston to suggest that everyone needs to connect his or her life with something bigger. Houston writes:

> By Great Story, I mean story that enables us to see patterns of connections, as well as symbols and metaphors to help us contain and understand our existence... Consider those teachers who see the child as the pattern of infinite possibility, a crossroad of biology and cosmogony: they work with passionate commitment to call forth the wonder dwelling within that child... Great Story is powerful and primal, capable of unlocking levels of the deep psyche. Engaging it produces an intense force, which in turn produces a mutation in consciousness. You become who you really are—and you know it. At these times when you are open to a sense of your own deeper story, coincidences multiply; suddenly there is energy for even tedious tasks, everything feels hallowed with meaning. This is the Pattern that Connects.[5]

Houston is referring to the need for people to make sense of their existence and is stating that if existence seems meaningless or trivial, people get worse, not better. When I first came across her thoughts on Great Story years ago, I had a difficult time reconciling her perspective with my knowledge of the depth of wounding of people with neuropsychiatric conditions. I felt that she was stating a principle that might be fine for neurotypicals but did not apply to children with deep brain issues such as autism or bipolar disorder. Now, having practiced in the field for twenty-five years, I see in the lives of my most successful clients a pattern of Great Story. Specifically, I see that the parents of these children continually affirm the "just rightness" of their child's condition. These parents understand that the wound of being born AD has the potential to take their child toward an awesome destination. They know that if he can learn how to rise above the extreme stress of the situation, he will come to know his genius.

Box 3.2 In the Crucible: Seattle Times, North West Afternoon

When Greg was eight, he asked us how to contact a newspaper. We told him to write to the *Seattle Times* and he typed a letter to Mary Elizabeth Cronin, telling her that he has Tourette syndrome and is a regular kid. Cronin called us and said, "I have to interview him." Her front page article led to an hour-long *North West Afternoon* TV appearance a month later, and the video of this show, taped and sent around the country by viewers, gave dozens of children an earlier diagnosis than they would otherwise have had. For five years we got calls and letters thanking Greg for his courage. He knows better than the rest of us how important it is to know—and be known by—one's Great Story.

I know from my experience as a therapist that each session must be a positive installment in a child's Great Story. It does not matter if his main issue is dealing with the "hairy-handed ankle grabbers" that hide under the bed of all six-year-olds. In session he will celebrate his victory over this darkness and so prepare himself to deal with the darkness and light of his own genius when it emerges.

To evoke a child's genius we need to help him develop a positive story that shows him how to have better control of his life. Invariably we will put together his Great Story as a historical narrative that begins when he was very little. Going back to the beginning in this way is similar to how Hopi medicine people heal those who come to them.

The Hopi believe that to heal someone you must first tell him the story of his people's origins and how they triumphed over the challenges that they faced. This leads to the healing of the sick person's psyche (he now puts meaning around his ailment), strengthens his immune response, and thus helps him heal his body. This effect would not occur if the medicine person treated the disease sufferer as a bundle of symptoms—a victim of circumstances beyond his control.

The important thing is to listen to a child's story, note the formative events in his life, and wait for the story line to begin to form. This is how you and he start seeing the face of his daemon, his genius. Along the way you will encounter the malevolent side of it. Most likely this aspect, the "obnoxious, dangerous, or terrified child," is the first persona that the AD child uses when in contact with people he does not know. It is important to listen over time to get the whole story, the Big Picture.

The atypical neurology of AD children may make for some interesting themes in Great Story. Dr. Temple Grandin, who wrote the book *Thinking In Pictures* about her life as an autistic person, describes how she visually conceptualized her progress through her college and her career as a world-renowned engineer.[6] She visualized herself going through certain doors at certain times. She writes:

> The really big challenge for me was making the transition from high school to college. People with autism have tremendous difficulty with change. In order to deal with a major change such as leaving high school, I needed a way to rehearse it, acting out each phase in my life by walking through an actual door, window, or gate. When I was graduating from high school, I would go and sit on the roof of my dormitory and look up at the stars and think about how I would cope with leaving. It was there I discovered a little door that led to a bigger roof (being built) while my dormitory was being remodeled… When I was in college, I found another door to symbolize getting ready for graduation. I had to actually practice going through this door many times. When I finally graduated from Franklin Pierce College, I walked through a third, very important door on the library roof.

About her graduation from college, Grandin notes:

> I went through the little door tonight and placed the plaque on
> the top of the library roof. I was not as nervous this time. I had
> been much more nervous in the past. Now I had already made it
> and the little door and the mountain had already been climbed.
> *The conquering of this mountain is only the beginning for the next
> mountain.*

In this last sentence you see how Grandin used Great Story to overcome
the difficulty people with autism have envisioning the future. Many autis-
tics are virtually paralyzed by the inability to anticipate what is coming
next. They become emotionally frozen in place when required to change
their routines or circumstances. Temple Grandin used a visual, symbolic,
Great Story to overcome what is probably a brain-based future apraxia
(inability to plan movement). Using this method she was able to link completion of one stage in her development automatically with the beginning of the next stage. This is a powerful comment on the ability of Great
Story to transcend even the most profound neurological limitations.

Jeremy's case

Jeremy's example illustrates the idea of the importance of how Great
Story can help you "become who you really are." Jeremy was a
fourteen-year-old with a huge bush of red hair, diagnosed with Tourette
syndrome and co-occurring bipolar disorder. I worked with him several
years ago while he was in high school. He is now a straight "A" student
majoring in biology at university. When I first met him, he was taking
medication to control his rage, oppositionality, and severely distorted
thinking. Without the medication in place, Jeremy's mind would become
psychotic. His mother had scheduled him with me to get a second
opinion on his diagnosis. I knew she viewed my intervention as part of a
medical procedure, but my work with Jeremy took the turn of recognizing part of his genius as well as giving his mother my clinical opinion.

Jeremy came in under the cloud of his mother's disapproval. In her
eyes he was the spitting image of her ex-husband whom she detested, and
she admitted that she did tend to identify Jeremy with her ex. He just

could not do anything right in her eyes and he did a good job of hassling her and making her life miserable.

In session, Jeremy was not the obnoxious kid I had been told to expect. He would range around my office examining things intently. "Now look at this," he would say partially to himself. "What do we have here?" All my little rocks, pinecones, scientific toys, all of them were examined. Jeremy also had an excellent memory for taxonomies—categories of things. As we worked for several sessions more, I shared my impressions with him that he had what I term a "call", if he chose to follow it, and that was to some kind of natural science, possibly entomology as he was most fascinated by bugs. "You are a person who has intelligent eyes," I told him. "The kind of person I would want to be making the decision about which wire to pull if someone had to diffuse a bomb." Teenagers love this kind of hyperbole and I could tell that it benefited Jeremy greatly to have his visual genius recognized.

By the time we were finished with our sessions, Jeremy's mother had a qualified confirmation of the presence of a bipolar-like condition in her son. And I made sure that Jeremy had an explanation for his life. On one hand were the "fiery" aspects of his personality, the oppositionality, wildness, and occasional hypomania. On the other hand were his positive qualities—his intensity of vision, intuitive analytical ability, and phenomenal memory. He left counseling with the understanding that, as a child challenged by bipolar disorder, he could summon great amounts of energy toward *any goal* that he chose. The important thing was that it was *his* choice. He could choose to lead a life of science, or direct his life energy into combat with authority figures. The choice between these two life paths was up to him.

Jeremy's mom dropped me an email several months after they stopped coming in to tell me that he was doing fine. Still having his ups and downs, but he was also getting more observer perspective, could understand the consequences for his actions, and he seemed to be listening a little better. It was hard to say if his medication was finally working or if my work with him had made any difference. At least I knew that he had an explanation for himself, a way to see himself as part of a world that might welcome his gifts. He knows he belongs. His people are science people.

Children like Jeremy need to connect the "little story" of their lives to the "Great Story" of their dreams, what they can give their culture and the world, and they need inspiration to dream big things for themselves! I deliberately worked in session to help Jeremy identify and confirm his own exceptional strengths.

Importantly, our kids need an explanation that takes *all* of their gifts and challenges into account, that considers the pluses and minuses of having an attention difference, and that moves them to be respectful of their own limitations, be that a tendency for temper dyscontrol, fighting, hyperfocus, oppositionality, or obsessionality. I often tell kids that these qualities are their "dragons" and they need to behave respectfully toward them, to recognize their power, but not let themselves be controlled by them. In truth both their challenges and gifts are aspects of their personal genius. Legend tells us that dragons do have treasures, but they guard them fiercely.

How to listen for a child's Great Story

Learning a child's Great Story involves listening to him with one's heart, more than with one's head, or analytical intelligence. Here are six ways to listen from the heart:

1. *Clear yourself.* Take a moment to relax and temporarily put your troubles and worries about the day behind you. Take a few deep breaths and imagine that you are putting all of your hassles in a large canvas bag, that you tether up and put by the door ready to pick up when you leave. Get a sense of your feet on the ground. Move around a bit.

2. *Center on your heart.* With your thumb and forefinger tap yourself on the sternum several times. Sub vocalize: "Back to heart now. Stay in the heart." If you feel oppressed by your life, deliberately call up a positive memory or think of something positive that you will be experiencing in the next couple of days. Put your focus on your eyes and deliberately let them relax and soften.

3. *When you are listening to the child, suspend your analysis* of what he is saying and just let his words in until you have the intuition to speak. Speak just enough to keep rapport with him.

4. *Ask him to tell you his life story as the plot of a movie or book.* Ask him to imagine that all his life experience has equipped him to deal with the challenges he faces right now—all of it has been a learning experience that gives him the capability to proceed toward his potential in some important way. Tell him that he is the hero of his own life and that you are interested in the "wounds" he has sustained in his journey and how these wounds have changed him for the better. Ask him about the experiences that have "marked" his life. If he is an imaginative child, ask him to project his life path into the future, into his growing up, to describe his potential vocation and contributions he will make to the world.

5. *Remember his narrative.* As he speaks, note to yourself positive aspects of his strengths and let yourself remember things you know about him from his history. You might remember dreams he has told you, or moments of triumph and tragedy in his life. You are remembering themes in the plot of his life, listening with your heart, in the same way that I was able to remember themes in Jeremy's life about his skill in noticing things.

6. *Tell him the story he is telling you.* When you summarize a child's narrative the way you see it in your heart, you help him remember who he is and where he is going. In a similar way, your AD child loves to hear your ideas about the central themes in his life. It helps him move forward to have a Great Story that is positive, purposeful, and powerful.

Explore your child's nighttime dreams to discern his Great Story

The AD child's nighttime dreams are a rich source of information about his Great Story. When you listen to your child's dreams and help him understand them, you serve as a catalyst for his change on spiritual, emotional, and intellectual levels. So much change is possible because the wisdom of the dream comes to the child from within himself. It is as if you are introducing him to the Old Wise Man or Old Wise Woman who lives deep inside his own heart, and who has all the answers he will ever need about his Great Story and what he must do to realize all the gifts that he possesses.

Box 3.3 In the Crucible:
release of Thomas the Dragon

When Greg was four he asked us to call him Thomas the Dragon, because "dragons breathe fire and guard their secret treasures." When I wrote the poem (on page 9) it ended up more or less in the shape of a dragon.

In the Chinese tradition, to paint the eyes releases the dragon from the scroll. I realized that the day would come when Thomas the Dragon and I would both be released from this page of our mutual Great Story. Now he is twenty, and I'm painting as fast as I can.

To some extent the face of a child's genius will show in his dreams. If there is a voice that says "Look at this instead of that," in dreams, it is probably the voice of the guiding spirit about whom this book is written. Special capabilities, such as the ability to dream at will, may show some of the talents of the genius.

It is important to understand three facts about the dreaming mind (as a convenience, I use the term "Dream Self" to describe the agent of the dreaming process in the child's mind, the Great Projectionist):

1. *The wisdom of Dream Self paces what you know by showing you what you do not see.* A child's Dream Self may help him overcome gullibility by telling him that one of his "friends" does not have his interests at heart, but it will not tell him what he should do about it. Dream Self is always watching. The

information it holds is gained from what it observed that the child himself did not observe or remember. Dream Self remembers seeing the "friend" do something devious out of the corner of the child's eye. The child himself missed the little betrayal altogether. Dream Self can give the child the instant replay (often in metaphoric fashion) but cannot tell him if it is a good idea to invite the other to his birthday party. Given the fact that Dream Self always brings into conscious awareness things that we did not know before the fact, it will always be surprising.

Daniel Siegel suggests that dreaming is required to consolidate memory. Great Story is essentially a series of memories that come together as the child's concept of himself. It makes sense that this process would include what Siegel terms "implicit" memory, which comprises those events that the child's body remembers but that he cannot recall consciously.

2. *An important function of Dream Self is the telling and retelling of Great Story.* Thus a child will dream that he is in an audience and everyone is waiting for the show but no one goes up on the stage. Dream Self uses this scene to tell the child that he is not "showing up" in some important way or does not realize that "his time has come." The moment when the child realizes that Dream Self has invited him to the stage, because that is where he belongs, is a moment of change in his Great Story.

3. *Dream Self communicates in symbols and "word symbols", or metaphors.*

   ○ A house is a symbol for a life. If a child's entire dream is in a crowded house, there is a good chance that either his mind is crowded with views on a subject, and/or his real life is crowded with people.

   ○ An eye is a symbol for "I"—the self, the ego. A child dreams that he cannot quite open his eyes, they are stuck shut. Then he realizes that, in a particular situation, he does not want to open himself to a new experience, or does not want to learn something painful or sticky about himself.

○   A figure of speech is a metaphor for a more important
    wisdom. A child dreams that he sits at a table with a lot
    of people unable to talk. At the head of the table a big cat
    eats something that the child knows is his own tongue.
    Now the dreamer knows that in some situation in his life
    "The cat got my tongue," or "I did not stand up for myself
    when I should have."

Dream communication is done with visual symbols because
deep "pre-verbal" areas of the brain are responsible for
generating dreams. Animals, humans, and reptiles all dream.
Dream Self is an ancient persona and has command of an
incredible library of remembered images that go back to our
origins.

To understand the wisdom of Dream Self, ask it the right questions

Use these six questions to help the AD child understand a bit more about
the meaning of a particular dream. At the end of this short query, suggest
to him that he write the results down in his "dream journal." Encourage
him to use this medium to record other dreams, especially repetitive ones.

1.   Begin with an invitation to share dreams or to hear one that
     he has dreamed.

2.   Encourage him to talk free form about the dream, and silently
     note events in the chronology or aspects of the dream that you
     find particularly interesting. Resist the temptation to analyze.
     Just listen and encourage him to talk.

3.   After he has had a chance to detail as much of the dream as he
     can remember, ask him what the dream felt like.

4.   Ask him if it reminds him of anything that has happened to
     him in the last few days.

5.   Ask him if he often has this particular dream.

6. Sometimes it's interesting to have the characters in the dream deliver their message themselves. Ask him to speak from the "I" position—"I am Max's bicycle. In order to stay upright, I have to keep moving forward."

Note a few of his responses to these questions and as you do, let broad themes mix around in your mind to give you a hunch about what the dream is saying. Share that hunch with the child and encourage him to comment on it and/or reject it. Remember that he is the final authority on the true meaning of the dream.

At some point the child may indicate the acquisition of some new awareness as a result of thinking about the dream. This is pleasant intuition, light-hearted wisdom. Intellectual analysis of symbols might contribute to his understanding of the dream but its meaning will probably come to him as an afterthought without much effort.

It is important to draw out your child's Great Story as he grows older. A wise person once said, "That which we focus on grows." Understand your child's life and help him grow through the turbulence of his youth toward his genius. Great Story helps him unveil the mystery of his life and shows him the moments, here and there, where his genius came out. As he tells the story and gets greater insights on the predicaments that he faces, he comes to understand who he truly is and form himself to that potential.

Guard against giving your child a negative Great Story

In my first book, *Survival Strategies for Parenting Your ADD Child,* I describe the work of psychotherapist Lisa Lieberman, from Portland, Oregon.[7] Lisa makes it a point to bring out the "shadow" feelings of the parents of AD children she works with, so as to remove the stigma of shame from these very normal reactions to the stress of parenting very difficult children. "Sometimes I wish he were dead!" is one such feeling that is often articulated by parents who sob deeply with tears of remorse for having said the words. "I wish he had never been born. I think about killing myself to escape the stress of raising him. I hate him sometimes. I just hate him!" Lisa points out that getting these feelings out often makes it easier for parents to stay positive in their relationship with their AD child. Holding in these "shameful" shadow emotions often leads to parents' putting them out to the child as his very own negative Great Story:

> You will never get it, will you!

> You are a loser and always will be.

> You should be ashamed of yourself for treating your mother like that!

> You hurt everyone in your life who tries to help you and you always will.

> You never listen to anything I tell you!

> I am so disappointed in you.

These are examples of negative Great Story lines that go in deep into a child's psyche and often result in the creation of a self-fulfilling prophecy of failure in his life. Though in the moment he may seem defiant and may shout back a barrage of foul profanity at you, every one of your words may be hitting the target, driving home the Great Story of his failure as a human being.

Another common example of negative Great Story is pessimistic medical prognosis, and the idea that a child must always be dependent on medication and can do nothing to help himself. Medication can be seen as the "scaffolding" for healing, the structure upon which the child's genius grows, but it is also very important to emphasize and affirm the child as an individual who is working hard on his own to change. Doctors will tell you that psychiatric diagnosis is a very imprecise process. It is extremely difficult to predict what will happen in terms of worsening or improvement of his symptoms as he grows, and his expectation of being able to handle his life will have a lot to do with his ability to realize his potential.

A negative medical Great Story may move a child toward greater disability. In terms of research on the human stress response, it is well established that a person's *perception* of his situation has an enormous amount to do with the healing process itself. Research with cancer patients shows that those who participate in positive and optimistic activities such as meditation, have a better prognosis than those who believe they are doomed to die and have nothing to do but wait until the end. Studies of the power of Voodoo point to the fact that if a person believes he is doomed, cursed, out of control of his own life and health, his immune system function is impaired.

It's never too late to help an AD child find his Great Story

The human brain continues to develop throughout the person's twenties. There is evidence from the early studies at Stanford, on obsessive-compulsive disorder, that how we handle difficulty in our life has a direct impact on brain structure. Other studies show that if we see a stressor as controllable, brain function tasked to handle the stressor will improve. If we see the stressor as overwhelming, brain scans show shrinkage in brain structure and abnormalities in firing patterns of neurons.

Thus we see that the wisdom gained from medical research and from mythology informs us that Great Story has the power to heal. Jean Houston says that Great Story calls forth the wonder dwelling within a child. What a lovely metaphor for the potential it has to open the door to his genius!

1. Realize the importance of your child's positive autobiography, Great Story, to his healing and the realization of his gifts.

2. Practice strategic dialogue skills to evoke his Great Story:

    (a) Clear yourself.
    (b) Center on your heart. Think of something or someone you love.
    (c) When you are listening to the child, suspend your analysis and wait until you are moved to speak.

(d) Ask him to tell you his life story as the plot of a movie or book.

(e) Remember his narrative.

(f) Tell him the story he is telling you. Help him remember who he is and where he is going.

3.   Help him develop his Great Story by teaching him how to understand his nighttime dreams.

CHAPTER 4

Fourth criterion

Caregivers build the AD child's participation in a community

This is the bright home
in which I live,
this is where
I ask
my friends
to come,
this is where I want
to love all the things
it has taken me so long
to learn to love.

David Whyte, from "The House of Belonging"[1]

In the legend of "The Spirit in the Bottle", the boy finds the spirit in a bottle entwined among the roots of a tree. The myth informs us that in order for a child's genius to emerge, the child must have *roots*; he must have a place where he belongs, rooted in a certain soil in a certain place. His spirit can only fly as high as his roots are deep. The attention different (AD) child gets roots from his *community*. Having a sense of community is a requirement for his development. To develop neurologically and emotionally, the AD child needs the opportunity to interact with others who are important to him, who are there to support and guide him. Here are some typical examples of an AD child's community:

- his immediate and extended family
- the people in his hometown
- his classmates and the professional staff at school
- employees of the local grocery store where he works on weekends
- his special interest group or athletic teammates
- his personal and online friends and gaming opponents
- his church or spiritual community, to include its teachers living and dead
- his ancestors; their country of origin
- his imaginal ancestors—those long-past dead who are his heroes or antiheroes.

Tragedy and transcendence: Al and Joe's story

I use the story of Al and Joe to illustrate the importance of community in the AD child's life. These two teenage AD boys were best friends. Al was diagnosed with bipolar disorder, Joe with severe attention deficit disorder (ADD) (inattentive type). Al was a gifted musician, challenged by extreme impulsivity and a tendency to dark depression. He sought refuge in illicit drugs. He had no community to speak of. Joe, not as gifted as Al, had a community of friends loosely gathered around his mother's church. And he was on his high school's baseball team. Through these activities, he came to know many people in town, both adults and other teens.

Joe's participation in these communities helped him deal with the chronic low-level depression he had experienced most of his life. People knew him. They accepted his moodiness and helped him laugh about things and not take himself so seriously. This was important "medicine" for him.

But Al was not so lucky. In a depressive funk over a girlfriend's rejection, Al overdosed on methamphetamine and died. Sometime later, Joe came in to my counseling practice to deal with his grief around Al's passing. Early in the conversation, he admitted that, contrary to his squeaky-clean public image, Al had actually gotten *him* addicted to meth about the year before. Joe was clever enough to hide his meth symptoms—the loss of weight and chronic irritability as "part of his ADD," but he quickly got to the point of realizing that meth was trashing his life. He felt that people in town whom he ran into were telling him to take better care of himself. Everyone knew something was wrong.

Things came to a head when Joe's baseball coach, Don, called him aside and confronted him on his meth use. Don had seen the telltale signs of methamphetamine addiction in some of the kids at school: the gaunt, unkempt appearance, the lack of appetite, the petty thievery practiced to get money to buy the drug, and the puzzling reports from Joe's parents about strange paraphernalia they had found in Joe's room, which consisted of burnt light bulbs with their bases removed (these are used by meth addicts to cook the substance for inhalation). At first Joe denied the charge. But there was a part of him that wanted to survive and it moved him to turn to his coach and tell him, without admitting to his meth use, that he had a problem and that he would deal with it. Being seen and encountered on his behavior told Joe that someone cared enough about him to recognize the difference between the valued aspect and destructive aspects of his behavior. It was not easy but eventually Joe ended his meth dependence. Soon his health came back and with it a healthy dose of gratitude for his coach taking the risky step of confronting him.

Joe needed his community to help him overcome his addiction. As an AD child, he needed its strength to bolster him to meet the challenge of dealing with the very personal struggle he faced to keep focused and upbeat in his life. Joe's ADD did make him vulnerable to substance abuse. Getting instant gratification, the endorphin rush that meth delivers, is tantalizing to depressed adolescents. Joe's community gave him the courage to do whatever it took to get off the drug.

As Joe and I talked, it become clear that he and Al had always been different in this regard. Joe had always known where he belonged. Al did not. Al felt like a wandering soul, never quite *here*.

Part and parcel of Al's life was his neurological constitution. His bipolar disorder gave him brilliance. It also gave him an explosivity and impulsivity that he could barely control. He needed older males around him, brothers, uncles, or father-substitutes (his father had left the picture when Al was five) who could help him temper himself. He needed someone to give him a strong "no," to tell him that he had reached his limit and needed to calm himself down and get his perspective back.

Al went to the well of drugs for relief from the pain of his mood shift and social isolation. He had burned all his bridges and had nowhere to turn when he was on a downward spiral. Because of his isolation no one noticed his life and his suffering.

Both boys carried an impaired sense of self because of their neurological development. Both had suffered damage to self-esteem because of inability to pay attention, difficulty in controlling impulsivity, and mood issues as they grew up. But one had the rock of community upon which he could position his body and mind to do combat with the monsters in his life. The other did not have the support of community.

Al's genius, his guiding spirit, his spirit, delighted in taking risks for new sensation, understanding, or exploration. But his genius was uninformed: it did not realize that balance is needed, conservation is needed, or the thrust of genius to its own fulfillment could be self-destructive. Having a guiding genius does not mean that one is enlightened. If a fifteen-year-old has the emotional IQ of a ten-year-old, his genius is ten years old.

Al's individual genius needed to be in dynamic interaction with the genius of the community. The genius of the community holds the rules for belonging. It is stated in unwritten ways, and shows how people treat each other. It lets you know that people care about you. It contains general rules of conduct. It gives children the feeling of belonging. The natural *hubris*, the egocentric extravagance of Al's bipolar symptoms, pulled him away from feeling that he belonged with other human beings at a time when this may have saved his life.

Responsibility and community

Oftentimes in my dealings with AD adolescents the question comes up: "Why should I do what you want? Why should I do chores or stay out of my sister's stuff? Why should I go to school? I can just refuse. What are

Box 4.1 In the Crucible:
visibility in the community

It wasn't until Greg spent six months in a residential school, at seventeen, that we realized the extent of the community in which we have lived all of his life. Many people in our small suburban city know Greg by sight, or from school, or have had short conversations with him in the computer stores he haunts. So many people asked us where he was and how he was doing, that we realized that he—and we—are not invisible as we had thought, but highly visible, an accepted and integral part of our community. In the neighborhood where he has gone to school since he was four, in libraries, parks, coffee shops, YMCA, computer stores, garage sales, the Safeway where he worked as a courtesy clerk, or in games arcades, or riding his bike, or walking the streets, Greg has been visible. And George and I along with him. The quick sideways glances at us all these years, that we thought were always negative, have turned out to be often curious, a little shy, even afraid. But once people approach us, it's plain they like Greg and want the best for him.

Visible he is, and visible we are. It's natural, I suppose. We have dealt with public tantrums and meltdowns since Greg was two, and our near neighbors in particular have been privy to our neurologically involved family life. Most people are both judgmental and accepting, more the latter as we talk to them, and as they get to know Greg. It helps that Greg is beautiful, smart, kind, likes people and loves animals, though his autism keeps him from wanting friends.

you going to do about it?" Parents dealing with a big strapping AD teenager who is flexing his muscles and letting out the energy of his genius in the world may feel at a loss. How do you assert your authority in a situation in which your child denies your right to do so? If you cannot answer this question, your relationship with your child is in jeopardy of losing equilibrium. You are about to be overpowered. When this happens, love goes out the window and emotional anarchy comes in.

This is a good time to begin teaching your AD child about community. The word is derived from Latin to mean "common fellowship." Fellowship connotes that there is an ethic of sharing in the relationship—straight across—this for that. This is a very concrete and useful way to communicate with AD teenagers about why something you want them to do is important, so that they are more apt to comply with your wishes. You tell the adolescent, "You give to the community, and you take from the community. If you damage the community, you must give something back."

The child's AD genius may not want to hear these words for it has a tyrannical aspect by nature. The genius is compelled to dominate the situation as a condition for its growth. But it needs the restraint of the community. Healing begins when the child understands that he needs resources in the community to realize his potential.

Many "wild, odd, and oppositional" children do not give their parents moral authority. That is, they do not believe that their parents have the right to tell them what to do and do not take their parents' advice. One of the advantages for parents of being in a community is that there are others, whom the child respects, who get can through to the child and back the parents up by advising the child to comply with parents' wishes and follow their guidance.

At the outset it must be clear that most AD children can be quite pragmatic when it comes to getting their needs met by their parents. They are typically willing to comply with a requirement if a quid pro quo is included that is acceptable. So the problem becomes, how do parents create a norm of "worthy exchange" in the family? The paradigm of "family as community" is a useful way to shape positive reactions from rebellious children.

The paradigm of family as community is expressed as follows:

> The family is a community. As is the case with any community, everyone brings something to the community. We bring things in and take things out. If anyone, including a child, damages the

community, such as taking its peace of mind or property, restitution is required.

Once an infraction is stated in these terms it becomes easier to establish a consequence for any behavior. If you take something out of the community, you must give something in-kind back to it. Here are some typical situations:

Situation: An adolescent does not contribute to his automobile insurance. He is tapping the financial resources of his primary community (his family) without giving back.
Solution: Parents revoke the child's driving privileges until he gets a job and contributes to the cost of insurance. He may not be able to go the whole cost, but he makes a substantial contribution to it.

Situation: The child breaks into his parents' room and steals money.
Solution: The door is taken off the child's room for some period and a dead bolt is put on the parents' door. The message is clear: "If you violate our privacy, you will have no privacy yourself and we will protect ourselves from you."

Situation: He damages some part of the family community (such as punching a hole in the wall).
Solution: He repairs the damage.

Situation: The child takes the peacefulness from the community by tormenting his sibling.
Solution: He does not receive benefit from others (such as his mom chauffeuring him around) for a period of time.

Whatever the consequence, it should remind the child that he is a valued member of the family community and is expected to carry his load, even though he also carries a psychiatric diagnosis.

Children diagnosed with bipolar disorder, the wildest pattern in the diagnostic lexicon, tell me that adults in their lives have to be in charge or they (the children) will take the place apart. The child's genius must learn its limits if it is not to explode "out of the bottle" and do damage to itself and others. Keeping firm boundaries helps the child by taking away the necessity for him to put energy into fighting authority. This approach disciplines the child in the Latin sense of the word (from *discipulus,* meaning "to learn"): it teaches him how to be a responsible adult. And it gives him the boundaries and structure in his life that he needs to grow to maturity.

Box 4.2 In the Crucible: community back-up

When he was fifteen Greg suddenly, over a month or so, became irascible, and nasty with it. His wild speech became more violent, and more and more often the violence was directed at us. Eventually the verbal abuse became physical abuse. The first time he punched me I let it go. The first time he assaulted George he let it go. But we knew we had to draw the line. The second time he punched me I called the police and he was arrested. The second time he hit George he was arrested again. Greg needed to learn that even small violence is not tolerated in our family, and—most important—our community backs us up. We couldn't have stopped his violence ourselves.

The importance of mentorship

The presence of teachers other than his parents or primary caregivers is essential if the AD child is to realize his potential. This daemon or "seed-self" needs different people to nurture it at different times in order for emotional and spiritual growth to occur. Parents cannot do it all *because* they are parents, and to some extent must share their child's issues. They provide the initial field for his development—their love, devotion, firmness, and honesty give him ground to stand on. But he needs other teachers to get him through crisis points that may be invisible to his parents.

My son Gregory has benefited greatly from different teachers in his life other than his mother and me. From his Aikido teacher he learned that carrying the diagnosis of high-functioning autism does not prevent him from excelling in physical endeavors such as the martial arts. His participation in Aikido gave him body confidence, and his observation of her gave him another example of a strong woman, besides his mother.

When he was fourteen, his eighth and ninth grade teacher taught him that despite all his "symptoms," he is a good kid, a teenager, and his teacher would not take any guff from him. The man held the line impeccably with all the AD children he taught. And because he had a specialty teaching kids with high-functioning autism and Asperger syndrome, he taught Gregory that his own mind was capable! These small breakthroughs came at a time when Gregory badly needed a social group and gave him the little bit of boost in morale and courage it took to seek out and acquire friends at his school. The social breakthrough, a rite of passage in itself, helped push positive change in Gregory's academic life and relationship to adults.

Some of our kids will find the teachers they need in the cops who, grim as their jobs are, help the terrified child get through the experience of breaking the law and get motivated to change their lives. One police officer I spoke with told me that he was ADD himself as a child. He knows how vulnerable kids with the condition are to impulsivity and behaving like little hotheads, being an ex-hothead himself. He is a gift in disguise to all the ADD-like "punks" on his beat.

Other caregivers such as the family doctor may become ad hoc guides for the child's successful management of crises. I advised the parents of one teenager I worked with, a boy suffering from obsession and depression, who was becoming anorexic, to stop pushing their child to eat. I told them that they should ask their family doctor to handle the situation by getting a physical done for their son, advising the physician that the boy was anorexic, and asking for his help. In a visit that followed the boy's physical, the doctor detected bone-loss and gave the boy a week to put on five pounds or face involuntary hospitalization under the state's public health law. This snapped the youngster out of his quixotic quest to become the thinnest living human being on the planet. He decided to start eating again. With that decision, and the boy's acceptance of low-dose antidepressant medication, his depression and obsessionality lifted. The boy's parents could not have achieved this resolution of the situation—someone else had to become involved.

There is another important reason to cultivate outside mentors in the AD child's life, and that is that children grow to maturity by watching mature adults around them. Recall from the Introduction, the idea that the first step in growth happens when the child becomes disturbed in some unhappy, symptomatic way. This is what I termed "the wounding." The wound opens the child to the possibility of learning, if the right teacher is present. Typically the child will listen and watch that teacher very closely. He will imitate the teacher. Then he will incorporate the actions and perspective of the teacher. The human psyche needs to "imprint" in this way to draw it to the next step in its movement toward self-realization.

Attunement between the AD child and his parents is an essential condition for the development of observer perspective in the child. AD kids also need other adult mentors; people who are not locked into the complexities of the parent–child relationship and can provide a fresh view. The poet Robert Bly, in discussing the developmental needs of male teenagers, says that older men, about the age of the teens' grandfathers, are needed to become "male mothers" to the teenagers so as to give them the deep nurturing that men are capable of expressing later in life.[2] Mentors model maturity, self-control, compassion, and honesty. Presence of mentorship is important because without this template for growing up, the child will not be able to control the negative aspects of his genius—the tendency for impulsivity, tyranny or extreme high anxiety.

The task of parents and adult mentors is to teach the child how to nurture three essential qualities in his life. These are the same three qualities that I will suggest are essential to wholeness and health in adults. The right teacher will give the child a sense that he belongs somewhere, that he has a *purpose* in being, and a contribution to make—he will give the child Great Story. The teacher will help the child develop his ability to handle *freedom*, to behave responsibly, and deal with his (the child's) tendency toward impulsivity. And the teacher will demonstrate the essential gift of *love* by listening, truly listening, and truly seeing the child. In this way the child is able to open his heart, relax his chronic hyper-vigilance and learn about himself.

Why having a sense of one's ancestral community is important

The community of the AD child has *temporal* as well as spatial compo-nents. His peers, supporters, and mentors go back in time as well as being present in his life right now. This ancestral community is an important feature of the child's sense of identity. It includes his actual blood ances-tors, and those with whom he identifies who are members of his people, his clan, and his ethnic group that have come before him. His ancestral community is both real and imaginal.

An AD child derives a sense of strength from knowing who his people are and how they survived. In the discussion in chapter 3 of Great Story, I noted that the belief that we heal ourselves in the present time by going back to our beginnings is seen in most of the ancient wisdom myths. It comes to us in the form of the ancestor worship of the Japanese Shinto religion and is seen in the medicine ways of the Hopi. If you are stuck, or sick, or disturbed, it helps to go back and learn how the ances-tors dealt with the situation. It helps to ask them.

The easiest way for a child to get to know his actual ancestors is to help him discover his genealogy. Fortunately we live in a time where we have access to the Internet, which can give us this information easily. To begin the search for your child's ancestry, encourage him look up the fol-lowing website: http://www.genealogy.com

There has been a quantum jump in the quality of information derived from genealogical sources in the past few years. Finding an ancestor, perhaps finding the city that he lived in, or the address of his house is a delightful surprise! Here are some ways that this knowledge helps the AD child develop a sense of self:

- For Stacy, an AD girl struggling with timidity, low self-esteem, and extreme shyness, it was useful to know that some of the women in her bloodline were suffragettes who figured in the struggle to write the nineteenth Amendment to the US Constitution, giving women the right to vote.

- It was helpful for Lawrence, miserably isolated and lonely because of the chronic crabbiness and obsession with perfection related to his AD diagnosis, to trace his ancestry back to Scotland, and learn that his line contained several people who fought the English with William Wallace in the fourteenth century (as in the film *Braveheart*[3]). It was a relief to know that he was more than his negative symptoms—that his temperament also showed strength of character.

- It was a powerful experience for Don, the only ADD Asperger African-American boy in his elementary school, to find out that he was a distant relative of Booker T. Washington, an African-American geneticist who contributed greatly to the progress of agriculture in the late nineteenth century. For the first time Don had a clear picture of someone in his line who was like him and who had changed the world.

The domain of the imaginal ancestor

Imaginal ancestors are people you may have heard about or read about, who, though deceased, can give you the wisdom of their lives. You can use your imagination to gain inspiration from people who are not your blood ancestors, by choosing to relate yourself to them *in spirit*.

The imaginal ancestor is somewhat like a spirit guide, angel, or "invisible," to use Findhorn founder David Spangler's term, but he or she is also very *human*. Dr. Oliver Sacks' boyhood love of chemistry got him in touch with the imaginals, whom he terms "honorary ancestors," in the lives of the ancient alchemists and early chemists.[4] These were the spirits who guided young Oliver in his studies in chemistry from the age of ten to fourteen. The imaginal is a seasoned traveler in our dimension and now, having passed over, is accessible to all for the wisdom and life example he provides.

In the course of my counseling work, there have been numerous occasions when it has helped an AD child to discuss his relationship to the persona of the imaginal. At these times I will ask the child to imagine that the imagined ancestor is in the room with us, simply observing benevolently. The child will often report that wisdom was gained from the imaginal about the situation we are dealing with in therapy. It does not concern me if this phenomenon is simple psychological projection or "mystic vision." The result is the same: an addition to the child's Great Story that makes him stronger.

Talking with an imaginal is very similar to the religious custom of praying. My experience as a clinician is that there is no one deity or imaginal to whom one need pray. One may choose to pray to "the spirit of the mountain," or Jesus. It does not matter. The process is useful because it provides a sense of *temporal community* to the child so that he may relax into insight about his predicament.

Denn, a very bright, highly anxious fifteen-year-old who worked with me in counseling, found such an ancestor in the presence of Ernest Shackleton, an early twentieth-century explorer who led an ill-fated expedition to Antarctica. Shackleton's ship was lost and he and his team were stranded on the ice for over eight months, before finding their way to a remote outpost. Many feel that it was Shackleton's compassion, strength, intuition, and raw leadership ability that brought all the men in his group home from this hell.

Denn imagined Shackleton's presence and consulted with him in imagination to give him the resolve he needed to make decisions in his own life, at home, and at school. He related to Shackleton not by blood, but by dilemma, and admiration for the imaginal's skill and character. He received marvelous and right-on wisdom about changes he needed to make to control the excesses of his brilliant but extremely thin-skinned genius.

Patrick, an AD thirteen-year-old of Caucasian ethnicity diagnosed with generalized anxiety disorder, was a gifted writer. In session, he told me that he was "Japanese at heart." Patrick was writing a powerful story about ancient Japan that involved the journey of a young hero-warrior to find his master, or Shogun. Patrick wrote his hero as having to deal with many obstacles and dangerous challenges, often virtually unarmed except for the power of his wit. This "unarmed hero" motif is often found in myth. In many stories, from ancient to modern, the hero is counseled to "let go" and trust the forces of the universe to help him.

Patrick suffered debilitating panic attacks that prevented him from going to school. I pointed out that his experience of panic was similar to the experience of his hero who was often faced with out-of-control situations in his life. I asked Patrick if this imaginal ancestor had wisdom for him in this regard. He told me that the imaginal advised him to forgive himself for not being in control of his panic reaction This was a useful piece of wisdom for him for it enabled him to stop feeling so deeply embarrassed and ashamed of himself for not going to school. He now accepted the fact that the panic he experienced was similar to having a seizure, something that was not his fault. This new awareness decreased the stress he felt and strengthened him to deal with the situation.

When I work with children like Patrick in psychotherapy, I try to sense if they have the free imagination and interest to benefit from discussion of imaginal roots. I have discovered that regardless of diagnosis, some children are ready to benefit from entry into this domain. Some are not. A child whose personality is very concretistic, highly scientific, or naturally skeptical may not benefit from this method. One child may derive strength from the experience of an imaginal ancestor. Another child may find this strength in his special interest, scientific, or artistic pursuit. Children realize the power of their imaginations differently.

My AD clients have taught me that the experience of imagination is required for the expression of genius. You have to be able to imagine yourself having a capability before you can develop and express that capability.

Building community one meeting at a time

Communities are not just static entities such as classrooms or social groups. You build community in a child's life by your example and affirmation on a daily basis, as opportunities present themselves. A brief example from my son Gregory's life illustrates this idea that community is as much a *process* as an end result.

Joanne, Gregory, and I recently attended a meeting convened to plan Gregory's educational process post-high school. Though all those who attended were committed to Gregory's well-being, and highly professional in their approach, there was a tendency to focus on Gregory's learning disabilities and miss his positives in the discussion. As the meeting went on, it became clear that Gregory, the person we knew, would get lost in the discussion. Joanne, seeing the direction of the discussion, took the floor. As she spoke, she changed the analytical tone of the discussion to make clear that it was primarily the presence of *support-ive communities* in Gregory's life that has helped him get through.

Joanne told Gregory's story from the beginning, describing the many supportive circles of community that have been part of his life—family, friends, school, neighborhood, professionals, and the wider circle of the community that knows Gregory from articles, books, and television. She highlighted the successes he had experienced as well as the awful moments. She thanked by name several of the professionals from his past who had helped him. She described Gregory's strengths and most impor-tant, how he has benefited from his interaction with all the communities that had touched his life—the schools, the social service agencies, the police, and the people in her church who pray for Gregory. She finished by thanking those at the meeting for being Gregory's community now. She made it clear that the most important two things that they could do for Gregory were to respect him, and to work together on his behalf.

We mark this meeting with the date on which it occurred because it is now part of Gregory's Great Story. The meeting could have been just another unpleasant experience for Gregory; having his personality dis-sected in public by people who did not know him. But as a result of Joanne's reframe of the group as a part of Gregory's community, it assumed a new energy—one marked by optimism, acceptance, and affir-mation. In the long run it will be these three essential qualities of commu-nity that will guide Gregory's positive genius into the world.

1. Develop communities in his life to which he must answer for his choices.

2. Help him take strength and example from his relationship to both his real and imaginal ancestors.

3. Seek appropriate mentors for him.

4. Take the opportunity to build ad hoc communities among your friends and the professionals who serve your family.

Box 4.3 In the Crucible: "Odd Duck"

At fifteen, Greg's favorite walk was a small park on the shore of Lake Washington. Dogs play there, and one day Greg got down on all fours, chasing a friendly German shepherd. Greg barked and growled, and the poor dog bristled and cringed away from this two-legger running on four legs. I briefly explained Greg to the dog's owner, a pretty teen, who told me her nephew has Tourette syndrome. I meet them everywhere, this network of support for our collective Odd Ducks. She warned Greg of dog poop in the grass and he barked with laughter, his body twisting in four-legged tail-wagging contortions. She was kind, and she was knowledgeable. I bless her and her Tourettic nephew. I bless all this community. To each other, our Odd Duckness is acceptable, even endearing. We need this nurturing and acceptance that is often rare in our lives.

And we need each other to find the genius in our Odd Ducks. We exchange our stories and feel less alone. Sometimes we laugh and cry together, friends, strangers, recent acquaintances. We are a community, though we link up haphazardly.

Support groups don't always work—our try with Touretters and their families, when Greg was eight, was a bust. The kids were so different in their symptoms and co-existing diagnoses and meds, that we found little common ground. Always some, though. Being an outsider is being an outsider.

And we do link up and hear each other's stories. There is no greater gift than to be visible, and acknowledged as good. Good child, good parent, good person. We give each other that.

Odd Duck

I'm an odd duck, Duck,
> *dicky dock dicky duck,*
I listen for the strange, for
  cheery quirks, *dicky duck,*
    quick quips.
Dancing in the sun, singing fun,
    I hear the song clear, hear it rare,
    hear it everywhere!
      Poem like a prayer.
You learn it with the ducks, Duck,
  dicky ducks.

I sing it with my son,
> *singy song singy son,*
sing it in the rain, *singy rain,*
  with cheery awe, *dicky duck,*
    brisk wit, giddy
    miracle of fun, *singy son.*
      We sing it with the ducks, Duck.

Yes, Duck, an odd duck,
  dicky dock dicky duck.
  Odd duck.

Fifth criterion

Caregivers address physical factors and medication

*All the creation myths tell us that a little bit of stability
grows and spreads if you focus on it.*

Michael Meade[1]

The body is the instrument through which the child expresses his genius.
The body of the attention different (AD) child, more specifically his
central nervous system, may be out of balance. Possession of a particular
genius may be part of the problem. From "The Spirit in the Bottle" we
learn that the spirit or genie brings trouble. The genie's energy is great
and the small body of the child may not be capable of containing its
ferocity. The physical manifestation of genius in the AD child may
include the following:

- The orbitofrontal cortex, the structure above and slightly
  behind the eyes (especially the part over the right eye), may
  under-function. This dynamic leads to the under-functioning
  of the brain's attention and reward circuits. This may cause
  the child to behave impulsively, to have a tendency to be
  depressed, to lack the ability to recognize and interpret the
  non-verbal behavior of others, and to be unable to appraise
  the actions of others as threatening or benevolent.

- Because of abnormalities of function in a brain structure called the "lateral prefrontal cortex," the child's working memory may be impaired. This deprives the child of the ability to cross-compare a present stressor with a past strategy for handling that stressor and so he becomes more reactive, less flexible in his responses. Under-function in this area, and in a structure in the limbic brain involved in memory called the "hippocampus," may deprive the child of the ability to compose Great Story or to integrate stressful experience in his life. This may cause him to live in a perpetual state of unresolved conflict. It will inhibit his ability to reflect on his experience and organize his life from this reflection.

- The emotional center of the limbic brain, with its amygdaloid complex, composed of the amygdala and thalamus, is overactive. This creates emotional extremes and hypersensitivities to outside stimulation. The hyper-charged function of these centers in the limbic system is also involved in creating the unpleasant sense of drivenness and pent-up energy that powers hypomania in bipolar disorder. This energy and drive may some day serve the child well, but right now having it on board is like living in a blast furnace.

- The cerebellum in the base of the brain, the seat of control of the involuntary nervous system, may be less efficient. This structure gives us the ability to roll with the punches, to have good emotional rhythmicity. Impairments of rhythmicity show in the topsy-turvy energy cycle of bipolar disorder—the person activates at a time when he should be getting sleepy. This is a highly destabilizing challenge to one's being.

- A structure in the limbic system called the anterior cingulate gyrus is hyper-energized. This causes the child to experience difficulty shifting gears from focusing on one thought to focusing on another thought. When this structure is not functioning properly, there is a tendency for the child to get stuck, locked into negative behaviors, or be emotionally explosive.

A central feature of all of the challenges listed above is that they push the AD child toward instability. The challenge is to achieve stability as long as possible because in so doing, the child's brain is growing strong and stable neural patterns. The child's reward for managing this aspect of the wild energy of his genius is observer perspective. There is no other way to survive the wild mood swings he experiences. He must ride them as a champion surfer rides a wave. Once he has mastered this skill, he has something to teach us all about keeping our composure under stress!

How instability throws off the AD child's internal "gyroscope"

AD children are greatly challenged by the difficulty they have dealing with stress from their own overcharged nervous systems and from the outside world. Unlike neurotypical children, they do not bounce back easily from defeat or frustration. This tendency to become unstable attacks their ability to accommodate to the requirements for daily living, especially school.

One way to conceptualize the AD child's problem is to imagine that his internal emotional "gyroscope" gets thrown off kilter easily, causing his affectivity and behavior to become "unbalanced." As this occurs, he loses the ability to be introspective, to learn from his experience, and to integrate the experience into his life. Here are several examples of how this problem with instability manifests itself across several different diagnoses:

- Children who show features of a generalized anxiety disorder may become extremely anxious, oppositional, irritable, or tyrannical. Or they will collapse into agoraphobia (fear of going outside the home), school refusal and depression.

- Children troubled by the symptoms of bipolar disorder may fly into the rages and wild swings of mood that are typical of this condition.

- Children with a tendency to perseverance, such as is seen in Tourette syndrome or obsessive-compulsive disorder, may become obsessive-compulsive or show a great increase in motor and vocal tics.

There are usually clear precedents for de-stabilization, though they may be hard to identify. External (exogenous) stress may take the form of an upset in a child's life, such as his parents' divorce or the loss of a cherished friend.

Internal (endogenous) factors may also push a child toward de-stabilization. In some younger children, who are challenged by mood dyscontrol or high anxiety, instability may occur as the child's young mind struggles to make sense of what is going on. Usually these features of personality will be evident in babyhood—he will hold his ears around certain noises, scream, or push his parents away. This is not how all children destabilize. Sometimes a child will appear normal until a certain age and then one day will "snap" into an unstable emotional state.

Older children may destabilize as a result of the shock of entering andrenarche (boys) and menarche (girls) when their bodies begin producing the Adrenocorticotrophic hormone (ACTH), which mobilizes the body and mind to deal with stress. This typically occurs around age eleven and may happen as early as age eight for some children. These children cannot stand the pressure of hormonal change as they grow into adolescence and their psyches become unbalanced.

The dark side of genius is typically seen when the AD child destabilizes. He may become obsessive, even tyrannical in pursuit of his goals. He may become combative. He may become devious and manipulative. These qualities are obnoxious and destructive but each has a positive aspect that becomes clearer as the child grows older. Obsession and perseverance become resolve. Combativeness becomes courage to stand up for oneself. A tendency to be manipulative becomes the ability to understand others and to get one's needs met in a social context, or be a good manager. As the child matures, and his genius is nourished, he will express its qualities more positively in his life. Perhaps there will also be aspects of the darker side present. But if there are, they will be balanced by the positive features of his character.

Observer perspective is most often noted when the child is feeling sociable or safe. At these times he will be more apt to acknowledge his part in the situation, and to attempt to make things right or avoid causing a particular kind of trouble in the future. When a child is able to exercise observer perspective, he is stable. His psychic gyroscope is on station and is capable of keeping him upright, grounded, and confident in the face of any stress that comes his way.

Destabilization and the stress reaction

Another stress on the child's inner gyroscope is his tendency to live the general adaptation syndrome (GAS) as a chronic condition. The GAS, which is also known as the "fight or flight" response to stress, is the term Dr. Hans Selye coined to describe the automatic response pattern the body and mind go into during distress.[2] Selye observed that when the human body is stressed, it mobilizes for its own defense by creating a set of reactions in the body and the mind that include:

- an increase in respiration and decrease of blood flow to the extremities

- tightening of the muscles

- a shut down of the ability for complex thought

- an increased sensitivity to stimulation

- catastrophic thinking—seeing danger everywhere, along with frantic ideation around survival, which pushes the need to attack or flee.

As I noted in *Survival Strategies for Parenting Your ADD Child*, research shows that the brain's reaction to the GAS and the normal state of function of children who experience ADHD are quite similar.[3] Cognitive function and the brain's use of the neurotransmitter dopamine are very similar in both situations. Dr. Dimitri Papolos, author of *The Bipolar Child*, has also noted the presence of what seems like a chronic fight or flight response in children diagnosed with early onset bipolar disorder.[4]

Brain studies show that chronic stress, and the resultant release of the stress hormone ACTH, causes cell death in the hippocampus and other areas of the brain essential for self-control, introspection, and observer perspective. Thus we see that there is a second order impact of the child's tendency toward instability—the more chaotic and stressful his life becomes, the less his brain is equipped to deal with the stress.

Put yourself in any situation in which you have experienced extreme distress and you get a sense of what it is like for many AD kids. In the situation you probably appeared unbalanced, out-of-it, and your decision-making may have been impaired. In terms of gaining rapport with your child, it is useful to compare what you have felt like at your worst to what he feels every day. The term "unbalanced" points in the right direction, for your psychological gyroscope is truly out of balance at these times.

Prevent instability with positive family communications, "memory talk," predictable family routines, and adequate sleep

In chapter 2, I described the importance of attuned family communications in helping the AD child heal the excesses of his temperament and develop a sense of self. In terms of the content of brain-strengthening communication, I noted in chapter 3 that Dr. Daniel Siegel considers "memory talk" most important in this regard. This is the practice of active listening with the child, of empathetically tuning-in to his life experience, and reflecting that experience back to him in such a way that he gains the confidence to deal with the stresses of life. Research on the developmental process makes it clear that it is more important for parents to help children understand and organize their emotional lives, than it is to give the children advice, or prompt an account of the facts of their lives such as contained in their response to the dreaded question "So, how did school go today?"

Attuned interaction is the most important ingredient of family stability, but predictable routines and adequate sleep are also important. I always ask about sleep habits in my first interviews with the families of AD children, because I know that if a child stays up too late or does not get up in the morning, his circadian rhythm (sleep–wake cycle) will be affected. Sleep deprivation destabilizes the mood and cognitive function of the AD child, and it may cause him to lose motivation for going to school and impair his ability to do schoolwork. He may become hypomanic, depressed, or psychotic. Most elementary school-age children need eight hours' sleep a night. The child should be sound asleep before midnight to avoid mood-destabilizing effects. If early morning arousal is required to fit a very early start time at school, then adjustment in school schedule should occur and be included in the child's individual education plan.

Adolescents need more sleep than younger children and their sleep cycle is somewhat different. They are naturally inclined to go to bed later and get up later. Some teens will require up to fourteen hours of sleep a night. If they cannot get adequate sleep during the week they may sleep in on the weekends. But current studies suggest that "banking sleep" in this way is hard on the body's natural rhythms and does not refresh the immune system as adequately as does getting a good night's sleep every night.

Stability in family routines should be an ongoing priority. Due to economic need, both parents may have to work. This reality is a driving force for instability—it keeps parents on the go and makes it difficult to find family time. To offset this threat to stability, it helps to have weekly calendar coordination. It is also important to determine which parent will have responsibility for educational and social service coordination for the AD child. Parents should try to share this load. And they should share the more odious aspects of parenting, such as dealing with particularly unpleasant professionals or bureaucracies involved in the family's life.

Having little routines in place is very important. Children and parents might get together right before the kids' bedtime for the "daily debriefing" or "wrap-up." This is an opportunity to share both the good and the unpleasant things about one's day, and for children and parents to tune-in to each other. Or there might be a loosely scheduled walk time. One of my most enjoyable activities has been a walk I take with Gregory up to a local park and back a couple of times a week. It is easier for us to relate when he is loping along beside me.

Examples of stabilizing family routines are:

- for younger children, a daily "wrap-up" with parents at bedtime

- going for a walk at the same time every evening

- taking your child with you every time you go to vote

- a trip to a favorite vacation spot with one child and one parent at around the same time every year.

Medication: the essential scaffolding for the growth of genius

The correct medication for a child will stabilize his brain function so that he can meet normal developmental milestones and have control of his life. Contrary to some current folk wisdom, medication is not a demon potion that takes away a child's soul. Nor is it addictive. Nor does it teach him that "being on drugs is OK." It is a prop, a cast on a broken limb, sometimes a temporary one. Used correctly, it helps the child calm his chronic state of crisis so that he may experience observer perspective. Medication is scaffolding, similar to that used in building construction, or to give support to climbing plants. As scaffolding, it is an essential support for the emotional, cognitive, and spiritual growth of the child.

Mood stabilizers—lithium and the anticonvulsants

Lithium carbonate (marketed as several different brand names) is a naturally occurring salt, and has been the drug of choice for manic-depressive illness since the late nineteenth century. Now, medications in the anticonvulsant class have become the primary medications used to treat mood instability in children. The anticonvulsant medications stabilize mood but, unlike lithium, do not generally reduce depression. These drugs include valproic acid and divalproex sodium (Depakote), carbamazepine (Tegretol), gabapentin (Neurontin), topiramate (Topamax), and oxcarbamazepine (Trileptal). Lamotrigine (Lamictal) is an anticonvulsant that has demonstrated an antidepression effect similar to that achieved with lithium.

Antipsychotic medications

Antipsychotic medications are also called "neuroleptics" because they regulate the brain's use of the neurotransmitters serotonin and dopamine. These drugs, often prescribed for children diagnosed with bipolar disorder or Asperger syndrome, enable the child to screen out intrusive thoughts or emotions that can take over consciousness. Several of these medications also have potent mood stabilization properties. Drugs in this classification include risperidone (Risperdal), olanzapine (Zyprexa), quetiapine fumarate (Seroquel), ziprasidone (Geodon), and aripiprazole (Abilify). Parents inform me that these medications, of all those available, have the best chance of helping a child achieve observer perspective. For the first time, a parent hears an apology for violent behavior. For the first time, the child owns his part in a situation. For the first time, a child gives a parent a genuine, from-the-heart compliment. Weight gain is the most distressing side effect of this class of medication and Zyprexa is the biggest offender in terms of this factor.

Antidepressant medications

Antidepressant medications soothe the brain's vigilance centers (relieving depression) and permit the release of neurochemicals associated with a euthymic (good) mood. Antidepressants and stimulants should only be given *after* administration of a mood stabilizer for children diagnosed with bipolar disorder. The selective serotonin reuptake inhibitors (SSRIs) such as fluoxetine hydrochloride (Prozac), sertraline (Zoloft), citalopram (Celexa), and one of the powerful new antidepressants, excitalopram oxalate (Lexapro), raise brain serotonin levels and help the child put a brake on impulsivity. Atypical antidepressants that have the ability to energize focus while raising brain serotonin levels (and reducing depression), such as bupropion hydrochloride (Wellbutrin) or venlafaxine hydrochloride (Effexor), may strengthen the ability of the child to think clearly and control his mood at the same time.

Stimulants

Stimulants are used to strengthen the ability of the cortex to regulate attention and emotional states. Stimulant medications include dextroamphetamine (Dexedrine), methylphenidate (Ritalin), extended time-release methylphenidate (Concerta), and salts of dextroamphetamine (Adderall). Atomexetine (Strattera), the most recent addition to the group of medications used to treat ADD, has an impact on the body's use of the neurotransmitter norepinephrine, not the neurotransmitter dopamine, as is the case with conventional stimulants. For this reason it may be more effective when used for children who experience side effects from stimulant medication.

The omega 3 essential fatty acids (EFAs)

These naturopathic supplements improve brain efficiency and communication between neurons and reduce symptoms of ADHD and bipolar disorder. Research from the US National Institute of Mental Health shows that the EFAs may be useful for some children in limiting their tendency for mood instability. A typical EFA preparation for children challenged by bipolar disorder, such as OmegaBrite, contains a high ratio of the omega fatty acid EPA, extracted from fresh water fish oil, to omega fatty acid DHA, which is extracted from flax seed oil and evening primrose. EPA has shown promise for reducing symptoms of bipolar disorder, while DHA may improve executive function in ADD and has been shown to ameliorate the symptons of depression. Doses of omega 3 EFA—in the range of 1.5 to 2 grams a day—have been shown in some studies to be effective for easing mood swings related to bipolar disorder and ADHD hyperactivity.[5]

AD children refuse medication for good reasons

An AD child may need the brain strengthening that medication provides but may resist taking medication. AD children resist "meds" for any number of very good reasons. They may hate the side effects such as weight gain, acne, and cognitive dulling. Adolescents may loathe the loss of libido or sexual function that may occur from taking mood stabilizers, antipsychotics, or antidepressants. They may realize that their peer group values them for being impulsive, funny, and the one who always challenges authority. AD children, diagnosed with ADHD, may push back from taking the stimulant medications that act to limit the amount of time they spend being "the life of the classroom." They may hate being associated with the diagnosis of children who take the medication. A child may believe that the medication takes away the power of choice for positive change. As one ADHD ten-year-old put it, "When I'm bad it's me being bad. When I'm good, it's the medication making me good." AD children may feel that adults in their lives are trying to brainwash them or turn them into zombies. These are good reasons to push back.

I believe that the fundamental reason many children resist medication is that they sense that it is a direct attack on the energy of their genius, a direct attempt to quell their spirit. This causes powerful pushback. In a sense, the child is correct in this assumption.

Medication may enable the child to focus, control himself, and succeed at school, or may quell destructive impulsivity or psychotic thinking. But in having all these positive benefits it may deprive the child's genius of the wrestling match with natural consequences that it needs in order to grow. One twenty-two-year-old Touretter reported to me that he was put on an old-style antipsychotic (haloperidol) to manage his tics when he was fourteen. Because he was on the medication all through his teen years, when he ceased taking it in his early twenties, he had to learn all the lessons that kids learn about life in their adolescence. In the safe but foggy state of consciousness he lived in for eight years, he missed the opportunity to learn important social and personal skills that come as the result of the experience of adolescence. In the face of this understandable resistance, getting cooperation to take medication requires out-of-the-box thinking and a lot of patience.

Box 5.1 In the Crucible: balancing medication

To medicate or not to medicate—sometimes it's a life or death decision. On his nineteenth birthday Greg took himself off his antipsychotic medication, against everyone's advice, and within a month his hold on reality had visibly loosened. Within three months he was actively psychotic. He thought people were following him. He wanted the drapes pulled and lights kept low. He ate bizarrely, a stick of butter for dinner, half a pound of peanut butter for breakfast, one big bite of face soap for a snack. He couldn't go anywhere. He didn't shower for several weeks at a time. He stayed up most of the night, laughing and talking and raging to himself. He threatened us constantly and barely managed to keep his fists quiet.

Four months off meds and his school program fell apart because he never got to school. He threw out all his clothes, tossed his tools and computers into the garbage, trashed or threw away every Christmas present. He often stayed out all night, walking the streets of Seattle, dozing upright, occasionally leaning against a secluded wall to snatch a little sleep, until paranoia forced him to stay home. We were frantic. No one could do a thing—he couldn't be hospitalized until he did something to harm himself.

That day came soon after he threw out all his possessions. I still can't write about the days we spent in the intensive care unit, the weeks in the hospital. Nobody can figure out how he survived—luck perhaps, or youth, or prayers, or Tourette vitality, or autistic stubbornness. I don't care how. I'm merely grateful.

The crisis forced Greg back on an antipsychotic, and so far, nearly a year later, he is doing well. The next crisis will get him hospitalized much faster. Now the professionals have a history. We hope he survives again.

But on an antipsychotic Greg is on dial tone. His emotions are muted. His computer work is more focused, but less wildly creative. His intellect is focused, but his poetry, his eccentric and original playing with words, is gone. He seldom laughs. He is still quietly delighted with scatology but can't manage the wild rumpuses of repetition and echolalia. His rhythms are off, alliteration and assonance are accidental. His brain can learn when he is on an antipsychotic, but his brain doesn't play. When he is psychotic, his brain shrieks and rages and finds enemies where none exist. He loses his poetry then too—his rhythms become disjointed, his word play is limited to insults and swearing, his vocabulary is stunted, his metaphors are frighteningly bizarre.

When he is medicated I miss his poetry and playfulness, though I'm deeply grateful for the relief from fear. Greg hates feeling stupid and slow and it's just a matter of time before he refuses the meds again. I can't blame him. He looks half alive.

But alive. How do we balance this?

Clark's story: dealing with medication refusal

Though gifted intellectually, Clark had a nasty hair-trigger temper. He was verbally impulsive and aggressive—he would say and do things that were destructive to his relationships with people he cared about and who cared about him. At home he punched holes in the wall and pushed and shoved his parents. There were times when he just could not contain himself. Though Clark had the ability to have white-hot focus on his schoolwork he was unable to master his own emotional life.

Clark's psychiatrist suggested that he take medication to give him more control over his temper outbursts. He suggested several possibilities, starting a trial with the anti-hypertensive quanfacine (Tenex). Tenex turns down the brain's use of adrenaline and calms the central nervous system, and helps some children with severe temper problems. Clark pushed back hard against taking the medication and he did not accept the doctor's diagnosis of "ADHD with episodic rage." Clark was lonely for friends. In his mind, taking medication would distance him further from other kids. He did not need the reputation or the put-downs that were suffered by other teens with similar diagnoses and medication regimens at school. He loathed the side effects of the medication, including tiredness, and some slowing of cognitive function. He gave his parents a resounding "No Fucking Way!" to their attempts to get him on the medication. They felt trapped by his condition; unable to do what they knew would protect themselves and help Clark.

Clark had been to an anger management course but true to form, his severe ADHD interfered with his ability to remember to apply the instruction around self-calming in the appropriate context. Right after the training, several incidents occurred in which he went from zero to sixty on the anger scale without slowing down. My hunch was that Clark's problem involved deep brain structures in the limbic systems that were not moved by the teachings from the anger management course.

When I began work with Clark I asked him about the important kids in his life. I knew that beginning on the subject of medication refusal would be a waste of time. Clark had to make his own decisions in this regard. The most important aspect of a teen's life is the quality of his relationships with friends and peers. The social domain is the arena for his developmental learning and progression. I knew that the only way Clark would accept medication would be to have a positive effect on his social life.

He told me that he had only one friend, Gina, who understood him and with whom he had experienced both emotional and sexual intimacy. Gina, he asserted, was the only one who understood his issues, and he was the only one in her life who accepted her as she was.

The Chinese symbol for "crisis" contains two characters—one character shows "risk," the other "opportunity." Oftentimes letting a certain type of crisis push the situation to resolution is the best choice. Crisis came to Clark when Gina broke up with him. He had gotten jealous of one of Gina's other friends, a boy in one of the classes they had together, and had jumped the kid as he came down the hall. In front of hundreds of kids, Clark had proceeded to make a fool of himself, semi-hysterically throwing the other boy against a locker and running off. Gina was very embarrassed by this event and immediately distanced herself from him, telling him she did not want to be his friend anymore. Clark was hurting badly from the rejection that came on top of the disgrace of a week's suspension for his assault.

In terms of the Chinese pictograph, we are now at the point of opportunity—of looking at some creative ways to change things for the better.

We spent quite a bit of time looking at the issue as an aspect of brain function. I described how the ADHD in his nature decreased his ability to think things through, by decreasing the capability of his orbitofrontal cortex—I showed him where this structure was located over his right eye. And I talked about how the overactive emotional centers of his limbic brain increased the push to impulsive action. I did my best Jim Carey impression of several different animals to illustrate the function of the animal brain.

In our next session Clark showed a good command of the brain physiology involved in what happened with Gina. He wanted to know just how medication might help him. I explained how the medications used to treat impulsivity increase communication between brain neurons that inhibit impulsive behavior. I told him that these kinds of medications could normalize the lives of people who run on "extreme arousal" most of the time. I explained to him that medication that inhibits expression of impulsive anger, and turns down the force of depression, may be part of the picture for long-term healing, in that the brain conditioning known as the "kindling effect" is prevented.

Several sessions followed in which Clark came in with extreme bravado but I noticed he was not bad-mouthing his psychiatrist or the suggestion for medication. In fact he was still hurting mightily over Gina's breaking up with him and beginning to wonder aloud if there was any hope for him at all.

As he lamented his situation I suggested that he might want to revisit the idea, from our discussion of brain function, that there are some parts of his brain that over-heat too quickly under stress. I suggested that he was experiencing a functional health-related problem, not a psychiatric problem. I told him that there might be a physical reason why he was such a "hothead."

Clark told me that he had not quite looked at it in that way before. He was terrified of any of the other kids seeing him at my office. He had bought into the idea that he was mentally ill. It lightened him up to think of his problem as an inherited pattern of reaction, a problem with the way his central nervous system reacted to stress, but not a mental problem.

He made a qualified decision to try the medication suggested by his doctor. He would assess side effects and decide if he wanted to stay on it. At some point he thought he would want to let Gina know that he was taking charge of the situation.

As it turned out, the medication worked well for him. He was not overly troubled by Tenex's principle drawback, its tendency to make one sleepy. I suspected that he was metabolically faster than most people and so had a leg up on the sedating properties of the drug. Most importantly, the genie in Clark's bottle was finally under some control. He could still get angry but when he did, he did not trash his life. He was able to apply his energy and very high intelligence to his work at school and his life began to blossom.

Clark's sessions with me decreased to the point of an occasional check-in. I enjoyed getting into the "pesky-adviser" role with him and was happy to be out of the crisis management place. He confided in me that the medication did not dampen his genius for calligraphy.

I last met with him after he turned fifteen. He was in an arts high school designed for kids with attention deficit disorder. Gina and he were now "just friends," she had a new boyfriend and he had several girlfriends. He was tattooed, obsessive about his calligraphy, and happy. His instructors worried about his intensity and tendency to party too much, but delighted in his presence. His work was already becoming known in the artistic community. The energy that spilled out of him as a child as impulsivity and relentless anger was under his direction and contributing to his ability to do the hard work of learning about his art.

To deal with medication refusal, pull toward the child's goals

Clark's story illustrates the idea that sometimes you have to wait for your moment to suggest medication. Timing is very important, even though you must deal with uncertainty and the stress of knowing that your child is at risk. But once something happens that gives him inner motivation to try meds, you have the opportunity to have him look at the question with an open mind.

It is best at these times to relate taking the medication to specific symptoms and avoid diagnostic labels such as "psychotic," "bipolar disorder," or "oppositional." Instead treat the symptoms or learning disabilities themselves, and present the medication as a way to increase function and opportunity.

- If a child has a problem controlling his tendency to blurt things impulsively and push friends away for this reason, present the medication as one way to bring more friends to him.

- If a child suffers from the inability to put his thoughts in priority order—"disordered thinking"—and figure things out (such as is seen in psychosis, autism, and Asperger syndrome), let him know that neuroleptic medication will help him put his thoughts in correct priority, one after the other. Let him know that this will have positive benefits for making friends.

- If the child has attention deficit disorder and experiences learning disabilities, describe the stimulant medication he takes as the "work med." Given the dyslexia, dysgraphia, central auditory processing, short-term memory, executive function deficits, and many more learning problems that are noted in the Individual Education Plans of many AD children in Special Ed, it makes sense to try something that might help one pay attention and get through the boring work. The child can consider the issue more clearly if it is simply put as a choice to do schoolwork the hard way or do it a little easier. To have friends, or to push people away.

The AD child should never be directly penalized for refusing medication. Pushing a medication-resistant child to take his meds is like pushing an anorexic teenager to eat. The act of pushing makes the conflict worse. I have learned after working with many AD children that as distressing as their behavior may be, they want to succeed just as much as do neurotypical children. That desire for success, along with a bit more observer perspective that sometimes follows crisis, may be the factor that enables a child to let go of some objection to a medication and commit to giving it a chance.

Though a child may be possessed by powerful genius, it is necessary to have a high state of brain function to express that genius. The body can be seen as a most exquisite tool of the spirit in this sense. If that tool is out of balance in some important way, the expression of the genius will also be out of balance. Being attuned to the child and providing stability to him through lifestyle and medication management, are the best things that you can do to give his positive genius the chance to emerge strong and straight.

1. Identify the factors that throw his emotional gyroscope off its equilibrium and work to keep these things out of his life.

2. Prevent instability with positive family communications, "memory talk," predictable family routines, and adequate sleep.

3. Use medication wisely, researching both benefits and dangers.

4. Encourage medication compliance by trying compliance to access to privileges, such as use of the car.

Sixth criterion

Caregivers help the AD child re-member himself

Neurons which fire together at one time will tend to fire together in the future.

Donald Hebb[1]

In previous chapters, we suggest that underdevelopment of the brain structure called the orbitofrontal cortex in attention different children puts them at risk of losing their composure, losing perspective, and going too far when confronted with stressful situations. In order for their positive genius to emerge they need to learn how to control the brain's tendency to scream into "fight or flight" when stressed.

When the attention different (AD) child gets "beside himself" with rage or fear, he must be able to "re-member" himself. I use the term "member" here as one would to describe an arm or leg. In this case it is the child's psyche that is detached and the task is to bring it back into his body. In terms of the central metaphor of this book, the genie (his emotional self) is out of the bottle with no control.

Box 6.1 In the Crucible: more mud, less pool

Journal:

Age ten. Greg wades carefully into his favorite creek, hunting bullheads and frogs. He finds salmon eggs—"Brown, Mom! Air bubbles that never pop!" Secrets in mud reveal themselves to his avid eyes and gentle hands. At his request I record his catches—three today, bullheads, two to four inches, slipped back alive into the living stream.

Later at the swimming pool he throws his "goddamn goggles fucking *torture* mask!" I make him pick them up. I explain him to the teenage lifeguard. I'm too old for this.

When Greg is engaged in something he loves to do he is calm and functional. The swimming pool is overwhelming, with its shouts and echoes, and is a ridiculous place to take him. So more mud, less pool.

The psychosomatic dynamics of losing control at the moment of stress

Many AD children display very impressive self-awareness in their discussion in my counseling office of the troubles that they have with others. They will voice understanding of others' reactions, and understanding of their own foibles and how their AD temperament is part of the problem. But when they return to the situation that challenges them, be it a crowded classroom or a very annoying little brother, they will lose their composure and self-control. Why the child has a difficult time being resourceful has a lot to do with the way human beings are wired to respond to stress.

Stress is a mind–body phenomenon that involves three types of activity: mental, physical, and behavioral. When the AD child becomes angry, for example, his mental activity speeds up and begins pumping "catastrophic" thoughts through his mind such as, "I can't deal with this," or "I can't let (the other) get away with this," or "I feel overwhelmed." At this moment his physical activity will show aspects of the general adaptation syndrome to include muscle tightening, shortness of breath, a feeling of heat in the body, and sweating. And his behavioral response will express his mind–body distress in impulsive and destructive ways—yelling, throwing things, or fleeing in panic from the stressor.

In the heat of the moment, the mind and body feed information to each other in such a way that the situation is made worse. The mind picks up on the body's reaction and tells itself that things are out of control. As the situation worsens the child becomes more frightened, generates more catastrophic thoughts, and his body becomes more stressed. Around and around it goes in a worsening cycle.

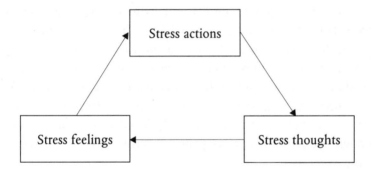

Figure 6.1 The psychosomatics of a worsening stress reaction

Five strategies to help the AD child cope with stress

Here are five strategies to help your AD child behave more resourcefully by staying "in his body," aware, and present in stressful situations:

1. Use body-state descriptive language.

2. Use affirmations, calming self-statements, and successful event recall to help your child be resourceful in difficult moments.

3. Get the AD child into joyful movement.

4. Use the wisdom of sports psychology to help your AD child develop personal resourcefulness rituals.

5. Build strength for self-control with "lion-hearted" parenting.

Box 6.2 In the Crucible: containing verbal tyranny

Greg has stayed awake until midnight from the time he was a toddler. During the evenings as his meds wore off, until his late teens, he became a wild animal. We tried everything, eventually sleeping pills—which didn't work—to get him to sleep and give us all some rest. George and I took turns with the evening and bedtime routines and fell into bed exhausted. Greg's symptoms tyrannized us all.

His wild rumpus of insults and name-callings and vicious threats lasted for hours, especially when we insisted on something that he didn't want to do. "Leave me *alone* fuckhead I'll take my shower in two minutes when I'm *done* I *know* the time I'm not *stu*pid fucking crusty old fart hag-bitch leave me *alone!*" And while the mother that I am stayed focused, adult and effective, refusing to be overwhelmed, the poet fiercely loved—and remembered and wrote down—his extravagances, his rhythms, his dedication to the exact word.

Over the years Greg has learned some restraint, and works hard to stop his verbal abuse. "I'm *going* out on my fucking bike you can't stop me asshole I *love* the dark I've got two lights on my bike buttpick so up your *butt* with a rubber *nut* you dickhead I'm sorry I called you that Mom you didn't deserve it I'm *going* out you can't fucking stop me. *Ass*hole." Sometimes an outburst/apology/outburst helped him stop, or slow down, his verbal roller coaster. Sometimes not.

George and I let Greg cuss at home as much as we can tolerate, to ease his burden in the company of others. It isn't possible for him to stop completely, so we help him learn when and where he can let it out. And we talk to our friends and neighbors, explaining his condition. Most people are supportive, once they know what's going on. Now he is twenty he swears much less, though people are more afraid of him than they used to be, because he looks wild.

Use body-state descriptive language

This is a communication technique that you, as a caregiver, can use to help the AD child get control of himself in difficult moments such as during meltdown or rage. Use language that alerts him to the state of his body, which is, now, hyperactive, excited, and possibly psychotic. Say: "You are frothing at the mouth and slapping yourself. I need you to stop slapping yourself. As soon as you can show me that you have control of your body, I will be glad to leave your room."

Instead of suggesting that he is a bad person, this way of putting it conveys the idea that he has forgotten how to control *his body* and the statement cues him to regain control.

Be aware that in times of crisis, your child's limbic brain is running the show—his cortical thought process is very inefficient at these moments. He is in his animal brain, so you must use simple and concrete language. Say: "As soon as you stop spitting and screaming at me I will talk to you about what you want."

Do not scold or lecture the child for this just enrages him further and pushes him further out of his body. He needs to come back. Again, the image of a wild genie out of his bottle is relevant here, and communication that calms the genie and gains his rapport is in order if we are to get the wildness contained.

There is a learning curve to using this kind of language and to setting up a rhythm that de-escalates the conflict. One parent told me that it took her several years to learn the technique. She was a fisher and used a metaphor borrowed from that sport. Getting control of the behavior of an out-of-control child is something like the way one plays a fish on the end of a line: use a little slack and back up when things are too hot, close the distance when there is opportunity to do so.

Use affirmations, calming self-statements, and successful event recall to help your child be resourceful in difficult moments

Affirmations, calming self-statements, and successful event recall work to change the child's perception of his capability to handle stress and affirm an expectancy of success.

Affirmations reverse the child's negativity and feelings of being overwhelmed caused by his body's fight or flight reaction under stress.

Affirmations are one-sentence, positively worded self-statements that the child repeats silently to himself twice daily and are used to build self-esteem and/or overcome self-limiting beliefs. Affirmations should be:

- personal

- positive

- present tense

- accurate and balanced

- indicate achievement "I am…" "I have…"

- describe change as EASY

- describe change as already happened

- reflect fun and excitement.

Here are some sample affirmations that follow these guidelines:

- "I feel warm and loving toward myself for I am a unique and precious being ever growing in wisdom and love."

- "Every day in every way I'm getting better and better."

- "I know what I know and I express myself easily."

Your child may want to write each affirmation down on a postcard. Each day he should read it to himself and vividly picture and experience the end result that he wants. He should repeat the affirmation several times, only affirming the goals he really wants. (It won't work if he tries to reprogram himself from a sense of duty or obligation.)

Calming self-statements are like affirmations but are specifically used during moments of stress and anxiety. What your child says to himself depends on the situation. Some examples are:

- "Relax, take several deep breaths; keep calm. This is really a minor matter that I can easily deal with if I keep my cool."

- "Nobody here is trying to get me; keep a sense of humor."

- "Relax. I'm in control. Take a slow deep breath. Ah, good!"

Successful event recall requires that the child deliberately recalls situations in which he functioned particularly well, felt at his best, and did a good job. It is effective to the degree to which he can vividly imagine and feel a previous success.

USE NATURALISTIC AFFIRMATIONS TO BUILD THE CHILD'S SENSE OF INNER STRENGTH

Because children may not practice affirmations as rigorously as is needed to change behavior, I shore up their power by using another form, which is introduced into conversation as a compliment, and which subliminally alters the child's perception of his potential. I use this form with children who come to me for counseling (and I teach it to their parents).

Using conversational affirmations, you bridge from a *known capability* to a *developing capability*. This is the process of helping the child see connections in his Great Story that are expansive to his sense of himself.

An example of this kind of naturalistic affirmation comes from my work with a twelve-year-old Tourettic girl who was badly teased at school for her vocal tics. This was the last thing she needed at this important time in her life and she was very depressed. I took the opportunity to affirm her resilience from her participation in Aikido, a pastime that was highly rewarding to her.

I said,

> I remember that you told me your Sensei (instructor) in Aikido said that learning to fall is the most important step in learning the art. She taught you how to roll into the fall and jump back on your feet. I don't mean to say I really know what you are feeling but it seems like you are dealing with those kids teasing you about your tics in the same way. You are hurt but you keep coming back. I am impressed with how you are dealing with it. Feels like you're making some powerful changes here.

It is relatively easy to find lots to compliment a person about, if you just listen with the question in mind about what they are doing *right*. As you do this you exert a powerful influence on the self-perception of the child and you strengthen his character. You give him courage with your words.

USE EVERYDAY LANGUAGE TO INTRODUCE AN AFFIRMATION INTO YOUR
CHILD'S CONSCIOUSNESS

1. Find an example of a skill that looked *impossible* to learn but
    which the child eventually mastered. Learning to ride a bike is
    a skill that many kids can relate to. "At first," you say, "it
    looked like you could never ride that bike, you would fall over.
    But you kept at it and you learned about balance, and now
    you're good at riding just about any bike."

2. Then bridge from this ability to some behavior change the
    child is working on, such as not hitting another kid who
    provokes him. "Controlling your urge to hit Matt must be just
    as hard as learning to ride your bike, but I see that you're
    changing in your ability to control yourself. You don't get into
    hassles anymore with a kid like him, who doesn't really
    deserve *any* of your attention."

AFFIRM THE CHILD WITH COMMENTS APPROPRIATE TO HIS STAGE OF
DEVELOPMENT

Affirmations are a language-based strategy and so they must be tailored
to fit children at different stages of development. Language is the basis of
thought and children *think* differently as they grow, with greater complexity and ability to form abstractions.

AFFIRMATIONS FOR AN ELEMENTARY SCHOOL-AGED CHILD

The basic challenge AD children face at this stage is in the development
of a *sense of self.* Amidst the turmoil of growing up attention different, it is
difficult to remember who you are. A child with a strong sense of identity
knows: "This is who I am. This is what I can do. This is how I deal with
the world. These are the ones who love me and whom I love and respect."
Development of a sense of self occurs when the child is out of crisis. This
may be difficult for an emotionally overwrought AD child. Here are some
affirmations that help children in this phase.

I know that this has been a frustrating year for you in school, but
when I saw how you got yourself together to get your science
project in, I knew you had reached an important change point in

your ability to get through your frustrations and keep on task. I'm so proud of you!

Jamie has invited you over to his house for a sleepover? Very cool! I see that you're really looking forward to enjoying your independence for the night!

You've told me that sometimes it feels like you can't control your body or your mind. I can see that you are now getting your brain and heart working together! Good for you!

AFFIRMATIONS FOR A MIDDLE SCHOOL-AGED CHILD

An AD child aged about twelve is especially receptive to affirming comments, because at this age he is negotiating the extremely important early adolescent identity crisis. How he comes to see himself at this time in his life will have a powerful effect on his sense of courage. He needs courage if he is to release his genius in a positive way. This child might receive and integrate into his self-concept comments such as:

I know the stress you have been through that led to your psychiatric hospitalization. Looks like you are getting things back on track now! Good work. How can I help?

I know you have struggled with the tendency to be a drama king around your friends. I am so pleased to see you having fun, and having greater control of yourself in social situations!

AFFIRMATIONS FOR THE HIGH SCHOOL-AGED CHILD

AD adolescents may be dangerously impulsive, hypomanic, or given to bouts of extreme depression. Or they may suffer in silence, without the comfort of a peer group. These children need affirmation of their ability to negotiate the extremely important identity crises that occur as they enter adolescence, around age twelve or thirteen, and then again around age seventeen. These are times when important questions must be resolved. As they enter their teen years the main question is, "What kind of a teenager should I be?" Later, toward the end of high school, the questions become, "Do I choose to be like my parents?" Or "Do I choose to be very different from them?" Or "Do I choose a way of life that I am learning from my peer group?" Or "Do I choose to put the whole thing on hold and slide along without deciding?" The child needs a rite of passage at these times, which may come in many different forms. A rite of passage is some accomplishment that requires the teen to dig deep within himself and find capabilities that he did not know existed before. It may be success in school or athletics. It may be meeting the challenge of an ordeal in the outdoors such as in the context of an outward bound or rites of passage program. The end result is that the adolescent's movement to adulthood is affirmed in such a way that his entire psyche knows it.

If the AD adolescent does not get the needed affirmation of his development, the manic side of his genius may take over. I have observed that if AD teenagers are not challenged in a way that brings out the positive aspects of their genius at the right time, the negative aspects will emerge. Typically the child will be given to flights of extreme emotion, impulsivity, lack of observer perspective, and a tendency to depression. Here are some examples of affirming language that help build his character strength at these important junctures:

> You know, you've gone through a rite of passage this last summer. The trek changed you. I can see that you have your priorities together!

> I am so impressed by your ability to see your relationship with Sharlene (his girlfriend) clearly. You have both your emotions and mind engaged. Very cool!

> I appreciate how hard it is for you to accept the idea that you need to take medication. I am pleased that you see it as helping you and that you choose to continue it. In my mind, being able to exercise this self-discipline takes a boy to manhood.

> I know kids with Asperger aren't supposed to be real bubbly characters, but I see you as the Happy Consultant. You just light up when you get the opportunity to help someone with computers! This is a very heartful side of you!

The power of using affirmations to boost kids' success in school has been documented in several studies. Cueing staff to deliberately give positive remarks to students, especially those at risk, has been shown in several study populations to be part of a marked reduction (better than 50 percent) in the number of children who dropped out of school. This result is powerful proof of a basic principal of human development, and one that has direct applicability to our discussion of the nurturing of genius in children: *what you pay attention to grows*. If you focus on the negative, it grows. If you focus on the capabilities of the child, these positive aspects will grow and become part of his genius.

Get the AD child into joyful movement

Participation in athletics, gymnastics, or a performing or martial art has saved the life of many an AD child. The embodiment that comes with participation in these activities greatly compensates for the tendency of the AD child to fly out of his body when stressed. Beneficial activities include the following:

- martial arts: Kendo (sword fighting), Aikido (the use of energy in physical encounters), T'ai Chi (the graceful Warrior Dance), Tai Kabuto (street fighting) and fencing, European style

- rock climbing

- skateboarding, skiing, and skating

- dance: ballet, tap, modern, jazz, folk, and ethnic

- yoga and pilates

- team sports: soccer, hockey, football, baseball

- wrestling

- swimming

- gymnastics.

In my counseling practice I have observed often that the healthiest kids I work with participate in activities that require extensive use of their bodies. The genius of the AD child is nourished by physicality. Being embodied, the child will feel integrated, capable, and brave. In joyful movement his anxieties lift, his intuition takes over, and his genius shows through.

Box 6.3 In the Crucible: balancing the body

I grew up with an undiagnosed mother. Ballet helped me through both her abuse and whatever neurological disorder I might have been born with—there must have been something, a touch of Asperger, a little Tourette, because these neurological disorders are genetically handed down from both sides of the family tree. Anything actively physical, especially something that balances both sides of the body, like ballet, or swimming, or gymnastics, or Aikido, helps to heal the brain's eccentricities. Learning lateral equality of strength and flexiblility helps many kids, and I was blessed with this accidental balancing of the body long before anyone knew much about neurological disorders and how to treat them.

Greg did exercises to balance the body when he was ten. He doesn't do well in team sports—I've never seen him do what everyone else is doing, except in mimicry. He can't tolerate the echoes in large rooms, like gyms or swimming pools, though he did very well in his early teens with Aikido, partly because the mat stifled sound. All his physical activity now is solitary. He used to walk and bike for miles, though on his latest med his muscles are stiff and slow and his walks are much shorter. He misses his normal physical activity.

Use the wisdom of sports psychology to help your AD child develop personal resourcefulness rituals

The destructive feedback cycle between stress thoughts, feelings, and actions described at the beginning of this chapter can worsen a child's coping ability *or* can be turned to his advantage. The secret is to devise personal rituals: learned habits that help him behave resourcefully at stressful times.

The use of ritual to increase personal effectiveness is an ancient human practice and is seen in all cultures. Rituals center a person, help him gather strength and confidence and move with awareness and precision. Rituals are seen in the ancient warrior societies of Africa in the form of traditional dances and chanting practiced by tribesmen before going into battle. They are seen in the use of meditation before martial artists entered into competition in Japan. In the modern armies of the world, they are formalized in military pageantry, and precise and complex battlefield movements that are initiated with a single command and followed without thought.

The model suggested here is drawn from the successful practice of sports psychology—the science of making winners of people who must perform under the most stressful situations imaginable.[2] Master sports psychologist Jim Loehr who has coached tennis champions and Olympic athletes to the winner's podium, teaches the use of short rituals as a way of countering the stress of competition and keeping focus on the game. Observing tennis greats such as Chris Evert, he noticed that these champions demonstrated little mannerisms such as (in Evert's case) plucking at the strings of her tennis racket while walking back and forth on the court between serves, all the while keeping an upright position and avoiding any distraction or indulgence in emotional display. Evert and other master athletes practiced what a famous Spanish matador called the "matador's walk," a proud bearing which the bullfighter says produces courage in a person.

Returning to the principle of psychosomatic feedback, we see that the choice of ritualistic behavior can powerfully influence mental attitude and the body's reaction to stress. In fact, the use of ritual enables the AD child to remember what to do without thinking *because* he has learned certain behavior at the *body* level and does not have to stop and analyze the situation. Effective rituals train automatic reactions in the three perceptual modalities of kinesthetic (feeling), visual (seeing), and auditory (thinking). Here are some examples:

Situation: an AD child is subject to bullying at school.
Ritual:

1. *Kinesthetic component.* Teach him the matador's walk, imagining that he has a string attached to the top of his head that holds his posture upright and confident. This enables him to walk

with power and confidence and, in so doing, project these qualities.

2. *Visual component.* Teach him to visualize himself walking past bullies, screening out their comments, avoiding eye contact, keeping his attention focused straight ahead on his destination.

3. *Auditory component.* Teach him to subvocalize "Power before me, power behind me, power to my left, power to my right, power above, power below."

Situation: entering a new social group for the first time.
Ritual:

1. *Kinesthetic component.* Have him carry in his pocket some memento of a friend, adult or child, and touch this memento as he walks into the social group.

2. *Visual component.* Teach him to remember a time when he enjoyed casual chitchat with another child or adult. It may be difficult for him to recall such an event but it is worth the effort to come up with just one resourceful memory. All he needs is one memory of social effectiveness.

3. *Auditory component.* Teach him to ask himself, when another child is talking about something happening in her life, "Has a similar thing happened to me?" When there is a pause in the conversation, relate the thing that he remembers that is similar to the other's experience. And provide an appropriate affirmation such as "No one in the world is more or less important than I am. They do their thing and I do mine." This affirmation gives the AD child greater confidence for social interaction.

Situation: taking a test at school.
Ritual:

1. *Kinesthetic component.* Teach him to sit upright, breathe deeply, and arrange the test sheet in front of him in a comfortable

position placing his writing instruments and calculator in an orderly fashion in front of him. Teach him to recall a time when he aced a particular test and remember how good it felt to see the good grade on the paper coming back.

2. *Visual component.* Teach him to see himself moving easily through the test, answering the questions that he knows first and then coming back to the more difficult items.

3. *Auditory component.* Teach him to subvocalize calming self-statements such as "This is no big deal, I can get through it." Or say to himself, "Noticing a bit of apprehension. Take a breath. There, that does it. No big problem."

Situation: dealing with frustration or anger-provoking situations. Ritual:

1. *Kinesthetic component.* Teach him to take his own pulse by pushing gently in on the artery just under his jawbone on the left side. While doing this, teach him to breathe down to his diaphragm. Then instruct him to walk away from the situation to a place where he can pace back and forth or walk for a short time.

2. *Visual component.* Teach him to see himself walking away from the anger-provoking situation noticing that the color of his body aura changes from red to a calming blue.

3. *Auditory component.* Teach him to subvocalize, "Walk it off. Walk it off" as he moves out of contact with the stressor.

MAKE SURE TO LINK PERFORMANCE OF A RITUAL WITH THE CHILD'S VALUES AND GOALS

Rituals train the AD child's "inner genie" to keep focused in the heat of stress but if a child is not motivated to achieve a certain goal, the most carefully devised ritual will not help him.

Learn about the AD child's basic values by tuning in to his Great Story. As you listen to his narrative of the trials and triumphs of his life, you begin to recognize his motivation and basic values. As he tells you about his struggles, you get an idea of what is meaningful to him—what was worth the risk, what really matters to him in his life. One child may desire academic success. Another may put a high priority on gaining friends or succeeding in some sports activity.

You get specific information by asking him how he wants to be seen by others, or who his role models are. Learning to perform a ritual is the same as learning a new habit and this takes work and dedication. It will not happen if the child isn't wholeheartedly committed to the process. As you listen carefully to the story of his life, you get a clearer idea of the kinds of endeavors that will benefit from the creation of a ritual. Ritual does not complement trivial pursuit. It is important that any ritual chosen addresses deeply felt needs and aspirations—things that really matter to the child.

Build strength for self-control with "lion-hearted" parenting

Most AD children are able to articulate appropriate behavior in a situation but do not remember to apply this knowledge. Typically, remembering what to do is forgotten under the pressure of stress. The ability to remember improves as the child grows through adolescence. This ability can be enhanced in younger children, with a very deliberate parenting and school approach that channels the child in a positive direction with rewards, boundaries, and consequences.

It is important that behavior be shaped by a trust-but-verify attitude. The genius of the AD child is powerful and becomes aggravated by attempts to constrain it. It is important to be strategic and certain in the imposition of consequences. I like Dr. Larry Silver's approach here.[3] He writes that parents need to have absolute control of the situation. He believes that all children, including those with neuropsychiatric issues, will respond to a parenting approach that is primarily loving, but also strict and unyielding. He advocates the use of natural consequences, such as the withdrawal of the parent from providing any service to the child until he complies with the adult's request. For example, parents are advised to stop making the child's dinner, stop doing his laundry, and stop getting him up in the morning and off to school. Silver reports that the loss of support quickly gets the attention of the most obstinate child and he becomes more amenable to behaving responsibly. Of course there are exceptions. It would not be safe to leave some children unattended. This would not be an appropriate strategy for a child who could not take care of basic needs unassisted.

Box 6.4 In the Crucible: "My Son Pulls Himself out of His Experiment with Anorexia"

Many Odd Ducks have qualities that would make them shamans in less industrial cultures. Shamans don't fit well in our noisy crowded cities but the impetus to experience the world of the invisibles is powerful. And one way to experience the transcendent is through fasting.

When I read Greg this poem he added the words "Experiment with" to the title, which opened up a new discussion about that phase in his life, and for me, a new understanding of why he stopped eating, and how he brought himself back to health.

> Since August he has starved himself to induce
> epiphany. Lost thirty pounds. Six hundred push-ups
> and chin-ups a day. He stops his meds. I give up
> all illusion of control.
> Today, after deep quiet under three blankets he tells me
> *Maybe I'm not healthy enough for visions.*
> His parakeets sing from opposite ends of the room.
> *I just ate half an egg and drank a glass of water.*
> *My stomach feels weird, feels good.* A northern flicker
> knock-knock-knocks outside the window.
> I tell him *Everybody's talking to you. Parakeets.*
> *Flicker. Your stomach.* His silence
> lasts all the afternoon.

But the central idea, of pulling back privileges that the child takes for granted, is sound. It is a reminder that he is a part of the family community and should do his part. Lion-hearted love strengthens the child's ability to contain his genius by giving the genius the message that strong as he is, the child's community is stronger, and will contain and control the Little Anarchist Within until he has developed the observer perspective to contain himself.

COMING BACK INTO HIS BODY, THE AD CHILD EXPERIENCES FLOW[4]

One AD child I worked with, a bright thirteen-year-old, was into rock climbing. He told me that when he was climbing it was like the face of the rock was flowing under him as he slowly moved up the side of the mountain. This is an apt description of the flow state discussed in chapter 8—a state of consciousness in which time stops and one's whole being is comfortably focused on the task. The strategies listed in this chapter are offered as ways to bring the AD child into a state of balanced intensity: aware simultaneously of his emotional state, and what is happening around him. Coming back into his body, the emotionally and energetically hyper-aroused child is able to take a breath, feel more in control, and behave more resourcefully.

1. Use body-based, concrete language when trying to help the child calm himself.

2. Use affirmations, calming self-statements, and successful event recall to help him be resourceful in difficult moments.

3. Use naturalistic affirmations that are appropriate to his stage of development to build his sense of inner strength.

4. Get him into joyful movement.

5. Use the wisdom of sports psychology to help your AD child develop personal resourcefulness rituals.

6. Build strength for self-control with "lion-hearted" parenting. Expect good behavior and provide reasonable and predictable consequences if it does not occur.

The seventh criterion in the field of nurturing: caregivers' practice of high-level wellness in their own lives

Introduction

What is genius? Genius is the desire to act upon what is already created or conditioned, coupled with the ability to do so and the strength of will to do so regardless of social constraints. Genius is despised close up, but the further you are removed from it in space and time, the more attractive it seems.

> Don W., an anonymous writer
> quoted in Strange Brains and Genius[1]

"Genius is despised close up, but the further you are removed from it in space and time, the more attractive it seems." This writer speaks of the fact that bringing up and tempering the genius of an attention different (AD) child may take a toll on our bodies. In *Survival Strategies for Parenting Children With Bipolar Disorder*, I described the case of Carol, the grandmother of a boy suffering from the severe episodic rage seen in bipolar disorder.[2] Carol educated me on the central importance of the caregiver keeping her own sense of control, love, and focus in the face of the furious assault delivered by a disturbed AD child. The wisdom "Physician, heal thyself," applies to all healers, including those of us in the role of parents. We have to be able to experience peace in our own hearts, even in the midst of crisis, before we can help our children find inner peace.

The idea of finding your own center is important here. This concept is drawn from martial arts such as Aikido, Karate, and Judo, and from many traditions of meditation. In these practices, one's center has a physical location close to, and just above, the navel. This point, located near the solar plexus, is called the "Din Tin" in Chinese, or "Hara" in Japanese. Masters of these movement arts train practitioners to put awareness on the center before every important move. To imagine that the movement itself and all the energy required is drawn up from that place in the body greatly strengthens the whole body and enables the person to accomplish dramatic, seemingly impossible, physical feats.

Sensing your center

Take a moment to imagine that your body is rigid, board-like, and that you have a balance point so that if you were stretched out horizontally, your body would be exactly level if supported at this point. The place on your body where you imagine you would balance is your center.

Now take a moment to send a deep, slow breath to that place in your body, breathing to your diaphragm so that your belly goes out like a small balloon. Relax into the experience and notice what you feel. Most people report that doing this kind of focusing relaxes them, clears the mind, and allows them to be more mentally effective in any task.

Parents who achieve a sense of being centered tell me that they "feel their feet on the ground" at all times. Or that they feel "fully in their bodies." They are learning to reverse the human tendency to panic, and get into emotional fight or flight in the face of stress. They are using stress as an isometric to strengthen themselves.

If you are able to achieve this feeling as you go into an encounter with your AD child, you may notice that he calms much quicker and is able to behave more resourcefully. Our children tend to notice intuitively our own sense of distress or confidence as they are provoking us. Though they may not have the "executive function," the intellectual capability to control themselves, they do instinctively read us and will tend to react accordingly. If your child reads you as being out of control, his loss of control will be worse. If he reads you as being in control, his behavior will tend to be less explosive, and his return to a resourceful state will arrive in a shorter period of time.

How stress challenges your ability to stay centered

The ability to stay centered is a litmus test of your overall hardiness. If you are on the verge of burnout, and feel exhausted, unable to cope, overwhelmed by your situation, you will have a difficult time staying centered under stress. You will be given to fight or flight and this is the energy that will invade your interaction with your child. You will fight him or run from him in distress. To prepare for the encounter with your child's genius, you must be strong in body, mind, and soul. You cannot stay in your heart and help your child return to this centering place unless you are able to do so yourself.

Given the constant pressure on you, there is a good chance that at some point you will break down physically and emotionally. Dr. Hans Selye said that we are given a finite amount of personal energy in our lives and that stress uses this energy up unless we renew it.[3] Borrowing from the Chinese martial arts, he used the word *chi* to describe this vital energy.

Chi is attacked by the relentless crisis of raising an attention different child. This is a crisis marked by the excruciating boredom and hair-raising terror you experience as a way of life. The boredom comes from never having the time to tend your own spirit or to do the things that you enjoy. Instead, you are involved in an endless sequence of doctor's appointments, hassles with the school system, or the police, or insurance companies. In many ways you have to function as the "frontal lobe" of your AD child, being his "executive function"—his day planner, friend finder, and defender before a hostile world. The other aspect of stress is crisis. As the parent of an AD child you must develop the intuition of an emergency room doctor and exercise this judgment more times than you can count. Crisis may be caused by his inability to control his rage, impulsivity, psychosis, or dangerous behavior. There is no let-up.

Typically this assault on your psychological, spiritual, and physical well-being begins before your child reaches the age of five. If you are the child's mother, you had thought that around this age your child would begin school, and you could return to doing the things that made your life enjoyable by way of vocation or work. But this return to normalcy is stopped as your child becomes symptomatic, and your life goes on hold. Your opportunity for personal renewal goes by the wayside and there is no let-up. You must forget your own goals and aspirations and become a full-time "special needs mom."

If you are not able to renew your *chi*, eventually you will reach the point of physical, emotional, and spiritual burnout. You will get sick and you will get depressed. You will stop caring. You will lose the ability to stay centered, and blow up when your child is having what can be euphemistically termed a "psychiatric moment." You are exhausted past your limits and yet still have to carry on. This is not a healthy situation.

It is interesting to consider the meaning of the word "burnout", for understanding this term gives us a clue about how to avoid it. Burnout is a term used by stress psychologists to indicate the state of mental disorder when a person feels physically, emotionally, and spiritually out of *chi*. People at this stage of burnout have lost the will to live. Life has become meaningless, a purposeless drudgery. But there is a way to avoid burnout, and in fact to prevail wonderfully, as did Carol, in the near-combat environment encountered with the darker aspects of your child's guiding spirit.

Selye pointed out that the body's ability to deal with stress is limited. Eventually the system gets exhausted and shuts down. In extreme cases this would mean that the immune system stops functioning, a person goes into shock, or dies. In terms of psychological dynamics, burnout can be seen as the emotional expression of the endpoint of the general adaptation syndrome. Burnout is another name for major depression and this state of consciousness expresses a person's feeling of being overwhelmed. Burnout is a dangerous condition, because it telegraphs the message to the body that it has been overwhelmed, and the body responds with a predictable shutdown response that may encourage the development of disease.

There is a way to renew yourself so that you prevail over stress and renew your *chi* so that you do not burn out, but rather that you "burn brightly" in every thing you do.

The three essential ingredients of high-level wellness

In 1979 University of Chicago researchers came to some important conclusions about the connection between stress and disease.[4] Their work showed that there is a group of people who live longer and better despite the stress they face. These "hardy" personality types may spend their days in very high stress occupations, as emergency room doctors, CEOs of huge companies, soldiers in combat, or have been through horrendous experiences such as German concentration camps during the Second World War.

Stress research tells us that the lives of these people are remarkable for the presence of three qualities: *purpose, freedom,* and *love.* As the parent of a

Box II.1 In the Crucible: the last day of respite

By the time Greg was eleven, I could no longer find respite care, though I paid babysitters three times the going rate. My friends helped out, but even they couldn't manage him anymore. The only person in our lives who consistently gave us time without Greg was his sister Kelly. She insisted on her right to have her brother with her for a couple of weeks every summer. She is still very much involved in Greg's life though she lives three states away, has two active toddlers and teaches high school full-time.

The last day of respite, apart from Kelly, came on a sunny Tuesday, when my friend Donna took Greg for a few hours while I went to yet another school planning meeting. Donna's house is big and full of dogs and cats, and her small gray barn has three horses. Greg loved going there. But when I got back from the meeting, I saw him walking the rail of the barn fence beside the street. He was stark naked and gathering stares and comments from passersby. Donna was calm as always, but told me she had had no control over him and couldn't take him again. I understood. And Greg was fine. He went to Donna's house with me the next month to see her new puppies.

But I was stuck. George could get away every working day for ten hours, but I had no time off my work with Greg except to go out in the evenings for a few hours when George came home. Weekends we tried to have some time together as a family and as a couple. Over the years as Greg became more and more floridly symptomatic, nearly all our time was taken up dealing with his uproar.

very difficult child, you must have a reason for living, you must enjoy freedom from oppression at work and home, and you must have the opportunity to give and get love in abundance.

Your ability to prevail when challenged by the aggressive aspects of your child's genius depends on the state of your psychosomatic health. If your foundational strengths in purpose, freedom, and love are strong, you will have the "juice" to behave confidently and effectively—to stay in your center. Having these three features in your life makes you an all-around stress-hardy person, and is a powerful inoculation to the burnout that may occur from struggling for many years with negative aspects of a powerful child's genius.

Importantly you must have a balance of all three qualities in your life to achieve high-level wellness. You cannot achieve a sense of freedom or love in your life without a sense of purpose. Freedom without overriding purpose becomes dilettantism. You have to know where you stand and what is meaningful in your life. And if you are not moved by a higher purpose, your ability to love is curtailed. You settle for shallow expressions of affection that pace your sense of withdrawing from the world, of making do. These three features must *all* exist in sufficient quantity if you are to experience hardiness, creativity, and the ability to persevere in the encounter with explosive aspects of your child's genius.

To renew your energy, your spirit, and to stay centered in your heart and power when your child is challenging you, you need to be able to lift yourself out of the day-to-day crisis and discover your own purposes; what gives your life meaning. You must be able to free yourself from the oppression of your parenting job. And you must be able to renew your love for yourself and find love in your work and life. When you achieve balance of these criteria you are able to experience delight and begin actualizing your own genius, your own reason for being alive. In the chapters that follow, specific suggestions are offered to help you experience more of these three essential qualities in your role as a parent and in your life at work and home. As you bring these qualities into alignment, you gain the energy and courage to free *your own* genius.

Practice enlightened selfishness to avoid burnout
Cultivate purpose, freedom, and love in your life.

CHAPTER 7

Self-care rule number one

Live on purpose!

Man is a goal-seeking animal. His life only has meaning if he is reaching out and striving for his goals.

Aristotle[1]

Do you believe that you deserve to have a purposeful life? Some people take the position that life is inherently meaningless, or that having the life you want is impossible, a luxury afforded to only a few. If you subscribe to this view your health is in danger! Stress research is clear that people who thrive, despite high stress in their lives, are committed to something that both challenges them and gives back to them. What is your challenge? What gives your life meaning?

We humans seem to be hard-wired to need a purpose. Having a purpose informs the body and mind that expansion and growth is the order of the day. If a person does not see his existence as meaningful, his body will take this as a message that it is time to shut things down. To stay healthy, you must have a reason to live. You must have something in your life that gives you a reason to get up in the morning. You must have a value system or a spiritual system, or work, to which you can offer your energy and your creativity. Living on purpose means that you have something you love to do that makes life worth living, that gives you what the hardiness researchers term "appropriate challenge."

Your attention different (AD) child gets great benefit from seeing you live the life you choose. One of his inherited characteristics is that he is "inner-directed." He moves to his own drummer. He may suffer in school because of his natural tendency to non-conformity. His work in life will most probably be along the "road less traveled," toward goals that he chooses intuitively regardless of the wishes or laments of adults in his life. This way of being is harder to bear if the child does not have the light of your fulfilled spirit.

He will watch you. If he sees you pursuing a meaningless existence, his cynicism around his own life and school will deepen. "What is there to be gained, after all, by all this absurd busy work? To end up like my dad? The whole thing sucks. Why should I try at all?" As this attitude deepens in the child's psyche, his genius moves away from its interest in the more arduous tasks of school (for imagined long-term gain) to the easier task of being a system disturber. Living as a social outlaw gives your child the thrill of being a counterpoint to your value system, and his genius bends to the service of making your life miserable.

Embarrassingly, AD children provide a litmus test of your satisfaction with your life. If you are unhappy or angry in your job, your AD child will copy your attitude and put it out in his behavior whether you want him to or not. His attitude may cue you to the necessity of taking a close look at how you are choosing to spend your time.

"Follow your bliss," means find and follow your own purposes

Dr. Joseph Campbell, the man who coined the term "follow your bliss," said that the most important thing in achieving satisfaction in your life is that you have the faith to keep after the activities that delight you.[2] It is the *following* that is important, not the acquisition of some perfect state of being. The first small step to following your bliss: you must believe that you deserve to live a whole-hearted life, and that it is possible to change things. This small, quiet decision puts you on the right track in terms of your purpose: fulfillment.

You do not have to change your vocation every five years to have a meaningful life. You simply have to be open to make little changes to put pursuits in your life that satisfy you. It is important to develop your personal vision of the kind of work and life you want to lead, and do something every day to move yourself in that direction.

What gives your life meaning? It might be your work with some art form. It might be your work outside the home. It might be tending your garden. It might be working with an organization that furthers some positive value in the world. Whatever it is that gives you a reason to go on and delight in the journey, it is good for you to go for it!

Have you ever looked at the expression on the faces of orchestra conductors as they lead their musicians in the accomplishment of a symphony? Or the rapt attention on the faces of jazz musicians riffing with each other? If the music touches your heart, there is always a sense of total commitment—of being lost in the work. The conductor must be totally committed to the piece of music or it will not move the audience emotionally, or pull out the best performance of each musician.

I believe that the great conductors of the world and our greatest musicians are by and large the happiest people on earth. Look at the bearing and manner of the late Vladimir Horowitz at the piano, or Zubin Mehta conducting the Israel Philharmonic. Look at the joy in their faces. High-level wellness requires that you put this kind of commitment into your life—you must find what purposes you can commit to and follow them with all your passion.

Having a purpose, you perceive opportunity and move outside your everyday habit patterns and personal comforts, your "comfort zone." If you do not have a sense of purpose, you shut down the assimilation of new experience at the perceptual level—not having a purpose, you cannot "see yourself" risking new behavior. When you live on purpose you are moved to say to yourself, "This is scary but my life requires that I deal with the fear as the cost of moving forward." If you are not committed to your life in this way you will always pull back. Eventually you will stop reaching as the aging process begins to calcify your ability to undertake new action. Use it or lose it.

Becoming more purposeful involves listening for your call

"Call" is a word used to describe the particular voice of your own genius. Another term for it is "vocation," a word derived from the Latin for "voice." Your call comes to you as a "voice in your ear," an invitation to become involved in a particular life work. Your call may change several times in your life. You sense your call by following a few basic rules.

- Pay attention to the things that are so full of delight that you lose a sense of time in the doing of them.

- Consider how you want others to see you in terms of your values and deeds. Say it in a sentence or two: "Jane Smith is a calm, committed, and brilliantly inspired special education teacher with the ability to help her students succeed."

- Pay attention to meaningful moments. These are times when you enjoy a fresh view of things. Some term them moments of "peak experience." Perhaps a sunset makes you cry, or watching your child finally overcome some obstacle. Your heart is filled with love and awe at the same time.

- Look at themes within the Great Story in the events of your life. If, for example, you have survived a traumatic event, you may find a call in helping others who have experienced trauma.

- Pay attention to the qualities and accomplishments you envy in others or the benefits of their lifestyle. You might be attracted to teaching because you are at a time in your life where having the summers off would be great! Or you might want to have the impact on kids' lives that teachers have.

- Consider the activities that make you feel at home with yourself, that you do with easy confidence or that you are able to teach others.

- Follow themes in your nighttime dreams such as "wandering" (an invitation to explore your psyche?), "waiting to go on stage" (an invitation to accept your call and run with it?), or "fighting with dragons" (an invitation to explore and contain the "fire" of your passions?).

Eric Utne, founder of the magazine *Utne Reader*, says that making sure that his heart and mind are working together has been important in his own life pursuit of purposeful endeavor.[3] If you leave yourself open to inspiration, you will get an idea of your call first as a potentially interesting or worthwhile involvement. Then, following Utne's suggestion, give yourself time to mull over the dialogue between your mind and your heart until a path to the call opens up in front of you.

Find your purpose doing things that delight you

One of my teachers, Dr. John Enright, summed up this situation with a simple model that has stuck with me for twenty-five years.[4] Enright said that a person might choose to spend his time: in discomfort, in relief from the discomfort, or in delight. In the first two zones, one either suffers, or experiences himself just one step ahead of things going to hell. If you are living in Zones II and I you are probably living others' expectations of you. Going through the motions. Putting on the mask. Keeping your head down.

If you are living in delight, in Zone III, you are living your purposes. Your life has meaning. You do not have to be a great artist (or a great anybody) to live in delight. You do not have to be perfectly happy all the time. You may get angry or experience many "negative" emotions. But through it all you are following your heart's desire. You are living the kind of life you choose, doing the kind of work you love. And thanks to your genius, you are good at it!

This model has implications for the parenting of your AD child. The pressure from your child's behavior keeps you in Zone I most of the time. You become used to life being a series of battles with your child, or other caregivers and professionals. You do not have the emotional leisure to dream your life—to imagine what sorts of vocations would move you through relief to delight. In terms of the freedom dimension you are free to move around in the foxhole that has become your life, but you dare not climb out of it. To experience your own sense of purpose, you have to be able to experience relief from the tedium and stress of raising your child and have reasonable control of the situation.

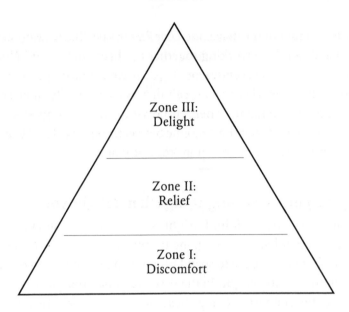

Figure 7.1 High-level wellness

To live in Zone III, identify your heart's desire

The first step is to listen to your call and let it lead you to your heart's desire—the work you *love* to do, the doing of which leaves you feeling whole, healthy, free. In terms of definition of terms, your call alerts you to the need to change your life path and your desire expresses the result of this change—your destination in terms of your life's work. Generally, we are taught that only a select few get to live their heart's desire. The rest of us have to lump it and do the best we can to achieve a little relief every now and then. It takes work to cut through the fog of this belief to identify what you really want to do with your life and to start doing it.

Your genius is directly expressed when you are doing the work that you love. You are lost in time. The Greek word *kairos* is used to denote this sense of total involvement. Hours may go by but you do not notice because in kairotic time, you are following your desire at every moment.

Children demonstrate what they desire in their delight in living, playing, and working in kairotic time. The child will show his gifts in his delight over his gem collection, his computer, or his phenomenal skill at motorcycling, rock climbing, acting, or music. Lost in his interest in these things, the child forgets the demands of his teachers or parents. Unfortunately the inability to adapt to clock time (the Greek word for this type of time is *chronos*) often results in the child being labeled as defective or deficient. In my counseling practice, I have observed that a predilection for living in kairotic time is characteristic of children with the diagnoses that are profiled in this book.

Box 7.1 In the Crucible: "Stalking the Wild Teen"

Over the years I've learned to savor and remember times of happiness. Sometimes a "short perfect October" is the only month in a year that is harmonious. The October Greg was fifteen, we had perfect Pacific Northwest weather as well as a respite from the disabling types of neurological eccentricities. We made the most of it.

Stalking the Wild Teen

Shaggy Manes are his first wild mushrooms—his eyes
finally know how to find them and they are suddenly
everywhere, tall clusters in hard-packed earth,
pale against the dark duff. When I was young
Shaggy Manes were eight-inch cylinders
of choice Gulf Island mushroom. Here, east
of Puget Sound, they hit four inches.
Fun to fry. Fat white rings browning,
picking up garlic and butter like a sponge.
Greg feasts on them days longer than I care to,
this short perfect October. He is fifteen.
Sporadic rain and sharp sunny days. Cold
nights. We hope to hunt down a chanterelle.

Your desire always expresses your love for being in the world. Loss of desire can be a harbinger for the development of depression in your life—the feeling of continual sadness, lack of energy, irritability, sleep problems or sexual difficulties. Depression is an indication that you are cut off from your purpose for being. This is a signal to look at how much satisfaction you are getting from your vocation, how much freedom you have in your life, and how much opportunity you have to give and get love.

Your desire may be seen in some secret longing you hold for some "impractical" vocation. One of my clients, a successful architect, had a secret desire to import fine fabrics with the art of the country of origin emblazoned on the cloth. She initially followed her desire with quiet delight, so as not to upset her husband and others who did not want her to pull her focus from her architectural practice. She used her frequent business trips abroad as opportunities to break away from her retinue of professional admirers and associates, to prowl local fabric markets and acquire fabrics and ideas for what eventually became a profitable import business.

Another man, a successful doctor, expressed his desire for freedom and unity with nature by nourishing a dream from childhood to be "a horseman"—to spend hours riding in the open country with the wind blowing through his hair, communing with nature and his trusty steed. Though he never had the opportunity to be around horses while growing up and establishing his medical practice, when he turned fifty he pledged to himself to realize his equestrian dreams. He bought a small place in the country where he could keep horses and (to use his term) "learn from them what I need to learn to become a horseman." This experience greatly invigorated him, changing his whole demeanor from that of the bored, pasty-faced city dweller, to a ruddy, rough-talking and joyous cowboy, and an even better doctor.

Deep desire is also expressed through the artist's way—in the visual arts, dance, writing, or music. The standard test for a writer is well known in the genre—"Is it possible for you not to write?" If you answer that question in the affirmative, there is a good chance this is not your vocation. But if you cannot keep from writing, you are probably a writer. This statement is true for all the arts.

Dr. James Hillman calls desire the "blue flame that purifies and trans-mutes" our spirits.[5] Thus defined, we see that accomplishing what we truly desire may not be painless. But taking the risk to "follow our bliss" may produce profound positive changes in our consciousness. To claim desire in your life you must first identify it and then you must live it. Here are three exercises to help you identify and live your desire.

Developing awareness of your desire: three exercises

Preparation: find a quiet place where you will not be disturbed. Put on some music that you enjoy that inspires and relaxes you. Breathe and ground yourself. Use your journal to note your thoughts as you go through this exercise.

First exercise

In a relaxed frame of mind, let your awareness wander back in time, first reviewing the past few days, then months, then years. Remember times when you felt yourself moving in the comfortable focus of kairotic time—when you were so involved in an activity that you lost track of the passage of time and experienced delight. Do not censor yourself. Allow the memory of any experience, no matter how impractical or mundane.

Once you have located several events in memory, choose the most powerful and take a few moments to enjoy it. Remember the delight. What was there about the event that was special? What made it luminous? Then let your memory float back to other similar events. When you are finished with this productive "day-dreaming," make a note or two to describe your experience. Take a moment to stretch and notice your energy level after this brief contemplation of your desire. If you were on track, you probably feel better, more alive.

Second exercise

Let your day-dreaming self imagine that there is a sudden knock at your door. A trusted friend enters to warn you that the Dream Police will arrive in twenty minutes. The Dream Police will take every memory you have except for those that you can write down in twenty minutes. What would you include on your list? Take a moment to consider what memories, thoughts, or important values you want to keep. Consider what is really important to you. Is it becoming wealthy or realizing love? Is it being successful? Is it being free? Your choice of memories will cast light on what is really important to you in life.[6]

Third exercise

Go back into the relaxed state of inner awareness. Breathe through your nose. Close your eyes. Imagine that you are standing outside in an open area that gives you a good view of the horizon and all around you, and above and below. Now bring images to mind that show you achieving your desire.

Imagine that these images are surrounded by other images, words, feelings, or colors that connote the values expressed by your desire—if you desire artistic accomplishment, for example, color the image of yourself doing art with a feeling of "being free," "living my truth," or "giving to the world." If you desire discovery and enjoyment of nature, surround that picture with value images that symbolize "love for the planet," or "helping the ecology."

Jot down a few notes in your journal about how you can manifest your desire. Do not censor. Just write down any hunches. Consider small steps and let a vision of your potential future emerge if you were to follow your desire. Watch for thoughts that say you are not entitled to actualize your desire. Note these "can't do" thoughts in a special place in your notebook.

When you are finished with this meditation, take a few moments to once again tune your awareness to your body and notice your level of energy. Change toward the positive indicates that you are on the right track in locating and moving toward your desire.

1. Know how to identify your own personal Call by looking at your dreams, values, and those things you have always enjoyed doing.

2. Pay attention to how much time you spend in the "discomfort to relief" zone in your life and try to move a bit more into the "relief to delight" zone.

3. Write down what is meaningful to you by imagining that you only have twenty minutes to write and that you will forget everything you do not write. What would you list as your most abiding interests?

4. Do something every day that puts meaning in your life. Little things are fine.

CHAPTER 8

Self-care rule number two

Live free!

I came to live out loud.

Emile Zola[1]

Live free or die! Stress research tells us that one of the leading causes of stress-caused illness in modern life is feeling out of control. People who stay healthy even under stress have some control over their lives—they are free to move, to react, and do not see themselves as pawns of adversity. Research tells us that people who feel out of control of their lives experience more health-related issues. And loss of freedom causes great stress to all mammalian life forms, from whales to humans.

Think back on the best times in your life. Chances are these peak experiences were times of consummate freedom—you moved and acted unaware of the passage of time, delighting in the moment. You may remember riding your bicycle down a hill at age ten with the wind in your face in the crisp morning air, or accomplishing something at school or work that required the full and joyful application of your talents.

Whatever the best experiences are, they happen in moments when we are in charge of our own lives. We don't have to fit into anyone's mold. At these times, our brains go through a considerable amount of strengthening and growth. Freedom is good for us over the long run! Experiencing freedom in some activity, we enter the state of being that Mihaly

Csikszentmihalyi calls "flow," and our body and mind are tremendously refreshed by the experience.[2] In moments of freedom we push our comfort zones past what we think we are capable of. We embrace new experience and build our capacity and strength for yet more new experience.

Five strategies for becoming freer in your parenting, work, and personal endeavors:

1. See your child's behavior as a challenge, not a curse.

2. Have a "BATNA."

3. Know that you deserve to live free of the tyranny of your child's symptoms.

4. Do not be afraid to "rock the boat."

5. Strive to communicate honestly in your personal life and at work.

See your child's behavior as a challenge, not a curse

You must see the situation as challenging, but not overwhelming. If you experience a sense of *futility* in your role as the parent of an attention different (AD) child, you will never get relief from your responsibilities or your child's symptoms, and you are on the road to burnout. The important thing is to feel that you are able to take action. You see a difficulty as a challenge, and wearying as it may be, you know you are not controlled by the stress in your life.

Have a "BATNA"

This term, borrowed from the book *Getting to Yes*, means the "Best Alternative To a Negotiated Agreement."[3] If, for example, you are getting nowhere with your local school district, your BATNA may be to put a good educational attorney on retainer. You may not want to take that action now, but you are willing to commit to it if necessary. Having a

BATNA, you can commit to decisive action. Having a BATNA you are able to stay in control of the situation.

You also need a BATNA when dealing with non-compliance of your AD child. Typically this is a fallback strategy, an ultimate consequence that you are willing to impose if necessary. An example might be to refuse to drive your teenage AD child to martial arts class until he agrees to take out the trash every day. Once you have decided on your final action, you can proceed with a great deal more confidence in your dealings with your child.

Know that you deserve to live free of the tyranny of your child's symptoms

Quite often parents, especially mothers of AD children, tell me that they do not have a life. Finish the sentence with "worth living," and you get the measure of their distress. The roots of the belief that "our lot is to suffer every day" are found in our own low self-esteem. Quite frequently AD children have AD parents, and those of us who are AD ourselves may have taken quite an ego battering growing up. It is not surprising that we do not believe that we deserve better. But we do. We deserve to follow our own dreams as much as our children deserve to have a chance to follow theirs.

Right now, pause reading for a moment and imagine your life as changed toward greater self-appreciation. If you were "really worth it," what changes would you make? Choose one area of your life in which you feel undervalued. Assign a current grade to the quality of your life in that area. Now think of a couple of things that are easy, effective, and immediate that you could do to raise the quality of life just one grade level. If you grade yourself with a "C" what would it take to improve to a grade "B"?

Do not be afraid to "rock the boat"

Changing things for the better can be a painful process and there are many good reasons why we might hold back from taking more control of our lives. Here are some typical examples of risk-avoidance expressed by the parents of tyrannical AD children:

We have never called 911 when he gets violent. When he picked up the knife and threatened me, I knew he didn't really mean it.

He has never been in a psychiatric hospital, even during the worst of it. I just took time off work and stayed with him.

We couldn't get services from the school's special education department. They told us that the district did not have the budget. I believe them.

I will home school him rather than put him on the medication the psychiatrist is recommending.

He's OK as long as he gets his way.

The problem is that all of these reasons deprive you of the freedom to make the changes that may be necessary to save your own life. In a way, all of these reasons may show that you are in the third stage of the grief process, the "bargaining" stage in which you deny consideration of options that take you out of your comfort zone. This attitude is entirely understandable given the powerful stress you are subject to on a day-to-day basis. People tend to hunker down under stress.

Strive to communicate honestly in your personal life and at work

Are you able, from time to time, to risk being your natural, vibrant, emotional self? Do you believe that people are communicating honestly with you, or are you subject to many linguistic semi-truth games? The quality of freedom manifests itself in honest communication. If you do not feel safe in communicating openly with someone, your relationship with that person is unfree. Knowing the truth of the situation gives you control. Being lied to or betrayed attacks your control of your life. Here are some examples of typical dishonesties in everyday life that undermine one's freedom:

- At work, managers lie to their employees, and employees lie to each other and to their managers.

- In long-term personal relationships, dissatisfaction and boredom between people in a relationship is not acknowledged or discussed. People have affairs to distract themselves from their misery.

- Businesses overcharge customers and deliberately mislead them.

- Politicians lie to voters to cover up the malfeasance of big contributors.

Being honest with others, being free at home and work, puts vitality in your life. Being unfree in either domain diminishes your vitality. If you work at a meaningless, oppressive job, you put your health at risk.

If you are free to say your piece and trust the information you get from people, you are better able to express your "natural child." If you communicate honestly, what you say is generally in line with what you feel. If you are happy, you express your happiness. If you are angry, you let the other person know your anger. People will tell you they feel comfortable around you because they know where you stand.

The mechanics of honest communication: using DESC scripts

You are free to the degree that you can be honest with people around you, but being more honest in your interpersonal communications may take a bit of practice. Being honest with another may hurt them or cause them to be defensive. It is important to know how to express your wants, thoughts, and feelings so that others hear you and feel safe in the exchange. In most situations it makes sense to behave *assertively*. If you over-control the situation, you put yourself in a win–lose position and make enemies. If you are passive, you risk letting yourself be used and manipulated. Assertiveness is the powerful middle ground that gets results without alienating others.

Asserting yourself

In stressful situations it may be difficult to remember the rudiments of effective communication. Writer Sharon Anthony Bower suggests that you actually write down what you want to say to another person with whom you have an assertiveness issue. She terms her method a "DESC script."[4] It is composed of four elements:

Describe behavior you want from the other.

Express your feelings from the "I position."

Specify the

Consequences that you want.

DESCRIBE BEHAVIOR YOU WANT FROM THE OTHER

People are not put off if you describe what behavior change you want in objective terms. If you use adjectives, such as "stupid," or "lazy," the other person will be more likely to turn you off or attack you verbally himself. If you tell your AD son that you are affronted by some obnoxious behavior, you give him something to work on. If you tell him that he is "rude," or "lazy," you give him an invitation to a fight because you indict who he is, his personhood (which he cannot change), not his behavior (which he can change).

EXPRESS YOUR FEELINGS FROM THE "I POSITION"

This simply means that you avoid the word "you" as in "you always," or "you never," or "I feel that you are…" (fill in the blank). Coming from the "I" position means that you are speaking for yourself and telling the other how you are affected by his actions, without putting an ultimatum on him. Saying to your child who has just insulted you, "What you said hurts me and makes me want to stay away from you," is more effective in terms of motivating him not to do it again than returning the insult in kind.

SPECIFY THE CONSEQUENCES THAT YOU WILL IMPOSE IF THE ACTION YOU DESIRE IS NOT FORTHCOMING

Writing out what you want to happen as a result of your communication precludes the possibility that in the heat of the moment your own emotionality will result in the encounter going nowhere. Voices are raised, positions are stated, but exactly what you want is unclear.

Here are examples of the use of DESC scripts in action:

- You might say to your AD teen diagnosed with bipolar disorder, who is smoking pot and has a driver's license: "I will not continue to let you use my car unless you submit to testing to make sure you are not driving stoned."

- You might say to your spouse: "When you come home from work, yell at our child, and get a battle going every night, my blood pressure goes up. It is not healthy for us to live like this. I am asking you to control your temper, or get help to control it. If you do not, I may choose not to live with you."

- You might say to your AD child who is in the middle of a rage and is throwing things and breaking things: "I will be happy to leave your room when you show me that you have control of your body. I do not want to be here any more than you want me here."

When you model assertiveness to your AD child, you let him know that you are immune to his tyranny and that you are in control. He needs to know that he cannot get his way by being a bully. Though his narcissistic genius may demand obedience, the Little Tyrant will not get his way.

Practice active listening skills

Using the DESC approach in your interactions, you approach your child and other important people in your life center to center. This way of relating deepens and strengthens your relationships. Daniel Siegel suggests that communications in attuned relationships show three characteristics. To paraphrase him: (a) people listen accurately to each other, (b) people strive to make sense of each other's communication, and (c) people are responded to in a timely and effective manner. Siegel says the best parents make it a point to evoke the child's feelings and thoughts about his life and the meaning of his existence.

Siegel's thoughts resonate a central theme in this book: *good listening is essential to bringing out your child's positive genius.*[5] Being a good listener is not rocket science. It simply means that you take the time to make sure that your child has heard your words and your meaning, and assuring him that you heard what he really wanted you to hear. Research done on the mechanics of good listening tells us that the verbal contents of our communications only account for about 40 percent of the meaning received by a listener. Better than 60 percent is communicated through tone of voice and nonverbal behavior. So it makes sense deliberately to make sure that you know where your child is really "coming from." To ensure active listening, ask directly for his interpretation of your words. Say: "It is important to me that you are hearing what I am really trying to get across here. Would you give that back to me in your own words?"

And to ensure you are accurately hearing the other's intention, ask: "I want to make sure I understand what you mean for me to hear. You are saying that you feel put-down and angry when I double-check to see if you have taken your medication."

When you practice assertive communication, you give the message to your body/mind that you are in control of your life. Remember again the central wisdom of stress research: if your mind picks up that you are no longer in control, it may initiate its own logic and begin a shutdown sequence in your body. It is common for unassertive people to become very depressed or develop other forms of illness.

If you feel that your lot is to be a prisoner, you will not be able to experience the inspiration to do things that will make you feel free and happy. This is not to suggest that you must deny the severity of the situation. It is to suggest that in order to be free of the oppression inherent in the situation you must believe that you deserve to live free—to "have a life."

Living free, you free the genius of your child

To free the genius of your child, live free yourself. AD children who have the best chance of making it through childhood and adolescence have parents who model freedom in their own lives.

I worked recently with one of the most adrenaline-charged kids I have ever met. Timothy, twelve years old, was diagnosed with Tourette syndrome and obsessive-compulsive disorder (OCD). He had a full-body tic, which he described as an "energy rush," that would totally straighten him out in his chair several times during a counseling session. Timothy was a wild and joyous child who few could accept because he said weird things, and acted baboonish from time to time. But he was a happy kid. Part of his foundation was the presence of his grandparents in his life. They lived in Alaska and Timothy regaled me with details of their exploits and incredible survival. He loved going to visit them and found the wilds of Alaska one of the few places big enough to support his wildness.

He came in with his mom before Christmas ticcing wildly but looking forward to seeing his grandpa and grandma. He had started on Prozac but had not responded to it. In session I affirmed his connection with his grandparents several times. I loved to get him talking about them and had let him know that he was in a "tic-friendly zone" in my office.

Several weeks later he came back, with his obsessional fixations greatly decreased. He had had a great time in Alaska and in the midst of it things just started improving. He talked hopefully about getting more control over the problems in his life. I knew he was very impressionable and I surmised that he had soaked up some of the hardiness of his grandma and grandpa. He needed the tactile proximity of happy old survivors in the persons of his grandparents. It was very important for him to have a sense of control, of agency, in his own change process. The Prozac could not have done its job if it were blocked by Timothy's will.

In terms of Timothy's genius, the Prozac can be seen as a structure upon which his genius can develop until he can make it in the world without the support of medication. I felt certain that Timothy had a path for his genius and that he is well served by the free-minded caregivers in his life.

Conclusion—the heart of freedom is your sense of connection with the universe

Whatever you do to manifest more freedom in your life, the heart of freedom lies in your belief that despite the hardships you face to gain autonomy, you are blessed by the universe and connected to it. Every ideology that has sought to suppress human freedom has first had to kill this spiritual connection. Though it is often difficult to remember this basic truth, no one can take your freedom away from you. Einstein said that each of us must ask the ultimate question: "Is the universe friendly?"[6]

Understand that living an unfree, restrictive, or oppressed life is dangerous to your health.

Practice these five strategies for building more freedom and control into your life.

1. See your child's behavior as a challenge, not a curse.

2. Have a "BATNA"—a "best alternative to a negotiated agreement." Know your backup plan.

3. Know that you deserve to live free of the tyranny of your child's symptoms.

4. Do not be afraid to "rock the boat" with professionals and at school. Learn how to do so effectively.

5. Strive to communicate honestly and assertively in your personal life and at work.

It is only when we answer in the affirmative that we experience the delight of being fully human and fully free.

CHAPTER 9

Self-care rule number three

Cultivate love in your life

*Love is a power which produces love; impotence is the
inability to produce love.*

Erich Fromm[1]

Love is necessary for the growth and development of human beings. The
brains of babies and toddlers who are loved have the best chance of
developing to their full potential. A loving bond between parent and child
is a prerequisite for attunement and the development of observer
perspective.[2]

Love is essential for adult survival. Interviews by the hardiness criterion researchers revealed that the people who survived Nazi concentration camps found ways to keep love alive in the midst of their hellish
lives.[3] In other situations, older people who have pets to take care of live
longer. People in high stress occupations such as air traffic controllers,
police officers, or military officers, who have the love and support of
family and friends, stay healthy despite the stress.

Love makes the heart and immune system function more efficiently.
Love clearly benefits the human nervous system. Call it "vitamin L," we
need it to survive, and to realize our gifts in the world.

Our children challenge our ability to love

Our attention different (AD) children are greatly challenged by the force of genius in their natures—the will to action, intensity, and impulsivity. These qualities cause them to be very self-centered. Given the enormous stress they experience, self-absorption is understandable. Living the stress reaction, they tend to be hyper-vigilant, selfish, and reactive. Their psyches have little room to give or get love. The struggle that they are in limits their perspective and prevents them from having the emotional expansiveness required for the experience of love.

AD children also deal with enormous amounts of failure and the chronically low self-esteem that results. As a parent, your AD child's lack of self-love will put pressure on *your own* self-esteem. You feel worn down by the stress. You have very little left to give. You may feel like a failure or the World's Greatest Chump who has given the best parts of your life to duty without getting much back. There is very little space for love left in you. You have much too much distress to feel like you can turn things around.

But there is a way to reverse this situation and move your own spirit toward renewal. My hardiest clients have taught me this lesson: if you are to reverse the downward spiral, you must rediscover love for yourself, and you must practice self-love in the relationship you create with your child. Love, well practiced, will detoxify your relationship with him and give him a model of being in the world in which joy and expansiveness are possible even for people as odd and disturbing as himself!

What does it mean to truly love yourself or your child? There are so many definitions, so many perspectives on what love is and, as parents of AD kids, we will experience many people trying to sell us their version of love. "If you love yourself at all get out of that toxic relationship!" "If you really loved your child, you would impose consequences every time he messes up. Tough love!" "You have caused his problems with your lack of 'attachment' to him."

In order to get through this confusion you need to have a substantial definition of love: a definition that provides criteria for taking care of your own spirit and for caregiving your child.

Box 9.1 In the Crucible: dilemmas of love

As Greg's psychosis* grew and infested our lives, I could no longer work at anything but care-giving, and dropped out of all writing activities. My friends were very worried and told me I had to get him out of the house. "You can't live with violence, Joanne. You can't write when you're scared. You have to get Greg out of your house." But there was nowhere for Greg to go, and no one else to take care of him. For several years I stopped seeing anyone, except for a few diehard best friends who acknowledged my dilemma.

I was trapped. I had no choice but to continue to mother my son. I mourned the loss of writing, but I couldn't find a way of working when Greg raged and threatened me all day and most of the night. He slept very little, and I often slept in the living room, one eye open (George did this duty on weekends) to keep him from burning the place down, turning on all the stove burners and walking away, experimenting with bare wires in electric sockets, mixing dangerous chemicals he bought on the sly—our resident mad scientist. Occasionally I fell deeply asleep and he would head off for a ten-mile bike ride at 3 a.m. Once he got completely lost and the police called. "Do you know where your son is?"

*Greg says that this diagnosis is incorrect. He prefers the term "disapproved-of behavior."

Erich Fromm's four qualities of love

In 1956, psychiatrist Dr. Erich Fromm wrote *The Art of Loving* in which he ventured a definition of love—one he had developed after working with hundreds of patients over the four decades of his practice.[4] Fromm was struggling to define real human love apart from the trivial. He was not

interested in romantic infatuation or the love one might profess for a
favorite pursuit or hobby.

He considered love to be the most powerful emotion because it
enabled two people (or more for that matter) to get together and in loving
each other deeply, call forth more love. He was not referring to sexual
love but to the emotional and spiritual connection between people.
Fromm suggested that four criteria must be in place in order for this
powerful, grounded love to exist. First, you must *care* for each other—you
must treat the other with kindness and attention to your relationship.
Second, there must be a norm of *responsibility* in the relationship. He
explained that this has to do with people being assertive with each other,
that it is a relationship of equals. Third, you must *respect* the one you love.
From the Latin *respicere*, "to look at," you must take a good look at the
other; you take the person in. You consider them. And finally, you must
have *knowledge* of each other. You must know his struggles, his shadow, his
spirit and his strength.

To summarize, Dr. Erich Fromm's four qualities of authentic love are:

- care
- responsibility
- respect
- knowledge.

Loving your AD child, you will be true to these four features in the way
you treat him. Loving him may be the greatest test of your ability to love
that you will ever face.

A word about care

The word "care" is given different meanings in English and Latin. In Latin
the word is *caritas* which means "dearness," or "affection" for another. The
Anglo-Saxon root of the English is *caru* which means "to suffer." Either
derivation suggests that care means one experiences deep empathy for
another. We know what it is to suffer and so we seek to prevent someone
we love from experiencing suffering. To use Dr. John Enright's term, we
live "in service" to the higher good of the other.[5] Erich Fromm extends the
word's definition to include the quality of putting *effort* into a relation-

ship. He terms care "the active concern for the life and the growth of that which we love." When you care for flowers, you water them. When you care for a child, you feed the child, bathe him, and give him physical comfort. Care is the active ingredient in love.

How much energy do you put into your own self-care?

Are you your own best friend? Do you put energy into taking care of yourself? The chronic stress of raising an AD child may inhibit your practice of this kind of self-examination but these are important questions to ask yourself. What changes do you need to make in your life so that you tend to your own suffering?

You may notice that it is difficult to think of ways to take better care of yourself unless you feel that you deserve to have your suffering eased as much as does your child. Just as you must know that you deserve to live a purposeful and free life, you must also know that your spirit, mind, and body also deserve loving care. Here are some examples of how you can practice self-care:

- Stand up for yourself with your spouse to insist that the duties of parenting your AD child are shared. As much as possible, neither of you should get off the duty roster because of outside work commitments.

- Take care of your body. Put awareness into what you eat. Drink enough water. Exercise regularly. Get a good massage from time to time. Get regular checkups.

- Have an activity in your life that gives you a sense of completion or enjoyment. It may be getting your hands into the garden, working on an art form, or persuing some other craft or hobby. Your genius will express itself if you let it.

- Attend personal growth workshops, or similar activities that contribute to the health of your body and mind.

In making changes like these in your life, go easy on yourself. Make small improvements that are easy, effective, and immediate. Start small and build from there.

Box 9.2 An exercise in self-care

If you do this exercise in the privacy of your retreat, you might light a candle, use essential oils, and put on some music that soothes you. Settle into a comfortable position, breathe down to your diaphragm.

1. Close your eyes and see an image of some being sacred to you, such as Jesus or Buddha or a beloved ancestor, sitting across from you, looking into your eyes with love and caring. Imagine that this being is sending you gentle affirmation and acknowledgement. Take a moment to let in this benediction.

2. Imagine that as you look at this image, its heart chakra (the area around the sternum) begins to glow a beautiful bright amber color. Now see the image slowly move its hand up to reach over and touch you on your own sternum, right by your own heart. As you visualize this, imagine that amber energy is flowing from the heart of the image down to the hand touching your heart. Just take in the energy and enjoy it for a moment.

3. Now move your own hand up and put firm thumb pressure on your sternum, and as you do imagine the amber energy increasing and spreading throughout your body, inhabiting and refreshing every cell from the toes to the top of your head. Let yourself be filled with caring, love, and grace.

Molly's story

Molly's story illustrates what one woman did to restore the quality of care for herself in her life and the impact this action had on her AD husband and son.

Molly was the mother of a bright sixteen-year-old Asperger boy, Darryl, with a mild but extremely stressful cyclical mood disorder. When Darryl was getting his way and in a good mood (when his genius had its belly full), he was fun to be around. When he was in a bad mood, he was a hyper-anxious, paranoid, ranting, critical tyrant. He was like sandpaper on her nervous system. Darryl refused to take the neuroleptic or anticonvulsant medication that could have helped him. He had seen the movie *A Beautiful Mind*[6] and its depiction of Dr. John Nash's loss of motivation after taking an antipsychotic drug, and had determined he would not "trash" his own intelligence that way. He did not like drugs, even if they might contribute to his independence, life success, and mood management. Having to deal with Darryl every day for all these years had almost killed Molly. Her hair had turned white. She had developed a low-level chronic depression.

Molly's husband was an Asperger-like engineer named Pat, a hands-off parent, who spent most of his time at the lab. Molly met Pat in college but her ambitions to pursue her interest in medical technology had ended when Darryl came along, and she had not completed her Masters. Her husband provided very little parenting help and zero interpersonal support. He could not communicate a sense of empathy to her. He tried to help by figuring things out logically, but he just did not sense when she was hurting. The brilliance that she found so attractive as a young woman now showed another hue—that as a person with Asperger, Pat could not give emotional reciprocity.

Molly now faced a predicament: "How can I be a good mother and at the same time save my own life?" Her first concern was for Darryl. She had taken the time to get her priorities in order. He was in need of twenty-four hour parenting care, but she got only token help from Pat and dealing with Darryl had worn her to a frazzle. She did love Pat but realized she felt more like his mother than his wife.

Molly gave herself a week in a cabin at a Northwest coastal beach to think about what she needed to do to turn things around. When she came to my office for a debriefing session with Pat and Darryl, I saw that the organizational genius that had powered her through college was helping her now. She had decided that two things needed to happen fairly soon if she were to stay married to Pat.

First, he would have to tell them at work that he needed more time off to deal with Darryl: that he had a sick kid at home who needed time under his sick leave coverage. His work, though important, had taken the easy front seat for too many years. Now he would have to learn some skills in fathering that were less familiar to him. And he would have to be more assertive with his supervisor at work.

Second, she turned to Darryl and told him that he would either get on appropriate medication or get another place to live. She told him that she would arrange through the individual education program process to have him placed in a residential school if need be. Molly choked back tears as she delivered this last piece of her "saving-my-life" manifesto. I knew it was the hardest thing she had ever said to anyone. Pat sat helplessly, looking at the ground, unable to form his thoughts about what to do.

Darryl surprisingly seemed to know just where his mother was coming from. He voiced understanding about how living with him had been so difficult for her. Still, he pleaded with her to change her mind. For the first time in many years, Molly saw him cry as he said that he did not want to take a pill that would "kill his soul." Molly wisely held her ground and though it did not happen right away, eventually Darryl got enough explanation from the family's psychiatrist to make it OK for him to accept medication on a trial basis.

I met with Molly several weeks after Darryl started on medication. She told me that the medication was working well, and contrary to the idea he got from watching *A Beautiful Mind*, neuroleptic treatment of his mood disorder and agitation did not result in his zombification.

I could tell that the predicament she faced had been resolved in such a way that her life was better for it. She had not decided how she wanted to change her relationship with Pat to make it more satisfying, but she knew something had to change and she was willing to put effort into the process. There was a possibility that he would accept short-term marital counseling to look at ways to wire around his difficulty on the emotional side.

She said the most important thing in all of this process had been her decision that she could and would turn things around—that her "life depended on it." Molly's decision to stand up for her life required that she face her own internal critical voices that said, "Do not be a bad wife and tell your husband he has to take time off work. Do not be a bad mother and tell your son you are ready to kick him out." She faced these voices with that of her True Call that, distilled by her suffering, said loud and clear (to paraphrase the words of poet Mary Oliver) "The only life you can save is your own! Save it!"

A word about love and responsibility

Responsibility is a word with two component parts, response and ability, which, taken together denote the ability to be able to respond to others. In terms of interpersonal relationships, responsibility points to a person's ability to stand up and be heard as an equal in the conversation. If responsibility is a strong value in a relationship, people will not seek to overwhelm or control each other. And they will also put a priority on responding to each other; they will feel that they "answer" (respond) to each other.

The opposite of seeing yourself as a responsible person is to see yourself as a victim. Others are doing things to you that you cannot control. The Latin derivation for this word is interesting; from *victima*, which means "beast for sacrifice."

Being responsible means that you see yourself as having choices in your life. You look straight on at the options you are faced with, even if they are not to your liking.

When it is in the child's highest good to let go

Sometimes the best thing to do is nothing at all. The most responsible action may be to let your AD child learn from natural consequences. The double-edged sword of being a great parent is that to the degree that you protect your AD child from the slings and arrows of outrageous fortune, you deprive him of the opportunity for learning. These are the difficult choices that you face every day as his parent. How much control is needed? When should I let him take a certain risk for the learning that is in it? When should I protect him?

Add to this situation the cruel fact that your AD child may resist your care, even denying his own condition. This may leave you, for example, in the position of having to deal with the abuse your child gives you as you take him to the psychiatrist and then deal with the abuse the psychiatrist gives you for "not following good parenting guidelines." Just getting through this experience requires great love, a great sense of service to your child.

It is clear that people develop emotional and cognitive complexity as they move through a succession of developmental stages. In adolescence, the big leap is to abstract thinking, the ability to have greater observer perspective, and control over one's own limbic impulsivity. A child needs to be somewhat independent of his parents to go through these changes.

It is often best to let the order of natural consequences be there for your child. If he refuses to eat what you feed him, have him prepare his own meals. If he refuses medication to control his impulsivity, let him deal with the consequences of his impulsivity. Let him come to terms with the fact that there is a part of him that is not quite under his conscious control. A strong kid has to learn his limitations.

It is important to know when to surrender to the fact that you do not really have an answer. Time to "Let go and let God." As the father of an AD child, I have learned that there is truth in the statement made by many sage philosophers and healers that the "creative give-up" may be the best route to the best outcome. At different points in my son's development, from his early years to his young manhood, I have come to realize that I really do not have solutions to many of the issues he faces, as a person with multiple neuropsychological diagnoses including autism. Despite my work with hundreds of AD kids, I have at times felt helpless in the face of my son's extreme behavior.

I have found that when I can relate to him with compassion, and give up devising plans to improve the situation, he is often able to develop mastery of the challenge. I have learned that sometimes I need to shut up and sit down. There is nothing more I can do. My son has taught me that sometimes the best survival strategy is no strategy at all. Sometimes the most responsible thing to do is let your child's experience in the world be his teacher!

A word about respect and love

"We never get any respect from him. He treats us like dirt!" This is a common complaint of the parents of many teenagers. Usually it translates to frustration over the teen's verbal rudeness and refusal to comply with parental requirements. AD children tend to be worse on this score. Though neurotypical teens can be very rebellious and obnoxious, most accept the fact that their parents are in charge. AD children will throw the gauntlet down. They will absolutely refuse to comply with any requirement, even refusing to go to school. They will insult and berate parents for hours, using the foulest insults, even in public.

Remembering the Latin derivation of "respect"—"to look at closely"—we see that what is happening in your parenting situation is that your child is not *seeing* you. He lives in crisis and from this perspective you are just one more annoyance to him. He does not see you as his mother or father in a way that cherishes you. Because he does not see you this way, he does not give you moral authority.

For him to respect you, his heart must be open to you. If it is not, there is nothing you can do to gain his respect. This is a great loss because though you may love him, in disrespecting you he is cutting himself off from the healing power of your love in his life.

How to encourage your child to respect you

To develop your child's respect for you, you have to build an emotional bridge with him; you have to cultivate trust. This process begins with your acceptance of your child's being and personhood apart from his behavior. Though you may revile his obnoxious or dangerous behavior, you value the person he is underneath. The first step is to tune in to the person you know he is and listen to him from that place. You do not talk; he does. Parents often think that good parenting means they spill their guts to their kids, that they reveal themselves. Self-disclosure can be helpful in facilitating interpersonal communications, but it can also get in the way, if what a child needs is the opportunity to tell you how it is for him. This gives you the opportunity to take out his Great Story and look at ways he can reformulate what is happening in his life.

It takes a bit of practice and skill to put your relationship on a positive footing. You will be tested by his disrespect many times. But each one of these encounters is an opportunity to turn things a bit toward the family value that could be stated as: "Around here we treat each other with respect." Table 9.1 shows some examples of language you can use to parry his attack and turn things in a more positive direction.

Table 9.1 Examples of positive language responses

The AD child's opening	Your response
"You never listen to what I say."	"You're right. I'm listening now."
"I feel like a loser. I do not have any friends."	"Yes. This is a time in your life when you are alone. Who knows how that might change as you change?"
"Fuck you and your chore list."	"I do not despise you, but I despise your language. We'll talk about chores later."
"You don't know me!"	"You're right. But I'm open to hearing who you are."
"You're pathetic. You know that? Just pathetic."	"So true! Our whole family is pathetic! At least that's probably what the neighbors say."

Notice that your response should not indicate that you are giving up your power in any way. You are simply hearing your child's anger at you and you are keeping your heart open at the same time. You are not taking it on. You may even find humor in the situation. Gaining your child's respect means that you stay clear on the behavior change you expect from him and you listen with all your heart at the same time. People who are angry or defensive are in a place of low self-esteem. You cannot compel or sell "good attitude" to your child if he is in this place. But you can listen, and as you do you may find the ice block that he has put between you begins to melt. The renewal of love is possible.

A word about knowledge and love

Joanne writes in this book how the experience of raising a very difficult child cooks the niceness out of you. It is a crucible experience that will either destroy you emotionally, or give you knowledge about yourself and those you love that you would not have gained if you were parent to a neurotypical child. In previous chapters I have described the idea that suffering in our lives, being wounded in some way, opens us up to change. The experience of watching your positive expectations for your child dissolve in the face of his symptomology is such a wound. You become as intolerant of absurdity as your child. You have more of a tendency to be assertive, even angry, with professionals who hinder more than help. You become more honest with yourself and your spouse. You simply do not have the luxury of pushing things under the rug.

Some, not all, of the couples with whom I work, tell me that their relationship has been strengthened by having to parent a very difficult child. They tell me that after years of the stress of it, they have worked through their calm exterior down to the parts of themselves that they would rather not show the world. These parts, the unknown aspects or "Shadow," have now been revealed. The stress of parenting first turned them into angry blamers, or tested their desire to run away from the relationship. If they survived this stage and kept talking to each other, they were stronger for the experience.

It is important for you to take the time to tune in to your misgivings, conflicts, and unspoken feelings, and express these to your partner. One way to do this is to schedule time to talk each week when you have privacy. Try to come from the heart, speak with honesty, and avoid pushing for a particular outcome. This is not a time to argue but to hold each other with compassion and acceptance. Ask your partner for honest feedback on some issue troubling you or give him your feelings about something he is doing. Sharing who you are and learning about the other makes your love stronger because it is based on real and true information.

Box 9.3 In the Crucible: tough mothering

Journal:

Noticeable increase in rages per day so I know he is spitting his pills. I watch him like the mother of all hawks, examining his cheeks and under the tongue with an invasive spoon. We both hate it. This morning I finally noticed the lump under his upper lip, the small oval tablet neatly tucked between lip and front teeth. He says he's been doing this "for a while."

Love is expressed through art, physical self-care, and contact with nature

If you define love as the presence of care, responsibility, respect, and knowledge, you see that the term has a much wider application than just one-to-one intimacy. In fact, so defined, you could see love present in an artistic pursuit, organizational context, in a social group, in your relationship to nature, or your relationship to your own body. Love expressed in each context will be different in terms of the depth and quality of care, responsibility, respect, and knowledge. You may, for example, experience very deep love of your medium when engaged in an artistic pursuit. You delight in creating a work of art, and find that the process pulls wisdom and intuitive knowing out of you that you did not see before. If love is present in your workplace, people will not have to wear psychological masks or hide their true selves from each other. Tears, joy, and the expression of other emotions will be accepted.

If you love your body, you will be guided by these four criteria in taking care of it. You will move with awareness. You will exercise and give your body the food that is right for it. You will feel good about the way you look. If you love nature, you will experience these criteria in your relationship with the ecology, taking a stewardship role toward its preservation.

Love furthers the life energy, the basic well-being, of both the lover and the beloved. Both giving and getting love makes us healthier. Deliberately cultivating love with your spouse and your AD child makes your family stronger and more stable, and gives your child's genius the courage to come out, full blossom, trusting the world!

Love must be balanced by purpose and freedom

You cannot achieve love in your life without purpose. Without purpose, you settle for shallow expressions of affection that pace your sense of withdrawing from the world. You make do.

Love is the great "Yes!" your spirit shouts to the universe in times of trouble. "Yes, I can make it and will pull through!" Having love gives us physical and emotional strength—stress research is clear on that point. And not having love, giving in to pessimism, surrendering to "the system," is dangerous, because when we give up the search for meaning and purpose in our lives, the first casualty is our aliveness and love for others and ourselves.

We all know the people who have made this bargain and lost. You feel a little tired and lonely around them. When you stop "asking the question," to use the term coined by one of my clients (who survived cancer) to describe giving up your search for purpose, you give up on love. This is dangerous to your health because your body and mind require that you have something to live for, as a condition for keeping you alive. Love helps sustain you as you work to build a meaningful life.

And love must be balanced by freedom. There is an old French saying: "L'amour c'est l'enfant de la liberté,"—love is the child of freedom. If you feel enslaved to someone or something, love is not possible. Love is a two-way street. Love can only exist in a context of profound equality and freedom for individual action.

Sam Keen says in his book *The Passionate Life: Stages of Loving,* "I gain personal identity only in the presence of another with whom I share myself."[7] Freedom is essential for the evolution of consciousness—we cannot share ourselves with another unless we feel free. Every time we do this we build more autonomy, more of a sense of ourselves as empowered beings. When freedom is present in a relationship, each person has the ability to move out of the orbit of the other and change on his or her own. Coming together again from this new place, the relationship is refreshed.

1. Understand the four factors involved in genuine love:
    care, responsibility, respect, and knowledge.

2. Care for yourself by taking care of your physical being,
    by standing up for yourself, and by involving yourself in
    activities that nurture you.

3. Practice responsibility by deliberately taking yourself out
    of the victim role in your life.

4. Build respect with your child by staying clear on what
    you want from him, listening from the heart, and keeping
    things positive.

5. Deliberately cultivate honesty in your personal
    relationships.

6. Practice love in your connection with nature and your art.

PART III

Special considerations

CHAPTER 10

The peril of neglecting to nourish the genius of the AD child

If the earth calls to the apple and it doesn't come, it tends to rot on the tree.

Gregg Levoy[1]

The paradigm for healthful living, described in the previous three chapters of this book—that healthy people have a life that is purposeful, free, and loving, applies to attention different (AD) children as well as to their caregivers. Our kids need to feel that their lives are important (the purpose factor), they need to be able to live free and go to school in the "least restrictive environment" (the freedom factor), and they need to experience self-love and the ability to give and get love from others (the love factor). Not surprisingly, if an AD child has these three qualities in his life he is also able to exercise good observer perspective. His genius is informed, and moves toward constructive ends.

The field of nurturing is the medium for the growth of the AD child's positive genius and hardiness. If the seven described criteria are in place in a child's life he will have the best chance of turning his attention differ-

ence to an attention *advantage.* To reference the wisdom of myth, he will
have the best chance of transcending the wound of atypical brain chemistry, to realize the exceptional gifts to which the wound gives rise. Thus
the obsessive, fixated, unhappy little boy becomes the obsessive, fixated,
very successful (possibly happy) computer scientist. The outcome does
not have to be heroic, but the conditions for helping any AD child remain
the same—the field of nurturing must be in place as he grows up.

The field of nurturing is the *soil* in which the *soul* of the child's genius
grows. If this medium is rich in the proper nutrients (the seven qualities),
the child's genius has a good chance of growing strong and straight, with
the capacity to reach for the sun (the child's potential) and make itself
healthier in the process.

If the field of nurturing is present as the child grows, he will enjoy life
as an adult, marked by purpose, freedom, and love. He will have a
vocation that nourishes him and does not over-stress or under-stress him.
He will behave responsibly, enjoying personal freedom while respecting
the rights of others, and he will know love in abundance. Look at the lives
of our great exemplars, such as Jacques Cousteau, Winston Churchill,
Eleanor Roosevelt, and Katharine Hepburn, and you will find attention
different people who worked through their wounds to live authentic,
productive, and interesting lives.

How lack of nurturing turns a child's genius away from positive purposes

Every AD child has a particular genius, a particular *daemon* (to use Plato's
term), and that daemon stays with the child his entire life. If the field of
nurturing is not present, the child will not express this daemon, his
genius, in positive ways. Given the explosive personality of the genius, or
genie, firm guidance and nurturing are needed to keep it from seeking
negative and destructive expression.

If the "soil" is not quite right, if one or more of the seven criteria of the
field of nurturing are not present in sufficient measure, the child's genius
may turn away from the "sun" toward different purposes. The development of the capacity to have a life marked by purpose, freedom, and love
will be "perverted" (from the Latin to "turn aside from the proper path")
toward another manifestation of the particular quality.

Take the case of Sam, an eleven-year-old diagnosed with Asperger syndrome. As is the case for many people with this condition, Sam tends to be obsessive about things, especially his work with computers. This wound of obsessionality could strengthen him or weaken him. If properly nourished, his penchant for not letting go of a problem until it is solved may give him a very positive reputation for resolve and persistence in his field. Or it could twist toward the pathological and be so consuming that he lives in dread of imperfection. A lot depends on how this quality is shaped by his caregivers as he grows to adulthood.

Carl, another computer whiz, is diagnosed with Asperger syndrome and also has a genius for getting around the Internet. But he is deeply bored with school and its inability to deliver any interesting educational experiences in computer technology. He sees going to school as absurd. None of his caregivers are able to deal with his feeling of under-utilization and he founders, experiencing life as a meaningless and lonely business. As is the case with Sam, he has no close friends at school. At some point it occurs to him that if this is all there is, why not make your mark (and have lots of online respect) *destructively*. His genius leads him to become a leader in a competition among hackers to take down as many websites as possible.

Or take the case of Tess, a bipolar fourteen-year-old with a genius for performance art, dance, and acting. She is unparalleled in her ability to portray many different emotional states but she does not have adult caregivers in her life who are attuned to her. Lacking the presence of people who love her, she becomes lost in her characters and loses sight of who *she* is as a person. Her depersonalization worsens and soon she turns her talent for acting to the task of becoming an expert shoplifter. Her genius, turned away from its purposes, works to give her little thrills and the admiration of her outlaw friends. This is a skimpy return on her potential but this is all she will realize unless some important caregiver attunes to her and helps her find herself.

Each of the seven criteria of the field of nurturing must be present if the child is to realize his genius. Typically, lack of a particular part of the nurturing system creates a specific characterological vulnerability or excess in the child. When a child's genius is not nurtured, it has a way of turning on the child to make things worse. Gregg Levoy notes in *Callings*

that there is a cost for refusing one's call.[2] Table 10.1 lists the criteria of
the field of nurturing and describes how a lack in any of these will impact
on the child. There is a cost to be paid for depriving the AD child's genius
of what it needs to grow and play its part in the child's life.

Table 10.1 The seven criteria of the field of nurturing

Field of nurturing criterion	If this criterion is not present for the AD child
One: genius is recognized	His genius works to fulfill a sense of "brokenness" in his life. He is not seen.
Two: caregivers are attuned to the child	The genius cannot love; it is domineering, cut-off, potentially brutal.
Three: Great Story is present	A lack of sense of self. There are feelings of rootlessness, depression, cynicism and high anxiety.
Four: community is present	A pessimistic worldview coupled with a sense of futility and loneliness marks the child's life.
Five: physical factors are aligned	The child's genius is disoriented, inattentive, vulnerable to psychosis, and self-destructive.
Six: the child is able to behave resourcefully	The child feels ineffectual, a perpetual "patient," with a lack of courage. Depression sets in.
Seven: caregivers live in high-level wellness	Delays in the development of the brain's attention system may occur. The child becomes cynical and depressed and sees himself as a victim.

First criterion: The AD child's parents recognize the child's genius

In chapter 1, I described how recognizing the AD child's genius enables
caregivers to provide the right nurturance for growth. Recognizing the
genius is also an essential aspect of meeting the child's developmental
needs. At some point in the child's life, usually in adolescence, the child's
genius will reach out for recognition. At this time acknowledgement is
required if the genius is going to develop to maturity. If the child's genius
is not seen, it may make its presence known in negative ways.

Let us return to Carl's case. His caregivers could provide recognition
of his genius for computers by enrolling him in coursework that builds

his computer-related skills. And they would do well to recognize his loneliness and his struggle to make friends. If Carl continues to see himself as flawed, a friendless loser, his genius may manifest this expectation of brokenness in reality. Becoming the "baddest hacker on the net" is, after all, recognition. It is something significant. Thwarted from positive expression his genius will choose destructive purposes.

Second criterion: caregivers are attuned to the AD child

If this criterion is not present, it will be difficult for the AD child to develop the neurological capability and self-discipline to pursue his own purposes in life. He will not be able to pay attention long enough to get anything done. Remember how important attunement is to the development of higher order brain function. If the child grows up without caregiver attunement, there will be a slowing of development, specifically of the child's ability to focus himself, attend to others and control his impulses.

Uneducated by love and attunement, the child's genius will realize its freedom by assuming the archetype of Little Anarchist. The child will become a captive of his impulsivity. His genius will be deflected in its task of bringing his gifts into the world, and go into the service of grabbing a little pleasure right here and right now. Growing up without a model for love and connection, the AD child may have serious problems being empathetic. The child's genius, uneducated by love, may become vicious and domineering with others.

Once again we come to the importance of *listening* to our children. Listening from the heart is the behavioral expression of attunement. In highly chaotic and dysfunctional families, there tends to be too much talking and yelling and too little listening. In this climate the AD child will learn how to get his way by manipulating others or browbeating them. Unfortunately the price to be paid for learning these strategies will be the underdevelopment of the ability to pay attention to what is really going on between people.

The emotional climate in which the child is raised has a direct impact on the expression of his atypical neurology and his genius. Attuned to his caregivers his brain grows and informs his genius along the way. He is connected to others and focused. If attunement is not present, the child's mentality may stay at a primitive level. His genius may still be present but it will have the moral tone of a troglodyte.

Third criterion: caregivers help the child discover a Great Story that moves him forward

Great Story is necessary if the child is to understand the patterns of his own giftedness. He has to know that he is on a hero's journey, and that the wound of being born with atypical brain chemistry is more than just a painful reality, it is a creative force for shaping an exceptional destiny. He has to have an autobiography, an understanding of who he is, to move forward.

Without Great Story, the child wanders through life feeling lost and ineffectual. He may become cynical. All the failures that come from growing up with atypical brain chemistry will confirm that he is nothing but one big problem and that is that. He will come to see himself as Better Off Dead. Life will become meaningless and in the face of this harsh belief, the child's genius will pull back and shrink away to be replaced by a sense of chronic anxiety. As pointed out in other places in this book, the experience of life as meaningless is dangerous to the health of human beings. We are wired to move forward or begin going downhill. Without Great Story the child cannot develop a coherent sense of himself. He cannot feel his feet on the ground to move forward. He does not feel at home anywhere.

The genius of a child without Great Story may find expression living vicariously, unconnected with others in any real way. The unconnected genius may seize on the latest fad and make decisions based, not on its own intuition and logic, but on what others think. The genius unedu-cated by Great Story may end up applying itself to the realization of others' values.

Sometimes it takes the wound of emotional disturbance to open a person's consciousness in such a way that he sees his Great Story. This is what happened to Arthur, a very bright, successful, nineteen-year-old with a talent for tennis and a diagnosis of ADHD. He came to me for help in dealing with a sudden rush of depression that had stopped everything in his life. Depression came to Arthur at a difficult time. He had won a tennis scholarship to an Ivy League school and the depression descended on him a few weeks before a critical match. All eyes were on him. Everyone expected a lot from him on the tennis court. But he cracked. He could not come through. He could barely get out of bed.

A few weeks later, Arthur dropped out of school and moved back in with his folks. In the meetings that followed it became clear that his depression would lift somewhat every time he talked about how he had been "living a role" for the past few years. He recounted that he had been an awkward kid in middle school but by the time he hit high school his tennis acumen had become a local legend. People paid attention to him for what he could deliver, and he liked the attention. The girls flocked round him. He was promised fame and fortune.

Arthur did have a genius for tennis but he also had another genius in him that wanted expression. This part felt hollow. Fleeing into fame and then into the prestigious school with a "full boat" (scholarship) Arthur realized that he had forgotten who he was, and had been on the path to becoming the type of person others wanted him to be. Once he realized this, his depression lifted quickly. He found himself spending more time outside, going on long hikes, and getting into contact with nature.

Arthur's Great Story might include his success as a tennis player but this vocation was not the one chosen by his genius. His genius did not want Arthur's Great Story to be "tennis star obeying his handlers." Arthur's genius stopped life with depression and as soon as it was given voice, the depression lifted.

The last time I saw Arthur he told me that he had changed schools and specialties. Instead of going to business school and majoring in athletics, he was going to become a teacher of environmental studies in high school. He told me that spending a lot of time outdoors had helped him deal with his depression. It had also provided the setting for him to discover his call: to protect the environment. He went into teaching, happy and committed whole-heartedly to his subject.

Fourth criterion: Caregivers build the AD child's participation in a community

If this criterion is not present, the AD child will not have a blueprint for dealing with adversity. He will not know what it looks like to be an adult in a positive way. He will not have the benefit and support of elders in his community to help him get through the hard times. Lacking a sense of connection in present time and ancestry, the child will feel rootless, alienated from all adult caregivers, and sad. He will have a difficult time reconciling his Great Story with that of his culture and may choose the Outlaw or Loner motifs for his Great Story.

Having a community in one's life is an essential requirement for the development of a sense of self. The lack of community in modern life has negative effects on both neurotypical and AD kids. But AD children are in greater jeopardy in this regard because it takes them much longer to develop a healthy sense of who they are.

The AD child lacking a sense of who he is, and lacking a connection with the community, may experience a deep pessimism and sense of futility in his life. Community buoys up his spirits and gives him support. Without it the child's symptoms and learning disabilities come down hard on him. In this situation the AD child's genius may go into hiding as the child drops into despondency. Or the genius may express itself in antisocial purposes—the child may become a bully or get in trouble with the law, or become deeply depressed.

Later on in life the AD child may harden his perception that no community is there for him (no one cares if he lives or dies). This move toward cynicism may express itself in a variety of ways, including criminal behavior, becoming a street person or a ruthless CEO, corporate criminal, or polluter. The AD adult, pushed by his genius, comes to believe that he does not have to answer to anyone or anybody. Growing up without community, with tremendous onboard impulsivity and aggressiveness, the AD adult has difficulty experiencing the reciprocity required in a love relationship and may become domineering and abusive.

Fifth criterion: Caregivers address physical factors and medication

If the AD child does not have stability in family and school routines, proper medication, good sleep and diet habits, the wounded aspect of the genius will take over the child's life. Without use of a strong body to express itself in positive ways, the genius will hitchhike onto every symptom the child has and make the symptom worse. To gain observer perspective, the child must experience stability in his life. If physical criteria are not addressed, he will not achieve stability. He will simply be a captive of the firestorm in his brain. His genius will have no limitation put on its power for destruction and will bedevil his life and push him to violence against himself and others.

Sixth criterion: Caregivers help the AD child re-member himself

In order to control his own life, the AD child must remember how to do the right thing when challenged by stress. He has to feel that he has a choice. He has to be able to bring his heart and mind together to come up with creative options. He has to have a sense of himself in his body, feet on the ground.

In order to become free from his parents, a child must know that he has the ability to exercise responsibility—he must know that he can respond to adversity and challenge in his life and be successful. Building this confidence for response invariably involves the completion of a "rite of passage."

A rite of passage is defined as a challenge that the child must meet by drawing on his own resources, with no help from others. If the child is to gain the benefit of the development of his personality, he must meet the challenge himself. In this process his genius is tempered, informed, and integrated.

The AD child will go through many rites of passage as he grows. These may range from getting himself out of bed and off to school even though he is living in a painful depression. It may mean that he attends his own individual educational plan meeting, and suffers the humiliation of listening to adults talking about his impairments so that he can have a say in the outcome. It may mean that he completes a more formal rite of passage in the course of a wilderness self-development course.

Each rite of passage gives him a sense of himself as one who has "made the grade." He will have been tested and passed the test. The gift he gets from this passage is the knowledge that he is the one who makes choices in his life—that no one else is to be blamed or credited. The gift he gets from the rite of passage is confidence and compassion for himself. In the process, he develops humility and compassion for others.

The task you face as the caregiver of the AD child is to provide him with as many rites of passage, as many opportunities to learn from his own experience, as you can. This is sometimes a painful duty. It is difficult to watch your child fail, but getting a certain number of failures under his belt, as well as successes, is part of how he succeeds, and develops the ability to respond to things himself.

If this criterion is not in the child's field of nurturing, he may come to see himself as the "identified patient" who really does not have the power to do much in his life. Or the child may develop a sense of entitlement; believing that others will always be there to take care of him. The genius of the AD child hates this kind of invalidation and will strike out angrily, thrashing impotently at authority figures and causing trouble mindlessly.

As an adult, a child who has not learned to become emotionally self-supporting runs the risk of becoming an emotional dilettante or narcissist. He expects things to be delivered to him and whines or blames others if they are not forthcoming. Or he may simply have such an impaired sense of self that he does not try to accomplish anything in his life. Either way he will be as angry as an adult as he was as a child, for he has not yet learned how to earn his own freedom and therefore must be dependent on others.

Seventh criterion: Caregivers practice high-level wellness in their own lives

This criterion is the cornerstone of the field of nurturing and is required if the field is to exist at all. The wisdom "Physician, heal thyself," applies to parents: if you do not have a field of nurturing for your own genius, you will not have the strength to create one for your child. Every one of the first six criteria is an important aspect of a wellness plan for you as a caregiver.

Though the field of nurturing is, in this book, a description of "optimum growing conditions" for the genius of the AD child, it also has applications for your wellness as a caregiver. If parents who are "walking wounded on eggshells" are raising a child, his genius will tend to take a path with some identifiable features:

- He will believe that his lot is to be a victim of circumstances (as are his parents). His genius will express itself as an underdog or a victim. "Poor me" will be his favorite game.

- He will be deprived of the emotional nurturing necessary for the development of his own emotional system. His genius will be guided by immaturity. It will take him longer to develop compensatory strategies for his symptoms.

- He will grow up with very low self-esteem. He may blame himself for his parents' troubles.

There is no better medicine for the AD child than to see his parents living lives of their own choosing, doing work that they love. This example gives the child's genius the blueprint it needs to guide him toward a positive future!

1. Recognize your child's genius so that it moves toward positive expression.

2. Attune to the child to enable him to meet neurological milestones, develop self-discipline, impulse control, and good relationships.

3. Recognize the child's Great Story so that he is able to avoid drift in his life.

4. Build his personal hardiness by insisting on healthy sleep, eating habits, and use of medication.

5. Build the child's sense of self-reliance and ability to remember how to behave.

6. Look for appropriate "rites of passage" for him that mark his progress toward success and realization of his positive genius.

7. Practice high-level wellness in your own life to encourage high-level wellness in your child's emotional life.

CHAPTER 11

How learning differences frustrate the expression of positive genius

Education is not filling a bucket but lighting a fire.

William Butler Yeats[1]

Children with attention differences tend to have cognitive weaknesses and specialized cognitive strengths. Their weaknesses are called learning disabilities and usually involve difficulty taking in information, processing it, and expressing it in such a way that tasks are completed. In the US, the term "learning disability" (LD) is officially defined by the National Joint Committee on Learning Disabilities to refer to a group of conditions in which children experience significant difficulty in listening, spelling, reading, writing, reasoning, or mathematical ability.[2] I add the emotional domain to this list because of the importance of emotions in making decisions and interacting with others to solve problems. Emotions give us valuable information about our environment and what action is appropriate in any particular situation.

Ten learning differences commonly seen in attention different (AD) children are:

1. central auditory processing disability: difficulty understanding others' words

2. visual processing disabilities: difficulty interpreting what is seen

3. non-verbal learning disorder: difficulty understanding non-verbal behavior of others; difficulty solving problems that require abstract thinking

4. impairment of verbal expression: the inability to put words to one's thoughts

5. dysgraphia: difficulty writing or organizing work on paper

6. dyslexia: reading impairment

7. impairment in short-term auditory, visual, or feeling memory

8. the "attention deficit disorder triangle:" inattention, distractibility, and activation—problems getting started on tasks that have no intrinsic interest

9. alexithymia: inability to label (thus understand) one's own and others' emotional states

10. athymia: very low emotionality (highly logical—does not reference emotion in making decisions) with inability to express emotion.

How children learn: the computer as a metaphor

Learning occurs as a child focuses on something in his environment, compares it to his previous experience, and upgrades his "data base," to include the new information. This permits the performance of some task (output). This process is akin to the way a computer operates:

Input (perception)—active memory—processing—output

Children take things in and process them visually (in pictures), auditorily (in words and thoughts), or kinesthetically (by feeling or touch). Each child learns differently. One might learn better from visual input.

Box 11.1 In the Crucible: visions of beauty

Greg's delight in visual beauty is quite different from mine. He can now tell me, a little dutifully, "That's a beautiful sunset, Mother." I had to teach him that most people think sunsets are enchanting. He has never understood why—though he sees the glowing purples and oranges transforming every few seconds, he doesn't call this beauty. When he was sixteen, he invited me into his room "to see something beautiful!" and showed me a small heavily soldered motherboard on his grubby carpet. "Isn't that beautiful!" he said. After some discussion I understood that in its functioning, as he had re-formed and re-soldered the board, it was extraordinary, so much more beautiful than a sunset, which does nothing. But it was a homely little piece of metal, indistinguishable from the rest of the scrap on his floor. I still can't always see the beauty in his boards, though I tell him dutifully, "That's a beautiful motherboard, Greg." Often he has to prompt me.

Another might need to hear words. One child might remember in sentence strings, another in pictures. Most people use a mix of the three modalities to process information with one modality standing out as a favorite. Table 11.1 describes how the modality that a person uses is expressed at each stage of the process.

Children think and solve problems differently

In modern educational parlance, children are said to have a learning disability (and identified for remedial services) if they cannot perform in the classroom in the auditory modality. This is the form that rules in most educational settings. Using the auditory modality, teachers require the child to sit still, listen to the lecture or explanation, take notes, and then recite what was said (as output) on exams, or graded papers. To prepare for listening and note taking, reading is assigned.

Table 11.1 How each learning modality is expressed

| | Modality | | |
	Visual	Auditory	Kinesthetic
Input	Takes in images	Hears, reads	Touches
Active Memory	Remembers images	Remembers words	Remembers feelings
Processing	Sees moving images	Thinks in word strings	Consults intuition

Typically, AD children favor one of the three primary sensory modalities; visual, auditory, or kinesthetic, and encounter problems thinking in another modality. Most AD kids balance a disability in one sense with an above average ability in another. Here are some examples of this kind of selective thinking pattern:

- A child diagnosed with attention deficit disorder may have difficulty taking in and remembering things that are said to him, but may have a superlative ability to remember things that he sees, or works with manually. He may also have a "play it by ear" talent for music.

- A child diagnosed with a non-verbal learning disability may have a very difficult time making meaning of others' non-verbal behavior, and may have an equally difficult time forming abstractions from what he sees, but he may also have a phenomenal memory for visual details.

- A child diagnosed with Asperger syndrome may not understand figures of speech, or read others' emotional states, but he may have a photographic memory for what he reads or sees.

I use the term "learning difference" to describe the kinds of thought patterns noted above because in reality, AD children are not learning disabled—they can function at a very high level given the opportunity to solve problems their way. They are "learning disabled" in the classroom but may be excellent learners in other environments. A more appropriate term to describe them would be "specialized learners." And they tend to specialize in "real world" types of problems and "incidental" learning. Many AD children, for example, disdain "toys," the kinds of manufactured plastic things you buy in a toy store. They want "real tools" (remember Barbara McClintock's girlhood demand of her parents (on page 49). And they don't learn well by being told facts that they must memorize. Learning occurs from having to wrestle with real world "incidents" in the course of their attempts to reach their particular goals.

Box 11.2 In the Crucible: mother and poet

Greg is skilled, though eccentric, in the fundamentals of oral poetry—rhythm, rhyme, assonance and alliteration. When he is angry, his rage roars in high drama. Sometimes he frightens me and I stand nose to nose with him, thrashing it out in words. He plays with threats and accents and insults and mimicry, up and down the octaves, loud, obscene, full of fire and joy and disgusting images. He makes me laugh. He makes me cry.

"Crap shit *fuck* I *love* this happy-happy new acid it burned my hand like a *laser* I could pour it on you Shit-for-Brains on your headily-head so *horri*-bibble burn your head right *off* so goodily-good-good-good I could *fart!*"

I push my limits because of him. One evening a few years ago, in a reading on the coast of Oregon, I read some poems that repeated Greg's most original and obnoxious swearing. My voice didn't break and no one walked out or threw tomatoes at me. I got my words to the back of the big room without a microphone. I've come a long way, mother and poet.

How unacknowledged learning differences bring out the AD child's negative genius

One of the primary causes of extreme behavior in AD children is the presence of unacknowledged learning differences. If a child cannot listen or reason through his problems, he will experience severe anxiety and frustration and may become depressed, enraged, phobic, or highly anxious. Once the learning difference is remedied, his difficult behavior may be greatly reduced and his success in school greatly enhanced.

The nature of the child's genius is continually to seek expression. If a learning difference blocks positive expression of genius, the AD child may seek the negative. Every positive feature of the child, his creativity, intolerance for absurdity, and ability to disturb and renew culture, has a shadow side. Creativity becomes inattentive hyperactivity and the inability to finish things. Intolerance for absurdity becomes oppositional defiance. The ability to disturb things for productive change becomes simply the ability to disturb and aggravate others.

Though he may be very intelligent and very gifted, the AD child's performance will be greatly limited by his learning difference and he will have a difficult time making a positive contribution. He will experience low self-esteem and a feeling of being out of control.

In addition, an undetected learning difference may cause important caregivers such as doctors and teachers to make the wrong decisions to help a child. A child who has several meltdowns a day, because his inability to process the non-verbal behavior of others prevents him from understanding them, may be misdiagnosed as having bipolar disorder, and he may be given the wrong medication as a result. Teachers of this child may assume that he is being willfully oppositional and recommend that he be put in a punitive educational setting that emphasizes behavior control at the expense of education. A child who cannot get started on things that are intrinsically uninteresting may be labeled "lazy," when the poor cognitive activation feature of attention deficit disorder is really the cause.

Our task as caregivers is to help the child find a path to his strengths. The child's brain is still growing and does not have the experience or wisdom to find strength. The probability that my AD clients have a learning disability on board prompts me to ask parents in my first interview to provide me with a copy of their child's most recent educational

Box 11.3 In the Crucible: stinks and bangs and heart-stopping play

Greg loves to play around with chemicals, creating what Oliver Sacks calls "the stinks and bangs" of alchemy[3] that lead us to science. When he was psychotic, his experiments were chaotic and dangerous and migrated from his room to the kitchen to the living room, all our carpets and floors showing burns and indelible stains. We kept a close eye on him, day and night, confiscating the latest forbidden chemicals and tools. When he is not psychotic his experiments follow his changing interests and are both safer and more thoughtful.

His laboratory is his body, and he plays with sensation—pain or pleasure, as long as it is intense. When he was twelve he gave names to a few dozen sparks, listing them by color, brightness, duration, intensity of pain, how far they traveled up his arm, and whether they left marks on the carpet. Or his skin.

We often get calls from friends and neighbors about Greg's escapades on his bike. When he was fourteen he created an electric current through the handlebars from the generator of his bicycle light, amping up the current as he pedaled. He headed down the big hill near our house, pedaling as fast as he could, until gravity took over and the current cramped his fingers around the handlebars, running up his arms. He was helpless. He fell down in time to save his heart and decided not to try that experiment again.

assessment. This is the series of tests used to identify learning disabilities. If the family has not had an assessment done, I strongly recommend that they arrange to do so. (See the excellent chapter on evaluation in Dornbush and Pruitt's practical manual: *Teaching the Tiger: A Handbook for Individuals Involved in the Education of Students with Attention Deficit Disorders, Tourette Syndrome or Obsessive-Compulsive Disorder.*[4]) Oftentimes health insurance will pay part or all of the cost. Whatever the cost, it is essential to gather this information at the front end. This information is the foundation for intervention planning that the child's school will use. It is also gives us important information about how we can be more helpful.

Education, not instruction, is needed

In the Introduction I noted that a common feature of the personalities and genius of the 100 most eminent people of the twentieth century was the dislike of school or the inability to succeed in school. Most likely the reason was that school, with its emphasis on conformity and standardization, is not a place where children with learning disabilities and attention differences will be successful. When one examines the lives of these most influential people, one sees that for most of them school was either a useless experience or a part of childhood trauma.[5]

Learning feeds the child's genius. It fuels expression of genius and gives it wing. If a child has a learning disability, his genius will be starved of attention. It was a measure of the strength of character and genius of the most eminent twentieth-century personalities that they could deal with the boredom and irrelevance of school and still develop their gifts.

The instructive approach, the idea that learning is about installing information in the brain, does not work for AD children with learning disabilities and differences. It is based on a standardized model of learning that assumes all children learn best in sitting positions, faced forward and upright, with note-taking pens in hand to sop up the teacher's words. If a child has a learning disability it will be difficult for him to learn this way.

The word education is based on the Latin educare—"to draw out." This is an appropriate definition of the best kind of teaching approach for our kids. Their attention differences and learning disabilities naturally create a wall that repels attempts to force in information. What is needed is a way for the child to be drawn out from behind the wall.

The educational (not the instructional) approach is the one most likely to result in the positive expression of genius because it is most *interactive*. It requires the child to reference his connection with the community at every step and pull out his strengths to meet challenges. It does not, as is the case with the instructional approach, make a *thing* out of him, a vessel to be filled. The educational approach tempers a strong child's genius and gives it positive expression even if learning differences are present.

Box 11.4 In the Crucible: autistic oasis or mess?

Except when he sits at his computer Greg sits on the floor for his work, putting computer parts together, experimenting with chemicals and electricity, soldering motherboards, reading. He has desk space, table space, bookcases, drawers, and shelving, but he organizes himself by placing everything around him in a circle on the floor. If anyone cleans up his room he flies into a prolonged rage because he is literally lost—he can't find the components for his work, and he has lost the patterns of how they fit together. To anyone else—to *me*—his room is a terrible mess, but for Greg it's an oasis of order and meaningful work. I've learned to leave it alone. We do a big cleanup when he has finished a project and needs help getting the next one set up.

Remedying the AD child's learning difference requires creative, positive, vision

In order to prevent a learning difference from blocking the genius of the AD child, the learning disability must be identified, the child must understand that he has a particular learning disability balanced by a particular strength, and an appropriate remedial (educational) approach must be implemented. All these interventions must be based on a positive vision of the child's potential and must pull on his particular strengths if they are to succeed. Education can be a powerful force in helping AD children to achieve this neurological balance. Education, the process of "pulling out wisdom," is what is needed because through this process, the child gets in

contact with what he does well to compensate for his challenges. Recall
Dr. Oliver Sacks' observation that

> A disease is never a mere loss or excess—there is always a
> reaction, on the part of the affected individual to restore, to
> replace, to compensate for and to preserve its identity, however
> strange the means may be.[6]

This quote affirms the ability of the child to have a meaningful life in the
face of his neurological impairment. And it suggests that the impairment
itself will cause the development of a different, but just as powerful, neurological capability. The body and mind are hard-wired to achieve
homeostasis and balanced function in the face of a maladaptation, by
enhancing the function of the nervous system in some domain. Human
beings are hard-wired to heal.

A child's genius is freed when (a) he is taught to be more efficient in a
modality that is giving him trouble (for example, a child whose visual-motor
disability makes handwriting difficult is given a computer) or (b) a
wire-around is developed with the child that brings in another modality
to help with the task (unable to comprehend what he is reading because
of inattention, but able to remember what he hears, he is given books on
tape). Here are several examples of how these two strategies can be used:

Example 1

LEARNING DISABILITY

Jerry, a ten-year-old, has an auditory processing disability that makes it
difficult for him to pick out his teacher's words from the noisy back-
ground of his classroom. At school, his teachers tell him what to do but he
does not seem to be able to follow directions.

CHALLENGE TO GENIUS

Not being able to follow directions, Jerry's high intelligence and creativity is redirected from academic accomplishment toward getting him
praise from other students for being the class clown.

REMEDIATION

Jerry's teacher suspects he has an auditory processing problem, and with his parents' consent, has him tested at school. Once the disability is identified, a new way of communicating with Jerry is devised. As part of Jerry's individual education plan (IEP) he is issued a laptop computer onto which teachers list their requirements for work completion, a syllabus for homework, and copies of overheads used in class. Jerry now has a reference tool to use all year round to guide him through his schoolwork. He becomes more successful in school and begins getting attention from the other kids for his positive contribution, not his ability to provide dysfunctional disturbance.

REMEDIATION TYPE

Greater efficiency in weak learning area.

Example 2

LEARNING DISABILITY

Angie, a nine-year-old, has a non-verbal learning disability (NLD) which prevents her from understanding the nonverbal communication of other children and forming conclusions based on her observations.

CHALLENGE TO GENIUS

Not being able to understand the emotional expressions of the other children, she laughs at them when they are hurt or misinterprets their friendly behavior as threatening. These reactions result in her social isolation. In reaction to their rejection of her, she withdraws into her own world and applies her genius for rote memory (a feature of NLD) to categorizing all the insults she has received from her social experience. This strategy causes her to become depressed and withdraw further into herself.

REMEDIATION

Angie's teacher talks with her and learns that Angie consistently misinterprets the non-verbal behavior of other kids. Suspecting the presence of an NLD, the teacher also tests Angie's ability to apply what she has learned in math problems and sees that she is deficient in her ability to accomplish this parts-to-whole reasoning, which is characteristic of NLD.[7]

The teacher talks to Angie's parents about her perceptions, and working with them, initiates testing toward establishment of an IEP. Children with NLDs need extensive one-to-one help in school and intensive help to develop social skills. As these changes are made, Angie pulls out of her depression and becomes more successful on the playground and in the classroom. A special enjoyment for her is working in the school library. Her NLD-related genius for archiving information comes to the fore.

REMEDIATION TYPES

Tutoring compensates for learning weakness in the group setting. The library job brings in her genius for rote memory to build her self-esteem and give her positive social contact.

Example 3

LEARNING DISABILITY

Tom, a thirteen-year-old, has an impairment of verbal expression, which prevents him from solving his problems with his teachers, parents, and other children at school. He cannot tell others what he wants or participate in solutions, but settles into monotonic answers to all questions, giving others a simple "Yes" or "No" without further elaboration. He is misinterpreted as being oppositional or a victim of some unknown trauma that has made him pull into himself.

CHALLENGE TO GENIUS

Tom is very creative and enjoys edgy performance artists such as Marilyn Manson. His creative genius steps to the fore to camouflage his inability to tell others what he knows and feels. He gets into the punk lifestyle, refusing to go to school, and sporting several tattoos, piercing his ears, nose, and tongue.

REMEDIATION

Tom is referred to a psychotherapist to help him deal with what is thought to be an emotional issue. After meeting with Tom, the therapist concludes that though Tom has a florid cognitive and emotional life, he could not express his thoughts or feelings verbally if his life depended on it. He communicates this to Tom, his parents, and other caregivers who, knowing what is going on, back off putting demands on Tom to be more expressive. This is the most important remediation.

Tom becomes more agreeable and interesting to be around. A few friends come into the picture for the first time. He also reacts positively to adjustment of his academic program to diminish the importance of verbal expression for his class projects.

REMEDIATION TYPE

Caregivers' understanding of Tom's genius and his learning difference ("disorder" of verbal expression), diminish their false assumptions about his emotional well-being and enable them to pull together to bring out his true genius (his creativity) in his life.

Example 4

LEARNING DISABILITY

Joshua is diagnosed with attention deficit disorder and experiences severe inattention, distractibility, and short-term memory issues. He is not succeeding in his mainstream classroom, primarily because he does not produce homework. Often he will do the work, but forget to bring it to school.

CHALLENGE TO GENIUS

Unable to get recognition for his schoolwork, Joshua takes his attention deficit disorder-related genius in the "Hunter-pathfinder" archetype to the streets and becomes involved with a group of kids who smoke pot and commit petty thievery.

REMEDIATION

Joshua's parents decide that as long as he is in an educational setting that does not let him move around and is not "hands on" in terms of learning, he will continue to have problems and continue to express his gifts in negative ways. They locate a program in their school district for children interested in environmental science, that features many field trips during the school year to study the ecology, and a staff who require students to perform scholastically in this action-based learning setting. Joshua thrives in this program following the ADHD dictums of "I do therefore I learn. I touch therefore I learn." In this setting, his genius is set free for productive purposes.

REMEDIATION TYPE

Joshua's parents put him in a learning environment suited to his genius and archetype.

Box 11.5 In the Crucible: the singing brain

The speech areas in Greg's cerebral cortex are slightly disjointed from the areas in his limbic brain that remember sequences. He repeats many sounds. He has a very small delay in processing what he hears, so understanding requires two separate operations— hearing the word, then knowing its meaning. As a result he requires quite a lot of repetition to remember auditory instructions. Under stress his speech becomes pressured—fast, giddy, full of repetitions and rhymes, almost a word salad. He strings words together in proper grammatical sequences, but he repeats, transforms, omits in his own syntax. His vivid emotions —anger and playful giddiness are the most prominent—color his voice and choice of words. Small talk is difficult for him, though spontaneous limbic utterances are natural and easy. Relaxed conversation with him is a feral rumpus of word play, expert mimicry, and his powerful intelligence. His language is organized in a wild way— perseverance of sounds plus the creativity of the limbic brain produce musical riffs of scatology, echolalia, violent images, cussings, and insults. His brain sings.

How to wire around a learning difference

Children will tell you why they don't do something well if you ask them. The biggest mistake we caregivers make is to jump to conclusions about what is going on. To begin planning how to help the child, sit down with him and ask him open-ended questions about his difficulties:

- What is it about math that is difficult for you? Is it remembering the facts, how to put them together to solve problems (math operations), or solving the problems themselves?

- Is it hard for you to write? Do your hands hurt when you try to write well? (This could be evidence of a visual-motor problem—the child is trying too hard to overcome his graphomotor issues.)

- What did you think when you saw the other girl crying after she fell off her bike?

- Is it more difficult for you to write or to think about what to write?

Keep going with your personal interview until you have a sense of the issues that the child faces. Look at some of his handwriting and math samples. It is important to get a clear idea of the problem because oftentimes a wire-around can be created on the spot:

- A child with handwriting issues may be given use of a computer.

- A child with homework memory issues may be issued with a laptop with his assignments for the entire year in its file system along with period check sheets.

- A child who cannot line up his math figures on a piece of paper is encouraged to use graph paper.

- A child who has a difficult time understanding social cues is paired with a Friendly Helper (another child who enjoys helping him decode what is going on with the kids at school.)

Another great way to identify learning problems and remedial strategies is to get a group of the caregivers together at school for brainstorming.

This is an informal meeting that can occur outside the IEP process that gives people at school the chance to talk about what they observe with a particular child in terms of his strengths and weaknesses.

At some point, the question should be asked, "What are some easy, effective, and immediate ways in which we could help this child?" The rules of creative brainstorming are followed. Everything goes into the list and the best options are sorted once the creative output slows. Oftentimes a one-page list of interventions for a child will be the most useful piece of a huge IEP file. Labor-intensive solutions may sound great in school staff meetings but after the meeting they may be forgotten. Too much work is involved. Keeping things simple is the key to success.

The specialized intelligence of AD children

One of the definitions of the word "intelligent" in the *Oxford Dictionary* is "able to vary behavior in response to varying situations, requirements, and past experience."[8] This definition points to the fact that "IQ" in any domain is raised by: (a) having a rich fund of memories and interests, and (b) having the opportunity to form as many connections as possible among them. This idea of intelligence does not exclude the gifts of AD children who may or may not register "high IQ" on standardized tests but who meet the test of high intelligence in some domain of endeavor. Be it the deep and piercing focus of the Asperger mind or the hot-burning creative passion of the bipolar mind, the AD condition will cause the child to have a more intense knowledge of the world in some extraordinary way than do neurotypical children. And it will be the child's tendency for *dysinhibition* of energy that will increase the number of significant connections. It will be his energy that gives him the life experience that fuels his intelligence.

There are two levels of action required of us as caregivers to bring out the soulful genius of our AD children. In the short term, we must ensure that educational assessment, both of the informal and formal kind, identifies learning disabilities, and that an appropriate educational program is created to address these learning disabilities. To do a good assessment the professionals with whom we work must be able to *listen* to the AD child and not see him as a bundle of symptoms. There must be a focus on capability as well as impairment. A central theme of this book is that in order

Box 11.6 In the Crucible: negotiating into autistic adulthood

Bringing up Greg is a huge intensity of emotions—joy, anger, denial, fear, acceptance. We cycle through them like the stages of grief. This is the crucible in which we live with our son. We never know how long, or how well, he will survive.

This summer, Greg is up in the air about what he wants to do in the way of school and work. We are helping him search for places for his genius with computers that will educate him for meaningful work that will support him. After months of discussion I have now told Greg that I will support his going off his current antipsychotic, because I understand a small part of his great loss—I see how his brain is different, and not quite himself. But—and this is the part that frightens me—he must keep himself and his father and me safe, and he must have a backup plan if he becomes psychotic again.

Our discussion is easier because Greg knows now that I see that he is right—he *has* lost some part of himself, some part of his genius, on this med. And he sees that I have the right—the right of mothers—to demand safety and harmony for the family, and a backup plan (back on a medication, hospitalized) if safety and harmony fly out the window.

It's a difficult negotiation. I have stopped rearing a child and started living with an adult son who still needs a lot of care and guidance. Greg's independence is our goal, and we do approach that in some ways, not at all in others. And that's the difficulty. Where can I stop being Greg's mother-to-a-child, and journey through this world with him, adult to adult? It's an ongoing quest, nurturing the spirit, uncovering the genius.

to help our children, we need to keep a positive vision of their potential. Caregivers promote healing with the attitude that if genius can't be expressed one way, it can be expressed another. Our tendency to pathologize our kids with labels can be poisonous to their spirits.

In the long term, we must push for the establishment of educational settings that *teach* our children. For many AD kids being put in "Special Ed" is a fate worse than death, because those so assigned are identified by other children as "retards" or "mental." It is clear what our kids need—structured, interesting, flexible, visual, hands-on experience with lots of opportunity for talk-aloud learning and lots of positive reinforcement. These new settings need to be truly student-centered rather than curriculum-centered. They need to provide ways for AD children and young adults to develop wisdom as well as knowledge. We also need to rethink how we create college-level learning environments for our children. The emphasis on the accumulation of specialized facts gained from instruction needs to be replaced with a focus on building the ability to learn from experience. This must be the ultimate educational goal with all subject matter wrapped around it.

1. Know your child's learning differences so that you can help him toward positive expression of his genius and appropriate medical and educational intervention in his life.

2. Realize that a good educational assessment is the first order of business to get him services at school.

3. Get teachers in his life who bring out his gifts and do not try to force-feed him information.

4. Know that every "learning disability" is matched with a compensatory skill. Devise remediation at school that brings out his best and wires around his worst.

Conclusion

Following the AD child's genius to the domain of the soul

There are demons in our lives who make us shrink in fear and revulsion. However, we need to look at them as bearers of gifts hidden under their wings! If we challenge them and make them yield up their gifts, they will be satisfied and will fly away leaving us to benefit from what they brought!

Julian Sleigh from Crisis Points[1]

Several years ago I had the opportunity to do a keynote presentation for the national conference of the Tourette Syndrome Foundation of Canada. I was describing the gifts in the wound of Tourette syndrome using Mozart's life as an example. Historical research shows the great composer to have been Tourettic. I began the presentation by playing some of his music. But the real music was the sounds of people in the room—all manner of Tourettic hoots, hollering, barking, and squeaking. One young man shouted "boom!" as he slapped his hand down on his notebook, every fifteen seconds.

There was such joy in the room. Later in the conference, at the banquet honoring Dr. Mort Duran, a neurologist and cherished in the Tourette community, several young men, all with Tourette syndrome, gave the participants an impromptu rendition of "Blue Moon" sung with the shouts, grunts, and other vocal tics of Tourette syndrome. Sitting next to me was a twelve-year-old boy diagnosed with autism. He had a gleeful, very autistic, look on his face. He was celebrating his enjoyment of the Tourette ensemble by scribing complex mathematical formulae on his napkin. A moment later he was up and dancing in spinning turns, a huge smile on his face, between the ticcing singers and the audience.

Such joy. At that moment I realized that the gift these Touretters and other attention different (AD) children give us is the gift of authenticity. They cannot help but be themselves! The energy in the room felt so clean at that moment. So inclusive. So fierce. It was a moment to remember.

There was no pretense in this group of odd people. No one was holding back or pretending to be neurotypical. There was Great Acceptance. I felt a spirit in the room at the time this was all going on. It felt like a huge loving inclusive Genius that held and protected the geniuses of all the children in attendance.

In dialogue with that collective guiding genius, I accept the fact that nature abhors straight lines and loves the crooked, interesting, soulful shapes. And further, that try as I may to make things orderly, straight-line, and predictable in my life, this is not the natural way of things. The spirit in that room taught me that to help our children and ourselves, we need to accept the simple fact that though there may be "standardized tests" for children in school there is no such thing as a "standardized child."

Some would take issue with this statement. They seek a certain ideal type of child and believe he can be created if only we keep at it. In fact there are some who say that the possibility for being born AD should be screened out of our gene pool.

Most of us see symptomatology as the enemy and see ourselves as soldiers in the battle. This is understandable: we and the professionals with whom we consult about our children, are conditioned to accept the medical model. And our children's behavior is often destructive. But it is also important that we do not write a negative Great Story for our children around their symptoms. We must be careful not to cloud our own vision of our child's potential in this way. This gets us nowhere.

In my counseling practice, children are directed to me by caregivers who work within the paradigm that there really is such a thing as a "normal" child—that you can measure normalcy with an IQ test and the tally of the number of birthday parties your child is invited to.

The notion that realizing one's potential involves achieving some mythical state of standardization is a modern invention. I think the ancient Celts had it right when they said that in times of great crisis, when conventional wisdom is useless, the *wyrd* shall save the day. The Celts defined the term *wyrd* to mean "destiny."[2] They were quite clear about it: when conventional wisdom fails, you had better have a dwarf or two on your side or you were done for!

In more contemporary terms, I believe that the genius of AD children is necessary for the survival of our species. It is intolerant of absurdity, wildly creative, and very disturbing. As the theory of dissipative structures suggests: the system needs disturbance if it is to remain viable.[3] Undisturbed, it begins to die. The system (culture) needs to be tested, pushed, and challenged, in order to remain vital.

Our AD children have gifts for us. Testing us with their behavior, they force us to get real. They teach us about the inevitability of trouble. They create a crucible in which the pretense is cooked out of us. This makes us see things clearer and more honestly. We need this clear vision to take care of ourselves in our personal and collective lives.

AD people disturb the system as children and will disturb it more as adults. We need people with these qualities to keep our minds clear, to challenge us, to come up with solutions that the best neurotypical minds cannot find. As distressing as AD children can be, they hold a powerful potential. In keeping with the mythical wisdom of the children's story of the "Emperor's New Clothes," someone needs to tell us when the emperor is buck naked!

As we nurture our children, we nurture ourselves

The genius of our AD child has another gift for us, much more personal, under its wing. The gift is that in meeting the genius we may come to know ourselves on the *spiritual* level. Perhaps to get in touch with our sense of *soul*.

The *wyrd* genius of the AD child makes us look where soul lives. It is not in the "up" place. The conventional understanding is that the direc-

Box C.1 In the Crucible: letting go

The day Greg's website server crashed for the second time in a week because of him, I got it. Last Thanksgiving, Greg set himself the task of getting more hits on happyspider.com than any other website on the Internet. By January he had hundreds of thousands of cumulative hits, and one day in early February he got two million hits. That day. And three million the next day. Everything he did was scrupulously legal and the server was pretty nice about it. They shut down Greg's domain for forty-five days and never let happyspider near a server again.

The writing is on the wall. Greg's relentless genius will take him far beyond my knowledge into his own life, and like all mothers I'll have to let him go, whether he is ready or not, whether he is independent or not, whether he is happy or not. Thomas the Dragon demands his eyes and will paint them himself if necessary, so that Greg can fly. And my own muse demands attention.

This summer Greg wants nothing more than unlimited computer time, and to grow his hair. It is already down to his shoulders, thick and wild, a rich dark brown. "Lumpy-dumpkins!" he warbles to me, grinning, as he lopes out to the balcony for a smoke, taking a break from his demanding muse. It's another moment, a whole summer ahead of us, to savor and remember. We're making the most of it.

tion to go in life is always "up." Success is measured as the attainment of a predictable, comfortable life—a house in the suburbs, and a job with good security. Advancement is the Holy Grail.

AD children bring us the wisdom that the development of one's depth as a human being may involve going *down*, as well as up. In mythology, down is the direction in which one finds one's soul, one's true nature, and one's genius. In mythology the wildest and wisest creatures live in dark places.

Robert Moore, in his book *Care of the Soul*, describes situations in which people spend their whole lives striving to better themselves spiritually and financially and only find real peace when they are facing a life-threatening disease.[4] He suggests that once hope fades, a new light may come on. In this place the person comes to perfect acceptance of the situation and stops living for the future. In this place he lives for the present and for the experience of meaning and love in the present.

In his column in the *Philadelphia Inquirer*, columnist and psychotherapist Daniel Gottlieb discusses the idea that having hope, holding out for the cure, trying hard to be normal, may actually retard the process of holistic healing in people with severe physical injuries.[5] He talks about his own experience of becoming a quadriplegic because of an automobile accident. He resonates with Moore's thesis as he talks about his descent into misery and depression after his accident. Being for many months in this place, without hope, brought him to a new state of being. He states, "There was something—that invisible hovering angel, perhaps—that wouldn't let me die. Something made me look for a way to find dignity and purpose. Something made me look for a way to give and receive love—to reclaim my very humanity." Gottlieb's sentiment is that we should be careful in how we pathologize conditions that afflict us, as they may be the opening to genius (the hovering angel), the royal road to our unconscious potential and wisdom.

In the story of the "The Spirit in the Bottle" the spirit gives the boy a magic cloth that has the ability to both heal a wound and turn ordinary metal into silver. This is a beautiful metaphor for the genius of the AD child: it has the ability to take your child, and you, the caregiver, from suffering to healing. To gain this benefit, you must get back to basics. You must go down to your own "roots," back to the place where your soul and genius live. In this place of true "observer perspective" you gain wisdom about what you need to do to save your life and further the expression of your child's positive genius. No illusions exist in this place. Just the truth held in the arms of compassion and respect for all the suffering you have gone through as a caregiver to midwife your child's genius into this world.

Pause for a moment here and close your eyes. Take a deep breath down to your diaphragm. Now send a breath to your heart area. Imagine yourself holding your child when he was a baby. Then in fast-forward, let images of the suffering and joy you have experienced with the child play across your inner image. Just sit with the feelings. Let the whole movie play.

Now imagine that from somewhere in that image, strong wings unfurl and wrap around you, holding you, cradling you, and bringing you peace. As you experience this feeling, imagine that you see your child's spirit emerging from your heart, flying to a future that is perfect for the child. Send blessing and acceptance for that future. Feel compassion for yourself, for all the things you have done to help your child realize this future. Know that he has his own genius, his own genie, and that you cannot be that guiding spirit. Just wish him the best possible outcome for his life, take a breath, and relax back into the sheltering comfort of those big wings.

Epilogue

We stopped writing and delivered *Genius!* ten days after Greg's graduation from high school. It was a good day, sunny and optimistic. But we all knew that this part of Greg's Great Story wasn't finished. He needed to find his own adult life, separate from his parents and in spite of his neurology, and we didn't know how to help him do that.

Greg took his independence into his own hands a few weeks after his twenty-first birthday. He threw his computers into the dumpster and slipped out of the house one September midnight, taking George's car. He had never driven a car before. We thought he had been lured away. We knew he might be dead.

He called from a pay phone with his second-to-last quarter, after three terrible days. It was close to midnight, everything was closed and his cell phone was lost. He was exhausted and dehydrated. He asked for the number of his counselor, but had nothing to write with and couldn't hold a number in his head long enough to hang up and dial.

I found the after-hours emergency number and he leaned over to the second pay phone—how many pay phones, let alone side-by-side pay phones, are left in Seattle these days?—and dropped in his last quarter. He dialed as I read the numbers, one by one. The moment his counselor answered Greg slammed down the phone on me, cutting the last tether to his mother. He grew up in that moment and I was privileged to be a witness.

Greg created his own rite of passage, because we couldn't provide one he could accept. He had to take this leap on his own, out of the nest, with or without the ability to fly. And we had to let him. We could guide him to safe landing but he had to make that first leap himself. Most important, once he left, we could not let him come home.

Seven months after his twenty-first birthday, Greg has moved out of the temporary group home he landed in after his rite of passage. He is living in his own apartment about twenty miles south of us, with professional support staff coming in every day to help him with the fundamentals of independence—paying bills, cleaning up, shopping for groceries. He continues to see his counselor and doctor, and is considering a new medication to help him focus. He is looking for work and planning a possible semester at a local college. We see him often and talk on the phone several times a day.

We have entered the adult-to-adult parenting years. Greg is no longer a child, and has embraced the responsibilities of taking care of himself. He still cycles in and out of frightening symptomology, and we are still the first to notice and alert his support staff. We are a very active part of Greg's care, but I have significantly fewer daily hours of care-giving. I do as much as I can by phone and email, especially with his caregivers.

George and I seem to have been successful parents. In spite of so many parenting mistakes, we see that our son is an adult; independent of us, ready for his life and willing to ask for help to get the life he wants. We have managed to provide a community of professionals who are learning to support him now and who can continue to support him when we are no longer alive.

It's helpful to lay out the map of our slog through the swamps and pitfalls of autism, psychosis, Tourette syndrome, and adolescence to Greg's independence, as we balanced him through his middle and late teens between life and death. We can see where we got off track, how long it took to find our way again, which shortcuts worked, and which didn't. Mostly we learned from our mistakes. When we didn't, we repeated the mistakes until we did. When we figured it out we wrote it down so we could remember, and possibly pass it on. It's hard-won wisdom. Here is how we applied the seven criteria of the field of nurturing to help Greg achieve success in his life.

First criterion of the field of nurturing—caregivers recognize the AD child's genius

Recognizing Greg's genius, his guiding spirit, has never been a problem for George and me, but we have learned to be surprised, and to accept his eccentricities. The neurological "wounds" that have formed him became beacons that led us through diagnoses and medications, to the under-standing of his absolute need for freedom in order for his gifts to emerge—freedom of thought and expression, freedom to move and vocalize, to eat and bathe, to mess about with his computers whenever and however he wants. As much we require that he stay alive, Greg requires his eccentricities.

We saw Greg's guiding spirit in his intense hyperfocus as a child, watching bugs, stalking crows, trapping a couple of animals in his backyard box-on-a-stick. (One memorably angry squirrel, one terrifying opossum. Greg decided, at nine, that he was no match for the rage and fear of a trapped wild animal, giving him the beginnings of wisdom and a lifelong metaphor running through his Great Story.) We saw it when he was two and three, figuring out the telephone lines and electric outlets, and we see it still in the intensity of his explorations of cyberspace and the guts of computers.

We see Greg's archetype as a Follower of Power, in the physical world through electricity and electronics, and in the world of ideas and culture, as when he learned how to mine the Internet for data. He realizes that information is power and has developed his genius to follow and manipu-late the flow of information, sometimes to excess.

We kept scanty records of Greg's infancy and early childhood. From birth he was an active, vocal, wakeful child and we had our hands full. We should have made time for those records. They would have helped our understanding of his development. His interest in power has always been pushed by a fierce, determined energy; a characteristic of his guiding spirit.

Greg's affinity with electricity and computers does not include much understanding of human relationships, or the ability to read facial expres-sions, tones of voice and body language. Teachers, who saw one set of his abilities and not the other, saw him as either highly intelligent or very slow. Both extremes are true of him, and both are inadequate to fully nurture him, without knowing how his autism shapes the action of his brain and body.

There is another archetype emerging in Greg's psyche that is part of his autism—he searches for Perfect Beauty. In his delight in a perfectly wired circuit board, or in his somewhat rigid sense of beauty in people, he finds seamless perfection enormously interesting. He has very high standards for his own work. This perfection-seeking trait, this interest in the beauty and function of natural and manmade things is seen in many people with autism and Asperger syndrome.

Second criterion of the field of nurturing—caregivers are attuned to the AD child

The essence of attunement is positive, contactful, communication. In parenting a child like Greg, we must understand his neurological limitations and work around them to nourish the part of him that *wants* to be in heart contact with us.

This is our hardest task, and takes a lifetime. We understand Greg's genius quite well, but for a long time we didn't understand its "wounds," and this interfered with our communications and led us to erroneous assumptions. We didn't understand that his hyperfocus is a part of the neurological "wounding" of autism, and results directly in his difficulties with transitions. Or that it is Tourette syndrome that gives him his giddy oral poetry and slightly scary ability to communicate with animals without words, as well as his feral insults and swearing.

So much of our learning about how to parent Greg effectively we learned by doing it wrong, noticing, and making changes. We learned to communicate one thing at a time. We learned when explanations had to be simple and concrete (explaining the non-verbals of other people) and when he could explore a subject with subtle distinctions and esoteric knowledge (computers, cyberspace, behaviors of animals in his childhood backyard, locations and qualities of the wildest campsites on the Washington coast).

Third criterion of the field of nurturing—caregivers help the child discover a great story that moves him forward

Greg has a natural understanding of the need for his own positive—and publicly known—Great Story. I've learned to focus on whatever I can praise, and to be specific, and give him words for his experiences and emotions.

The first time I saw Greg after he left I gritted my teeth and didn't say how scared and angry and hurt I was. Knowing the healing of a positive Great Story, I told him he had taken himself through a rite of passage that led him to his adulthood. I told him he had faced his dangers with courage and intelligence—I went into a few specific details. I told him I was very proud of him, and so happy to be with him again. Every time I saw him I repeated this praise. Sometimes I had to slip it into the moments between his rants. Now he tells me himself that he went through a rite of passage into his adulthood, and is proud of himself. He thinks of himself as strong and smart, and remembers this when he faces something unknown.

He could have seen his rite of passage as a failure. If I had talked exclusively about the nauseating fear his father and I went through for those three days, if I had focused solely on the dangerous aspects of his adventure, if I had seen his leap into adulthood as my loss and his selfishness, then he would see himself as a failure, and would not have the independence he has now won with such courage and strength. As his mother, I have a responsibility to tell him that he is good, and a success, and a loving person, every chance I get, and find the chances when they are difficult to see.

When we focus on the positive Greg flourishes. I've learned over the years to praise him profusely for whatever he does that is positive. Even in a contentious disagreement, I can find something to praise. Sometimes I wait until the disagreement has calmed down. Sometimes I slip it in, sandwiched between his rants.

Fourth criterion of the field of nurturing—caregivers build the AD child's participation in a community

I've learned to thank and acknowledge the little ad hoc communities that have come together so often for Greg, in school meetings, in his counselor's office, now in his home. I've learned to thank particularly the "angels." These are professionals who work from the heart, and can't sleep if a client is falling through the cracks. They work hard, and they work kind. They are a huge positive in every client's life.

George and I have nurtured Greg's bonds with our communities. He is accepted and valued in my church, and though he does not attend service often, he benefits from the good wishes and weekly prayers of the congregation. He was accepted and mentored by the men in George's 1990's men's group—the Tuesday Night Moody Bastards. They found him to be extremely exasperating and chaotic, but they admired his physical courage, and his insistence on speaking the truth as he saw it. The confrontation they showed him, as well as the respect, was part of his learning.

Greg's imaginal ancestors are unexpected. In his late teens his walls were bare except for a couple of small posters of Oscar Wilde and Marilyn Monroe. They inspired him, Greg said, because they followed beauty, learned to deal with their natural charisma, were deeply intelligent in spite of (or perhaps because of) their inborn flaws and gaps, and they couldn't help but tell the truth. And they were pretty. Greg puts high value on youthful slender beauty. He definitely prefers Wilde in his youth and thinks Marilyn died at an appropriate age, before she got old or fat.

Greg finds kindred spirits in personalities such as Nikola Tesla. This man, perhaps the greatest inventor who ever lived (one of his discoveries being alternating current), showed features of Asperger syndrome and obsessive compulsive disorder. True to his neurotype, Greg was more interested in building his own Tesla Coil than in the personality of the man who invented it. But he knew something of Tesla's life from reading online information about how to build the great coils that could throw lightning-like bolts of static electricity.

Almost every leap forward in science and technology in human history shows the presence of people like Greg. He sits with a proud, talented, and sometimes disturbed group of individuals.

Fifth criterion of the field of nurturing—caregivers address physical factors and medication

We have paid very close attention to Greg's medications over the years, and we are appalled at the long list of them. Few had been tested on children and some are now known to be far more dangerous than we knew. But overall, we're grateful to live in a time when new medications are developed that help neurologically compromised people. Some meds allowed Greg to function in school, some kept him alive.

It was always difficult to try yet another new medication for Greg. We researched each medication extensively, especially the side effects, and learned to balance the positives against the negatives. There were times when as parents we had no choice but to give Greg the med—half alive is better than dead. Greg needed us to make these hard decisions, so he could live to adulthood. We learned to start with the shortest course and lowest dose and pay very close attention to Greg's description of side effects. Our decisions were informed and right for that time. Then and now, we wish we hadn't had to make them. It was always difficult.

In terms of the Gyroscope Model, we are becoming more sophisticated in what destabilizes Greg and what brings him back to stability. Lack of sleep due to nighttime hyperactivation has been an enormous problem. Recognising the powerful impact of nicotine on his mood, awareness, and thought content, we do not confront him with anything too stress-producing when he needs a smoke. And we are quietly relentless in our efforts to help him quit cigarettes.

We discovered that physical activity calmed Greg's wild mind for up to an hour, though most sports were beyond him. We watched him turn into a giddy little gibbon boy at six, hooting and jumping at the constant echoes in the crowded gym—obviously basketball was out. But when he first walked into an Aikido class, at thirteen, he loved the visual and auditory quiet (white walls, thick floor mats) and stuck it out for a year, until he needed to be away from people again.

We have found that purposeful work greatly comforts Greg. If he finds something interesting, some new learning, or new fascination, we will typically run with his interest and nurture it. As we have noted in chapter 1, a special interest can provide continuity to a person's experience. For people with autism and Asperger syndrome, doing purposeful work is stabilizing, being bored is hugely destabilizing.

Sixth criterion of the field of nurturing—caregivers help the child re-member himself

Before Greg was born, George and I taught stress management work-shops to several thousand state, federal, and county employees. Remem-bering how to manage stress is essential and people like Greg find it almost impossible to come up with strategies on the spot. Teaching him to deal with the stress of his wild neurology was a huge challenge, even with our experience, and one we couldn't do without some talented professionals.

When we could drop our own models, we noticed that Greg knew ways to calm himself and we learned to simply encourage these practices. He has a lifelong love of small compact places to scooch his body into—a very autistic comforting. Coupled with this he has a deep loathing of being trapped, which comes from his basic humanity—no one likes being trapped—and is emphasized by his Tourette need for physical freedom, his need to tic and spit, to swear, to rant, to run.

He is more comfortable in forests and on the wild coast than any urban or suburban space, even home, because in the wild he can be wild—he can rant and scream and tic and throw things and no one will hear him or look at him or tell him to stop. His body teaches him, and us, the human need for wild places.

Throughout Greg's life we have helped him develop good habits around his care of himself. Living alone now, he is enjoying a lot more freedom to just be himself and we are heartened by his ability to manage his own stress. Greg is learning in his adult life that he really does feel better when he eats and sleeps properly. He recognizes (reluctantly) that medication sometimes enhances his life. He knows that going for a walk calms him, and tending plants on the balcony lifts his mood. We couldn't have said it better ourselves.

On quite a few occasions during Greg's growing up, until his late teens, he threatened us with violence. The genius of children such as ours often has a take-no-prisoners dark side. This is not an indication of malevolent personality. It is simply an aspect of genius that must be tempered by a connection with the community. We tried to model these values in our parenting approach.

We guided our response to his threats—and eventual punches—by the premise "violence begets violence," and were intolerant of any display of it. Greg tested our boundaries hard, and we needed the community to back us up. When we couldn't stop him from punching us, the police and courts did. He is a non-violent adult. We couldn't have achieved this without the community's laws—and police backup—against domestic violence.

I've tried a zillion ways to help Greg organize his time, his tools, and his living space. What works best, always, is the simplest. At his most symptomatic, he threw everything into a backpack, ignoring the small inside and outside pockets, digging out whatever he needed from the shambles of letters, money, bottled water, loose papers, and granola bars. His room was a larger version of the backpack. When he is stable, he can find places for important items like keys, wallet, and cell phone. He puts them in their designated place nearly all the time these days and is quietly delighted to find them there when he needs them again. Simplicity is still the best way, and Greg has lots of clear plastic bins in multiple sizes.

I can usually help Greg find ways around his extreme skin sensitivities. But his poor sore feet had me baffled for years. Greg needed his shoes loose, size 9 feet in size 13 sneakers, tightly laced, making him clumsy and unable to run, giving him constant blisters and calluses. All during his teens he couldn't bear the tight touch of shoes.

The summer he was 19, Greg asked to take ballet classes. He was enchanted by the beauty of ballet, and realized he might like the kinesthetic feel of it. He struggled with the glove-tight ballet slippers, nearly as difficult as the tights and dance belt. At the end of the summer he decided he would rather watch ballet than dance it, but his feet were transformed. He pushed himself hard to endure those ballet slippers and by the end of the summer he wore size 9 sneakers to school. Now his shoes fit and his feet are normal.

Seventh criterion of the field of nurturing—caregivers practice high-level wellness in their own lives

George and I are blooming these days, as well as Greg. It's good to be an adult again, doing the work I choose, instead of a perennial mother doing the work that has chosen me all these years. We're as happy to get our son out of our home, as he is happy to get into his own home. We like him so much more when we don't have to share a kitchen and bathrooms with him.

During Greg's childhood George's wellness centered around his active fathering, and his work—counseling, writing, lecturing. His mind and heart were engaged and his successful career reflects his success in self-care.

Like many women, I've done less well. According to the IRS, Social Security, and my own resumé, I've had no career and done almost no work in the past twenty-one years, though I am an accomplished writer and poet. But I have not had the time or energy to focus on turning my talents into income. The stress and boredom, the 24/7 duty, the lack of recognition of work well done, does take a toll.

In Greg's early teens, when his symptomology became florid and violent, I gradually dropped out of all out-of-home activities. Five years ago I recognized that I had no life beyond incessant mothering and shot out the front door half the evenings of the week, as soon as George got home from work.

What has saved me is art and community. I sing in two choirs, teach and sculpt found wood, co-chair an annual art show, organize and read in the occasional poetry reading, and take part in church activities, including the Board of Deacons. When I can find the time at home (these days I can) I write poetry, books, articles, and children's stories.

In hindsight I like to think that I should have done more of this, especially paid work. But hindsight shows me the price Greg would have paid.

When Greg was about twelve I met a woman in a writing class who had an autistic son and a well-paid career outside the home. I asked her how she did it, talking a little about Greg. She told me she and her husband had decided to place their son in a group home, at five years old, because she couldn't do her work and mother an autistic child at the same time. It was a very successful placement and probably lifelong. They saw him once a week.

We looked at each other in horror. There was no bridge between her choice and mine. In hindsight I could make no other decision. Nor could she.

George and I have successfully parented Greg through childhood because we have nurtured his guiding spirit. This is the most important aspect of parenting. It is always the spirit that shows what the child needs for his growth into a useful and happy adulthood. Our task as parents was to listen and observe, to discern what was nurturing from what was harmful, to form opinions and make decisions, to teach, to learn from our mistakes, to show up and keep going, to recognize when childhood was accomplished and move on to the new wonders of the adult son.

I'm so glad to be done.

Joanne Barrie Lynn
May 2005

The field of nurturing awareness checklist

Instructions: This is a personal awareness exercise. Rate the presence of each of the criteria in the field of nurturing in your attention different (AD) child's family and school environments. Each criterion may be rated from 1, which means the factor is not present in your child's life, to 7, which means the factor is present and is a dynamic part of the child's life on a day-to-day basis.

1	2	3	4	5	6	7
Factor not present			Factor moderately present			Factor very present

1. Caregivers recognize the child's genius

Significant questions:

Do caregivers:

1. Understand how the AD child's compensation for a "deficit" in social, emotional, or cognitive ability helps form his genius?
2. Study the child's *early interests* to glimpse his genius?
3. Understand how the child's *fears* point to his genius?
4. Have a sense of the child's *archetype?*

Approximate strength of this factor in your AD child's life: _____

II. Caregivers are attuned to the AD child

Significant questions:

1. Do family members accept each other's foibles?

2. Do family members demonstrate positive communication behaviors such as smiling at, assuring, and affirming each other?

3. Are there good listening behaviors in the family?

Approximate strength of this factor in your AD child's life: _____

III. Caregivers help the child discover a Great Story that moves him forward

Significant questions:

1. Do caregivers in the child's life listen to him?

2. Are caregivers able to help him make sense of his life?

Approximate strength of this factor in your AD child's life: _____

IV. Caregivers build the AD child's participation in a community

Significant questions:

1. Does the child have a community of peers?

2. Does the child know his ancestry and is he able to identify traits of his family?

3. Does the child have "imaginal" ancestors or heroic figures that he may reference to experience a sense of belonging?

4. Are there adult mentors in the child's life?

5. Is the child given consequences that affirm his connection to the community?

Approximate strength of this factor in your AD child's life: _____

V. Caregivers address physical factors and medication

Significant questions:

1. Is the AD child receiving the appropriate medication?

2. Is his sleep schedule stable?

3. Do his diet and exercise habits further his physical health and emotional stability?

Approximate strength of this factor in your AD child's life: _____

VI. Caregivers help the AD child re-member himself

Significant questions:

1. Is body-state specific language used in high-stress situations?
2. Does the child receive continual affirmation of his ability to self-control?
3. Does the child have opportunities for joyful movement?

Approximate strength of this factor in your AD child's life: _____

VII. Caregivers practice high-level wellness in their own lives

1. The domain of purpose

Significant questions:

- Do you have meaningful work in your life?
- Do you put attention on identifying your call, the kind of work that nurtures your spirit?
- Do you experience delight and awe in your life?

Approximate strength of this factor in your life:_____

2. The domain of freedom

Significant questions:

- Do you believe that you deserve to live free of your child's symptoms?
- Do you see your AD child's behavior as a challenge (not a curse)?
- Do you have a fallback plan (BATNA) to maintain control in your family?
- Are you afraid of rocking the boat to get services for your child?
- Are you able to communicate honestly at home and at work?

Approximate strength of this factor in your life:_____

3. The domain of love

Significant questions:

- Do you have the opportunity to express love for someone?
- Do you have people in your life you know deeply and who know you in the same way?
- Is there an ethic of responsibility, of equality in your important relationships?
- Are you surrounded by people who respect you?
- Do you take good care of your body?
- Do you have an art form in your life that nourishes you?

Approximate strength of this factor in your life:_____

Notes

The importance of identifying the genius of 'attention different' children: preface

1 Lynn, George T., *Survival Strategies for Parenting Your ADD Child*, Underwood Books, Grass Valley, CA, 1996.

2 Lynn, George T., *Survival Strategies for Parenting Children With Bipolar Disorder*, Jessica Kingsley Publishers, London, UK, 2000.

The Spirit in the Bottle

1 This myth has been told many different ways in many different cultures. This rendition is written by Joanne Barrie Lynn based on the Grimm brothers' version. Find the original in *Complete Brothers Grimm Fairy Tales*, Gramercy Books, Random House Value Publishing, New York, 1993.

Part I: Understanding and nurturing the positive genius of your attention different child

Introduction

1 Epigraph: Jung, Carl G. *Memories, Dreams, Reflections*, edited by Aniela Jaffe, Vintage Books, New York, 1989 (reissue).

2 Moore, Robert L., *Care of the Soul*, Perennial, New York, 1994. The Romans defined the male form of guiding spirit as "genius" or "animus" and the female form as "juno" or "anima"—the spirit, angel, goddess, that animates us and gives us wisdom, in the performance of our personal art form. Moore embraces this idea of the personal genius in this book, pp.298–301.

3 Bruun, Ruth D., *A Mind of Its Own*, Oxford University Press, Oxford, UK, 1994. Dr. Bruun, a leading authority on Tourette syndrome, describes her theory, based on an analysis of Mozart's life and work, that he had Tourette syndrome.

4 Dickinson, Emily, "Much Madness is Divinist Sense." *The Rag and Bone Shop of the Heart*, edited by Robert Bly, James Hillman, and Michael Meade, Harper Collins, New York, 1992.

5   Grandin, Temple, *Thinking in Pictures: And Other Reports of My Life With Autism*, Doubleday, New York, 1995.

6   Hillman, James, *The Soul's Code: In Search of Character and Calling*, Warner Books, NY, 1996.

7   Pickover, Clifford, *Strange Brains: The Secret Lives of Eccentric Scientists and Madmen*, Harper-Collins, New York, 1998.

8   Sacks, Oliver, *The Man Who Mistook His Wife for A Hat*, Touchstone Books, Carmichael, CA, 1998.

9   David Weeks and Kate Ward, in *Eccentrics: A Study of Sanity and Strangeness*, Kodansha International, New York, 1988.

10   Prigogine, Ilya, *Self-Organization in Non-Equilibrium Systems: From Dissipative Structures to Order Through Fluctuations* (with G. Nicolis), J. Wiley and Sons, New York, 1977.

11   Hillman, *The Soul's Code*. Hillman discusses a common denominator of the eminent personalities he studied: they all disliked school and most learned more outside school than in attendance.

12   Pickover, *Strange Brains*.

13   Hillman, *The Soul's Code*.

14   Moyzis, Robert K. *et al.* "Evidence of positive selection acting at the human dopamine receptor D4 gene locus," *Proceedings of the National Academy of Science*, January, 2002, vol. 99: pp.309–314. Provides an overview of the research behind the theory that leaders of early human transcontinental migrations possessed a variant of the DRD4 gene, the so-called "risk-taking" gene found in persons diagnosed with attention deficit hyperactivity disorder.

15   Kupzig, Robert, *Psychology Today*, February, 2004, pp.66–72, reviews Simon Baron-Cohen's development of his theory of autistic "systematizers."

16   Einstein, Albert, *The World as I See It*, Philosophical Library, New York, 1949. Einstein used to speak of his non-logical, intuitive way of reaching knowledge, as "tapping into God's thoughts." "The deeper one penetrates into nature's secrets, the greater becomes one's respect for God."

17   Ledgin, Norm, *Diagnosing Jefferson*, Future Horizons, Arlington, TX, 2000. Dr. Temple Grandin endorses Ledgin's theory that Thomas Jefferson showed features of Asperger syndrome. The author observes features of Asperger syndrome in Jefferson's poor social skills, sensory issues (he would often deliver speeches wearing his bedroom slippers), and presence of a series of special interests, the most famous of which was the building of Monticello, a project that lasted many years and resulted in a beautiful, but not very practical structure.

18 Hartmann, Thom, *Attention Deficit Disorder: A Different Perception*, Underwood Books, Grass Valley, CA, 1997 (revised edition).

Chapter 1 First criterion: caregivers recognize the AD child's genius

1 Epigraph: Jacobsen, Rolf, "Guardian Angel," from *Twenty Poems of Rolf Jacobsen*, translated by Robert Bly, The Seventies Press, Moose Lake, MN, 1976.

2 Moore, Robert L., *Care of the Soul*, Perennial, New York, 1994.

3 Pickover, Clifford, *Strange Brains: The Secret Lives of Eccentric Scientists and Madness*, Harper-Collins, New York, 1995. His study of the lives of the great inventers, Tesla, Edison, Darwin, and Johnson, reveals the genius of these distinctly "attention different" men.

4 Jamison, Kay Redfield, *Touched with Fire: Manic-Depressive Illness and the Artistic Temperament*, Simon and Schuster, New York, 1993.

5 Flaherty, Alice, *The Midnight Disease: The Drive to Write, Writer's Block, and the Creative Brain*, Houghton-Mifflin, Boston, MA, 2004.

6 Hillman, James, *The Soul's Code: In Search of Character and Calling*, Warner Books, NY, 1996.

7 Bruun, Ruth D., *A Mind of Its Own*, Oxford University Press, Oxford, UK, 1994.

8 Rilke, Rainer Maria, *The Lay of the Love and Death of Cornet Christopher Rilke*, W.W. Norton, New York, 1963. His narrative continues, "I want to beg you to be patient toward all that is unsolved in your heart and try to love the questions themselves. For one human being to love another human being: that is perhaps the most difficult task that has been entrusted to us, the ultimate task, the final test and proof, the work for which all other work is merely preparation."

9 Hillman, *The Soul's Code*, p. 23.

10 ibid., p. 198.

11 Pickover, Clifford, *Strange Brains*, p. 85

12 ibid., p. 289.

13 Jung, Carl G., *Man And His Symbols*, Laurel Leaf, Holt, UK, 1968 (reissue). Jung describes the importance of the acceptance of paradox and "loving the struggle" (p.59).

14 Lynn, George T., *Survival Strategies for Parenting Children with Bipolar Disorder* Jessica Kingsley Publishers, London, UK, 2000.

15 Hartmann, Thom, *Attention Deficit Disorder: A Different Perception*, Underwood Books, Grass Valley, CA, 1997 (revised edition).

16 Mesibov, Gary, "High-Functioning Autism or Asperger syndrome: Why the Controversy?" *Autism and Asperger Digest*, November–December 2000, pp.16–18.

17 Hobbes, Thomas, *The Leviathan*, London, England, 1660.

Chapter 2 Second criterion: caregivers are attuned to the AD child

1 Epigraph and content from Siegel, Daniel, J. *The Developing Mind: How Relationships and the Brain Interact to Shape Who We Are*, Guilford Press, New York, 1999.

2 Simoneau, Teresa, *et al.*, "Bipolar Disorder and Family Communication: Effects of a Psychoeducational Treatment Program," *Journal of Abnormal Psychology*, November, 1999, vol. 108, no. 4: p.588. Provides guidelines for best communication style to assist recovery of family members suffering from bipolar disorder and schizophrenia.

3 Maté, Gabor, *Scattered*, pp.72–74, Plume, New York, 1999.

4 Siegel, *The Developing Mind*, p. 70.

5 Marks, Tracy, "Rediscovering the Muse, Finding Our Personal Sources of Inspiration," *Woman of Power*, Fall/Winter, 1990, no. 15.

6 *My Big Fat Greek Wedding*, Gold Circle Films, Home Box Office, MPH Entertainment, Playtone Pictures, 2002.

7 Lynn, George T., *Survival Strategies for Parenting Your ADD Child*, Underwood Books, Grass Valley, CA, 1996.

8 Lynn, George T., *Survival Strategies for Parenting Children with Bipolar Disorder*, Jessica Kingsley Publishers, London, UK, 2000.

Chapter 3 Third criterion: caregivers help the child discover a Great Story that moves him forward

1 Epigraph from *Spirited Away*. Written and directed by Hayao Miyazaki, Walt Disney Studios, Burbank, CA, 2001.

2 Siegel, Daniel, J. *The Developing Mind: How Relationships and the Brain Interact to Shape Who We Are*, Guilford Press, New York. For autobiographical memory see p. 21 and for the function of dreams see p.52–54.

3 Silver, Larry B., *The Misunderstood Child: Understanding and Coping With Your Child's Learning Disabilities*, Random House, New York, 1998.

4 Lynn, George T., *Survival Strategies for Parenting Children with Bipolar Disorder*, Jessica Kingsley Publishers, London, UK, 2000.

5 Houston, Jean, *The Search for the Beloved: Journeys in Mythology and Sacred Psychology (Inner Workbook.)* J.P. Tarcher, New York, 1997. Chapter 9, "Of Story and Myth," is the basic cite for this discussion of Great Story.

6 Grandin, Temple, *Thinking in Pictures: And Other Reports of My Life with Autism*, Doubleday, New York, 1995, p.34.

7 Lynn, George T., *Survival Strategies for Parenting Your ADD Child*, Underwood Books, Grass Valley, CA, 1996.

Chapter 4 Fourth criterion: caregivers build the AD child's participation in a community

1 Epigraph: Whyte, David, excerpt from "The House of Belonging", from *The House of Belonging*, Many Rivers Press, Langley, WA, 1997.

2 Bly, Robert, interview with Robert Bly from the Public Broadcasting Service's special "No Safe Place," March 27, 1998.

3 *Braveheart*, Twentieth Century Fox, 1995.

4 Sacks, Oliver, *Uncle Tungsten: Memories of A Chemical Boyhood*, Vintage Books, New York, 2001.

Chapter 5 Fifth criterion: caregivers address physical factors and medication

1 Epigraph: from Michael Meade's workshop at the Seattle Art Museum on March 13, 2004 titled "Culture, Conflict, and Change: Native Spirit and Jungian Ideas."

2 Selye, Hans, M.D., *The Stress of Life*, McGraw-Hill, New York, 1978. Introduces the eustress and distress concepts, p.74.

3 Lynn, George T., Survival Strategies for Parenting Your ADD Child, Underwood Books, Grass Valley, CA, 1996.

4 Papolos, Dimitri, M.D., *The Bipolar Child: The Definitive and Reassuring Guide to Childhood's Most Misunderstood Disorder*, Broadway Books, New York, 2000, pp. 211–213. The observation that bipolar disorder in children expresses, in extreme form, the general adaptation syndrome ("fight or flight" reaction) was made during panel discussion with Dr. Dimitri Papolos at the *Jean Paul Ohadi Conference on Children and Adolescents with Bipolar Disorder*, Chicago, IL, December 1, 2000.

5 Kaplan, Arthur. "Omega 3 Fatty Acids Evaluated for Bipolar Disorder." *Psychiatric Times*, December 1999.

Chapter 6 Sixth criterion: caregivers help the AD child re-member himself

1 Epigraph: Hebb, Donald, *The Organization of Behavior: A Neuropsychological Theory*, Wiley, New York, 1949, p.70.

2 Techniques for building presence under stress drawn from sports psychology are reviewed by Katy Butler in "Living on Purpose," *Psychotherapy Networker*, September/October, 2003, pp.28–37.

3 Silver, Larry B., *The Misunderstood Child: Understanding and Coping with Your Child's Learning Disabilities*, Random House, New York, 1998.

4 Csikszentmihalyi, Mihaly, *Flow: The Psychology of Optimal Experience*, Harper and Row, New York, 1990.

Part II The seventh criterion in the field of nurturing: caregivers' practice of high-level wellness in their own lives

Introduction

1 Pickover, Clifford, *Strange Brains: The Secret Lives of Eccentric Scientists and Madmen*, Harper-Collins, New York, 1998.

2 Lynn, George T., *Survival Strategies for Parenting Children with Bipolar Disorder*, Jessica Kingsley Publishers, London, UK, 2000.

3 Selye, Hans, M.D., *The Stress of Life*, McGraw-Hill, New York, 1978.

4 Pines, Maya, "Psychological Hardiness" (an overview of the Kobasa/Maddi hardiness research), *Psychology Today*, December, 1980, pp.34–98.

Chapter 7 Self-care rule number one: Live on purpose!

1 Aristotle, *Nicomachean Ethics, Book I*, translated by David Ross, Oxford University Press, reprint edition 1998.

2 Campbell, Joseph, M.D. His "follow your bliss" quote is taken from the PBS Bill Moyers interview series, *The Power of Myth*, Doubleday, New York, 1988, pp. 120, 149.

3 Utne, Eric, "Long and Winding Road," *Utne Reader*, Nov–Dec, 2002, pp.66–68.

4 Enright, John, the delight model, provided during the course of Dr. Enright's participation in a workshop titled "Responsibility, Awareness, and Communication," November, 1978, Cold Mountain Institute, Vancouver, BC, Canada.

5 Hillman, James, M.D., *A Blue Fire*, Harper-Perennial, New York, 1991.

6 Metzger, Deena, *Writing for Your Life*, Harper, San Francisco, 1992. Contains the Dream Police exercise.

Chapter 8 Self-care rule number two: live free!

1 Epigraph, from Schom, Alan, *Emile Zola, A Biography*, Henry Holt, New York, 1988.

2 Csikszentmihalyi, Mihaly, *Flow: The Psychology of Optimal Experience*, Harper and Row, New York, 1990.

3 Fisher, Roger and Ury, William, *Getting to Yes*, Penguin Books, New York, 1981.

4 Bower, Sharon, *Asserting Yourself* (Second Edition), Perseus Publishing, Boulder, CO, 1991.

5 Beaulieu, Daniel, "Beyond Just Words," *Psychotherapy Networker*, Jul/Aug, 2003, vol.27, no.4, p.76.

6 Einstein, Albert, *The World as I See It*, Philosophical Library, New York, 1949. Contains quote: "Is the universe friendly?"

Chapter 9 Self-care rule number three: cultivate love in your life!

1 Fromm, Erich, *The Art of Loving*, Harper and Row, New York, 1956.

2 Ibid.

3 Pines, Maya, "Psychological Hardiness" (an overview of the Kobasa/Maddi hardiness research), *Psychology Today*, December 1990, pp. 34–98.

4 Fromm, *The Art of Loving*, p. 24.

5 Enright, John, *The Structure of Human Experience*, Pro Telos, Mill Valley, CA, 1980, p. 13.

6 *A Beautiful Mind*, Universal Studios, 2001.

7 Keen, Sam, *The Passionate Life: Stages of Loving*, Harper, San Francisco, 1983.

Chapter 10 The peril of neglecting to nourish the genius of the AD child

1 Levoy, Gregg, *Callings: Finding and Following an Authentic Life*, Crown Publishers, New York, 1997.

2 Ibid.

Chapter 11 How learning differences frustrate the expression of positive genius

1   Epigraph: Silver, Larry, *The Misunderstood Child: Understanding and Coping With Your Child's Learning Disabilities*, Random House, New York, 1998, p. 379.

2   The Website of the National Joint Committee on Learning Disabilities provides this set of definitions of learning disabilities (2003). http://www.ldonline.org/njcld/fact_sheet.html

3   Sacks, Oliver, *Uncle Tungsten: Memories of A Chemical Boyhood*, Vintage Books, New York, 2001.

4   Dornbush, Marilyn and Pruitt, Sheryl, *Teaching the Tiger: A Handbook for Individuals Involved in the Education of Students with Attention Deficit Disorders, Tourette Syndrome or Obsessive-Compulsive Disorder*, Hope Press, 1995.

5   Hillman, James, *The Soul's Code: In Search of Character and Calling*, Warner Books, NY, 1996.

6   Sacks, Oliver, "Losses," *The Man Who Mistook His Wife For A Hat*, John Curley Co., South Yarmouth, MA, 1986, p.6.

7   Rourke, Byron, *Nonverbal Learning Disabilities: The Syndrome and the Model*, Guilford Press, New York, 1989.

8   *Oxford Dictionary*, American Edition, Berkley Books, New York, 1997. On p.414 is provided the definition of "intelligent" as "able to vary behavior in response to varying situations, requirements, and past experience."

Conclusion: Following the AD Child's Genius to the Domain of the Soul

1   Sleigh, Junlian, *Crisis Points*, Floris Books, Edinburgh, UK, 1998.

2   Meade, Michael, *Men and the Water of Life: Initiation and the Tempering of Men*, Harper Collins, 1993. Details the origin of the term "wyrd."

3   Comings, David, *The Gene Bomb: Does Higher Education and Advanced Technology Accelerate the Selection of Genes for Learning Disorders, Addictive and Disruptive Behaviors?* Hope Press, 1996. Here a pioneering researcher ventures the idea that it is desirable to clean the gene pool of neuropsychiatric disorders caused by the D-2 (risk-taking) dopamine allele. This idea is less understandable from a systems view of culture that is informed by the theory of dissipative structures—the system will perish without significant disturbance.

4   Moore, Robert L., *Care of the Soul*, Perennial, New York, 1994.

5   Gottlieb, Daniel, "Against Hope: Misplaced Optimism Can Be A Curse," *Psychotherapy Networker*, March/April, 2003, p.80.

Subject index

Author index